Other Books and Series by Jeff Bowen

Applications for Enrollment of Chickasaw Newborn Act of 1905
Volumes I thru VII

Cherokee Intermarried White 1906 Volume I, II, III, IV, V, VI, VII & VIII

Visit our website at **www.nativestudy.com** to learn more about these
and other books and series by Jeff Bowen

CHEROKEE INTERMARRIED WHITE 1906 VOLUME IX

TRANSCRIBED BY
JEFF BOWEN

NATIVE STUDY
Gallipolis, Ohio
USA

Originally published:
Baltimore, Maryland
2014

Reprinted by:

Native Study LLC
Gallipolis, OH
www.nativestudy.com
2020

Library of Congress Control Number: 2020917307

ISBN: 978-1-64968-078-5

Made in the United States of America.

This series is dedicated to
Jerry Bowen
the Brave and the Strong.

Other Books and Series by Jeff Bowen

1901-1907 Native American Census Seneca, Eastern Shawnee, Miami, Modoc, Ottawa, Peoria, Quapaw, and Wyandotte Indians (Under Seneca School, Indian Territory)

1932 Census of The Standing Rock Sioux Reservation with Births And Deaths 1924-1932

Census of The Blackfeet, Montana, 1897- 1901 Expanded Edition

Eastern Cherokee by Blood, 1906-1910, Volumes I thru XIII

Choctaw of Mississippi Indian Census 1929-1932 with Births and Deaths 1924-1931 Volume I
Choctaw of Mississippi Indian Census 1933, 1934 & 1937, Supplemental Rolls to 1934 & 1935 with Births and Deaths 1932-1938, and Marriages 1936-1938 Volume II

Eastern Cherokee Census Cherokee, North Carolina 1930-1939 Census 1930-1931 with Births And Deaths 1924-1931 Taken By Agent L. W. Page Volume I
Eastern Cherokee Census Cherokee, North Carolina 1930-1939 Census 1932-1933 with Births And Deaths 1930-1932 Taken By Agent R. L. Spalsbury Volume II
Eastern Cherokee Census Cherokee, North Carolina 1930-1939 Census 1934-1937 with Births and Deaths 1925-1938 and Marriages 1936 & 1938 Taken by Agents R. L. Spalsbury And Harold W. Foght Volume III

Seminole of Florida Indian Census, 1930-1940 with Birth and Death Records, 1930-1938

Texas Cherokees 1820-1839 A Document For Litigation 1921

Choctaw By Blood Enrollment Cards 1898-1914 Volumes I thru XVII

Starr Roll 1894 (Cherokee Payment Rolls) Districts: Canadian, Cooweescoowee, and Delaware Volume One
Starr Roll 1894 (Cherokee Payment Rolls) Districts: Flint, Going Snake, and Illinois Volume Two
Starr Roll 1894 (Cherokee Payment Rolls) Districts: Saline, Sequoyah, and Tahlequah; Including Orphan Roll Volume Three

Cherokee Intruder Cases Dockets of Hearings 1901-1909 Volumes I & II

Indian Wills, 1911-1921 Records of the Bureau of Indian Affairs Books One thru Seven;
Native American Wills & Probate Records 1911-1921

Other Books and Series by Jeff Bowen

Turtle Mountain Reservation Chippewa Indians 1932 Census with Births & Deaths, 1924-1932

Chickasaw By Blood Enrollment Cards 1898-1914 Volume I thru V

Cherokee Descendants East An Index to the Guion Miller Applications Volume I
Cherokee Descendants West An Index to the Guion Miller Applications Volume II (A-M)
Cherokee Descendants West An Index to the Guion Miller Applications Volume III (N-Z)

Applications for Enrollment of Seminole Newborn Freedmen, Act of 1905

Eastern Cherokee Census, Cherokee, North Carolina, 1915-1922, Taken by Agent James E. Henderson   *Volume I (1915-1916)*
                                          Volume II (1917-1918)
                                          Volume III (1919-1920)
                                          Volume IV (1921-1922)

Complete Delaware Roll of 1898

Eastern Cherokee Census, Cherokee, North Carolina, 1923-1929, Taken by Agent James E. Henderson   *Volume I (1923-1924)*
                                          Volume II (1925-1926)
                                          Volume III (1927-1929)

Applications for Enrollment of Seminole Newborn Act of 1905 Volumes I & II

North Carolina Eastern Cherokee Indian Census 1898-1899, 1904, 1906, 1909-1912, 1914 Revised and Expanded Edition

1932 Hopi and Navajo Native American Census with Birth & Death Rolls (1925-1931) Volume 1 - Hopi
1932 Hopi and Navajo Native American Census with Birth & Death Rolls (1930-1932) Volume 2 - Navajo

Western Navajo Reservation Navajo, Hopi and Paiute 1933 Census with Birth & Death Rolls 1925-1933

Cherokee Citizenship Commission Dockets 1880-1884 and 1887-1889 Volumes I thru V

DEPARTMENT OF THE INTERIOR

Commissioner to the Five Civilized Tribes

Muskogee, Indian Territory, March 9, 1907.

NOTICE IS HEREBY GIVEN that the undersigned, the Commissioner to the Five Civilized Tribes, has been designated by the Secretary of the Interior, as the official to make and approve appraisals of the value of improvements upon land in the Cherokee Nation which were made prior to November 5, 1906, by white persons who intermarried with Cherokee citizens prior to December 16, 1895, and who have the right under the Act of Congress approved March 2, 1907 (Public 180), to sell improvements.

NOTICE IS FURTHER GIVEN that former claimants to citizenship by intermarriage who have made permanent and valuable improvements on lands of the Cherokee Nation and who claim the right to sell the same under and by virtue of said Act of Congress of March 2, 1907 (Public 180), must appear before the Commissioner to the Five Civilized Tribes prior to April 1, 1907, and designate the land upon which are located the improvements which they claim the right to sell by virtue of said Act; and if any such intermarried citizen shall fail to appear before the Commissioner to the Five Civilized Tribes prior to April 1, 1907, it will be considered that he makes no claim to the benefits conferred by said Act. Such appearance and designation of improvements must be made before the Commissioner at his office in Muskogee, Indian Territory, at any time between Monday, March 11th, 1907, and Saturday, March 30th, 1907, inclusive, or at any of the following named places between the dates named at which places the Commissioner will have a representative to receive said designations and hear testimony relative thereto:

Bartlesville, Ind. Ter., Monday March 18th, 1907, to Saturday March 23rd, 1907, inclusive.

Tulsa, Ind. Ter., Monday March 25th, 1907, to Saturday March 30th, 1907, inclusive.

Claremore, Ind. Ter., Monday March 18th, 1907, to Saturday March 23rd, 1907, inclusive.

Nowata, Ind. Ter., Monday March 25th, 1907, to Saturday March 30th, 1907, inclusive.

Vinita, Ind. Ter., Monday March 18th, 1907, to Saturday March 23rd, 1907, inclusive.

Pryor Creek, Ind. Ter., Monday March 25th, 1907, to Saturday March 30th, 1907, inclusive.

Tahlequah, Ind. Ter., Monday March 18, 1907, to Saturday March 23rd, 1907, inclusive.

Sallisaw, Ind. Ter., Monday March 25th, 1907, to Saturday March 30th, 1907, inclusive.

Designations must be made in person by the intermarried white claimants, or in case proper proof is made that he is physically unable to appear, by some adult member of his immediate family, or in case proper proof is made of the fact that the intermarried white claimant is physically unable to appear and has no adult member of his immediate family, by a person holding a properly executed power of attorney; provided, that in every case the designation must be made by a party familiar with the character, ownership, location and value of the improvements to be designated. At the time of said designation the testimony of any competent person will be taken by the Commissioner as to the location, character and value of said improvements.

No former intermarried white claimant will be permitted to designate improvements upon more land than he would have been entitled to take in allotment for himself had he been admitted to citizenship. If any intermarried white claimant has made a tentative selection of a full allotment he will not be allowed to designate improvements upon other land.

NOTICE IS FURTHER GIVEN that if any citizen of the Cherokee Nation entitled to select an allotment shall claim that the improvements on land tentatively selected by a former intermarried white claimant, or held by him, do not belong to said intermarried white claimant, or makes any adverse claim to said improvements, or to the right of the intermarried white claimant to sell said improvements under the Act approved March 2, 1907 (Public 180), said citizen must appear before the Commissioner to the Five Civilized Tribes either at Muskogee, Indian Territory, prior to April 1, 1907, or at one of the places above designated and within the dates above designated and make formal complaint before the Commissioner to the Five Civilized Tribes of his contention. At Muskogee, Indian Territory, between March 11th and March 30th, 1907, inclusive, and at the other places herein named during the hearings at said places as herein fixed, plats will be open for inspection showing the location of tentative allotments made by former claimants to citizenship by intermarriage and all other land on which such claimants claim improvements, so far as indicated by the records of this office.

All persons interested should take careful note of the limitation of time herein provided for, within which designations and complaints may be made, and that they must be made by appearance before the Commissioner.

TAMS BIXBY,
Commissioner.

This particular notice concerns the appraisals of improvements on properties held by Cherokee intermarried whites. You would have found notices like this throughout the Nation to bring in people to finalize the allotment question, of who belonged and who did not.

E.C.M.

DEPARTMENT OF THE INTERIOR,
COMMISSIONER TO THE FIVE CIVILIZED TRIBES.

In the matter of the application for the enrollment of
ALBERTIN HAMPTON as a citizen by intermarriage of the Cherokee
Nation.

DECISION

THE RECORDS OF THIS OFFICE SHOW: That at Fairland, Indian
Territory, July 9, 1900, Albertin Hampton appeared before the Commission to the Five Civilized Tribes, and made application for the
enrollment of himself as a citizen by intermarriage, and for the
enrollment of his wife, Jane E. Hampton, et al. as citizens by
blood of the Cherokee Nation. The application for the enrollment of
the said Jane E. Hampton et al. as citizens by blood of the Cherokee
Nation has been heretofore disposed of, and their rights to enrollment will not be considered in this decision. Further proceedings
in the matter of said application were had at Muskogee, Indian
Territory, September 3, 1902, October 14, 1902, and January 2, 1907.

THE EVIDENCE IN THIS CASE SHOWS: That the applicant herein,
Albertin Hampton, a white man, was married, in accordance with
Cherokee law, January 20, 1874, to his wife, Jane E. Hampton, nee
Thomas, who was at the time of said marriage a recognized citizen
by blood of the Cherokee Nation, and whose name appears on the approved partial roll of citizens by blood of the Cherokee Nation,
opposite No. 195; that since said marriage the said Albertin Hampton
and Jane E. Hampton have resided together as husband and wife, and
have continuously lived in the Cherokee Nation. Said Albertin
Hampton is identified on the Cherokee authenticated tribal roll of
1880, and the Cherokee census roll of 1896, as "Bert Hampton", an
intermarried citizen of the Cherokee Nation.

IT IS, THEREFORE, ORDERED AND ADJUDGED: That in accordance with
the decision of the Supreme Court of the United States, dated November
5, 1906, in the case of Daniel Red Bird et al. vs. the United States,

under the provisions of Section twenty-one, of the Act of Congress approved June 28, 1898 (30 Stat., 495), Albertin Hampton is entitled to enrollment as a citizen by intermarriage of the Cherokee Nation, and his application for enrollment as such is accordingly granted.

                Commissioner.

Dated at Muskogee, Indian Territory,
this JAN 18 1907

The above is an accepted decision of the Commissioner to the Five Civilized Tribes. The Attorney for the Cherokee Nation had fifteen days after the date of Commissioner's decision in which to protest.

Cherokee
58.

W.W.HASTINGS.
ATTORNEY

OFFICE OF

H. M. VANCE.
SECRETARY

Attorney for the Cherokee Nation,

MUSKOGEE, I. T.　　January 18, 1907.

The Commissioner to the Five Civilized Tribes,

Muskogee, Indian Territory.

Sir:

Receipt is acknowledged of the testimony and of your decision enrolling Albertin Hampton, as a citizen by intermarriage of the Cherokee Nation. Time for protesting said decision is waived and I consent that said person may be placed upon the schedule immediately.

Yours very truly,

W. W. Hastings

Attorney for Cherokee Nation.

The above is a notice of the Attorney waiving the time for protesting the Commissioner's decision (on the two previous pages) concerning Albertin Hampton's application and consenting to place the applicant upon schedule immediately.

INTRODUCTION

The *Cherokee Intermarried White*, National Archive film M-1301, Rolls 305-307, are found under the heading of Applications for Enrollment of the Commission to the Five Civilized Tribes. The genealogical value of this series concerning the relationships between many Cherokee tribesman and their marriages among another race is very important and virtually a treasure trove of information long sought after. While on the other hand what these cases are really about are the efforts of many to attain Cherokee land allotments. Referenced from the Supreme Court Decision, Cherokee Intermarriage Cases – 203 U.S. 76 (1906).

This collection of Intermarried claims involves two hundred and eighty-eight separate cases with a variety of scenarios from the divorced to the widowed to the deserving to the deceptive. During these times there were many that wanted what was rightfully only the Cherokees. You will see each case will be headed by the title from the first folder as an example: *Intermarried White I, Trans from Cher. 34*, the transfer number is the Dawes Commission number from the claimants spouse.

These cases are fascinating because of the generational bloodlines that can be verified by documentation rather than just word of mouth. From Kent Carter's book, *The Dawes Commission*, "The tribe also, continued to oppose the enrollment of whites who had married into the Cherokee tribe. That controversy dragged through the U.S. Court of Claims and then the Supreme Court, which finally ruled in favor of the tribe on November 05, 1906. The court upheld the Cherokee citizenship laws that denied rights to any white who had married into the tribe after November 1, 1877. It also upheld an 1839 law which stated that anyone who moved out of the nation lost their citizenship unless they were readmitted. The applications of 3,341 persons were rejected as a result of this ruling, and the allotment clerks were forced to undo a great deal of their work. With the issue finally settled by the courts, the commission was able to send the first schedule of Cherokees by intermarriage, containing fifty-five names, to the secretary of interior on June 10, 1907. Eventually only 286 people were enrolled as intermarried whites----far fewer than the number put on the rolls of the Choctaw and Chickasaw tribes, which had much more liberal laws on rights based on marriage." [1]

---

[1] The Dawes Commission and the Allotment of the Five Civilized Tribes, 1893-1914 by Kent Carter, pg. 121

In Cohen's Handbook of Federal Indian Law he states, "In the *Cherokee Intermarriage Cases,* the Supreme Court considered the claims of certain white persons, intermarried with Cherokee Indians, who wanted to participate in the common property of the Cherokee Nation. Such persons were permitted by tribal law to be tribal citizens with limited rights in tribal property. The tribe had also provided for the revocation of citizenship rights of a white person who intermarried with a Cherokee if the Cherokee spouse were abandoned or if a widower or widow married a non-Cherokee. The Court found that the Cherokee Nation had authority to qualify the rights of citizenship which it offered to its "naturalized citizens. Such tribal action defeated the claims of the plaintiffs:

The laws and usages of the Cherokees, their earliest history, the fundamental principles of their national policy, their constitution and statutes, all show that citizenship rested on blood or marriage; that the man who would assert citizenship must establish marriage; that when marriage ceased (with a special reservation in favor of widows or widowers) citizenship ceased; that when an intermarried white married a person having no rights of Cherokee citizenship by blood it was conclusive evidence that the tie which bound him to the Cherokee people was severed and the very basis of his citizenship obliterated."[2]

An important footnote that Cohen published within his pages for the above paragraph also needs to be studied. He noted, "Under Cherokee law white persons intermarrying with Cherokees before 1875 were tribal citizens for most purposes, including allotment of tribal land, but had no interest in tribal funds except those funds derived from tribal lands. A Cherokee law that became effective in 1875 provided that whites marrying Cherokees had no rights to tribal property but could obtain full citizenship by the payment of $500 to the tribe. In 1877 the tribe provided that no intermarried citizen could obtain any rights to tribal land or funds."[3]

During many years of study this author has found cases that should have been been accepted, especially with the particular documentation presented. All in all the outcome of the decision made should have rendered a different result. Also there have been many that numb the mind as to how they their cases were even considered. The years have given many the hopes that their ancestors were one of those that had a decent claim and an honest consideration. Like any time in history there are political struggles

---

[2] Felix S. Cohen's Handbook of FEDERAL INDIAN LAW 1982 ED. pgs 20-21.
[3] Felix S. Cohen's Handbook of FEDERAL INDIAN LAW 1982 ED. pg 21 footnote16.

and the human factor that points out man is not perfect. These pages were transcribed with the wish that another person somewhere along the line will find their relation from the past and give them the answers long hoped for.

Jeff Bowen
Gallipolis, Ohio
NativeStudy.com

Cher IW 248

◇◇◇◇◇

DEPARTMENT OF THE INTERIOR,
COMMISSION TO THE FIVE CIVILIZED TRIBES.
FT. GIBSON, I. T., AUGUST 27th, 1900.

IN THE MATTER OF THE APPLICATION OF James S. Harris and wife, for enrollment as citizens of the Cherokee Nation, and he being sworn by Commissioner, T.B. Needles, testified as follows:

Q What is your name?   A James S. Harris.

Q What is your age?   A Sixty five.

Q What is your Postoffice?   A Muskogee.

Q Are you a recognized citizen of the Cherokee Nation?   A Yes sir.

Q By blood?   A Yes sir.

Q What degree of blood do you claim?   A One sixteenth.

Q What district do you live in?   A Canadian.

Q How long have you been a resident of the Cherokee Nation continuously?   A About twenty one years.

Q For whom do you apply for enrollment?   A Myself and wife.

Q What is the name of your father?   A William Harris.

Q Is he living?   A No sir.

Q Was he a Cherokee citizen by blood?   A No sir; white man.

Q Did he die before 1880?   A Yes sir.

Q What is the name of your mother?   A Susan Harris.

Q Is she living?   A No sir.

Q Was she a Cherokee citizen by blood?   A Yes sir.

Q Did she die before 1880?   A No sir; died since then.

Q What is the name of your wife?   A Phirena Harris.

Q Is she living?   A Yes sir.

Q Is she a citizen by blood?   A No sir.

Q When were you married to her?   A 1872.

Q Her father and mother living?   A Both dead.

Q Die before 1880?   A Her mother died since 1880.

Q What was her name?   A Elizabeth Conley.

Q What District did you live in in 1880?   A Canadian.

(1880 Roll, Page 21, #592, James F. (S) Harris, Canadian District)

(1880 Roll, Page 21, #593, Pyrena Harris, Canadian District)

(1896 Roll, Page 34, #934, James S. Harris, Canadian District)

(1896 Roll, Page 88, #120, Pyrenia Harris, Canadian District)

The name of James S. Harris, appearing on the authenticated roll of 1880, as James S. Harris, and on the census roll of 1896 as James F. Harris; the name of his wife, Phirena, appearing on the authenticated roll of 1880, as well as the census roll of 1896; they having made satisfactory affidavit as to their residence, being fully identified

1

according to the page and number of the said rolls, as indicated in the testimony; he will be duly listed for enrollment by this Commission as a citizen by blood, and his wife as a citizen by intermarriage.

The undersigned, being sworn, states that as stenographer to the Commission to the Five Civilized Tribes, he correctly recorded the testimony and proceedings in this case, and the foregoing is a true and correct transcript of his stenographic notes thereof.

R R Cravens

Subscribed and sworn to before
me this 7th day of September, 1900.

T B Needles
COMMISSIONER.

Copy

◇◇◇◇◇

Cher-2030.

DEPARTMENT OF THE INTERIOR.
Commission to the Five Civilized Tribes.
Muskogee, I. T., October 18, 1902.

In the matter of the application of James S. Harris for the enrollment of himself as a Cherokee by blood of the Cherokee Nation, and for the enrollment of his wife Pyrena as a citizen by intermarriage of the Cherokee Nation.

James S. Harris, called as a witnes[sic], being first duly sworn and examined, testified as follows:

Q What is your name? A James S. Harris.
Q How old are you? A Sixty seven years.
Q Are you a Cherokee by blood? A Yes sir.
Q What is your wife's name? A Pyrena Harris.
Q Is she a white woman? A Yes sir.
Q Was she your wife in 1880? A Yes sir.
Q She claims her citizenship through you? A Yes sir.
Q Have you and yiur[sic] wife been living together ever since 1880? A Yes sir.
Q Have you ever been separated at all? A No sir.
Q Has the Cherokee nation[sic] been your home ever since 1880? A yes[sic] sir.
Q You have never lived anywhere else? A No sir.
Q Have you any children? A Yes sir.
Q They are all old enough to be on the roll themselves--to enroll themselves?
    A Yes, got families of their own.

--------------0--------------

Cherokee Intermarried White 1906
Volume IX

Frances R. Lane upon oath states that as stenographer to the Commissioner to the Five Civilized Tribes she reported the testimony in the above entitled cause and that the foregoing is an accurate transcript of her stenographic notes thereof.

Frances R Lane

Subscribed and sworn to before me this October 25th, 1902

BC Jones
Notary Public.

◇◇◇◇◇

E C M   Cherokee 2030.

DEPARTMENT OF THE INTERIOR,
COMMISSIONER TO THE FIVE CIVILIZED TRIBES.

In the matter of the application for the enrollment of PHIRENA HARRIS as a citizen by intermarriage of the Cherokee Nation.

D E C I S I O N

THE RECORDS OF THIS OFFICE SHOW: That at Fort Gibson, Indian Territory, August 27, 1900, application was received by the Commission to the Five Civilized Tribes for the enrollment of Phirena Harris as a citizen by intermarriage of the Cherokee Nation. Further proceedings in the matter of said application were had at Muskogee, Indian Territory, October 18, 1902.

THE EVIDENCE IN THIS CASE SHOWS: That the applicant herein, Phirena Harris, a white woman, is alleged to have married one James S. Harris, who was that the time of said marriage a recognized citizen by blood of the Cherokee Nation, who is identified on the Cherokee authenticated tribal roll of 1880, Canadian District No. 592 as a native Cherokee, and whose name is included on the approved partial roll of citizens by blood of the Cherokee Nation opposite No. 5297. Said marriage is alleged to have been contracted in 1872.

December 24, 1906 and again on February 13, 1907 the applicant in this case, Phirena Harris, was notified to appear immediately and give testimony tending to establish the date of said marriage. This, said applicant has failed to do. Said applicant, Phirena Harris, is identified on the Cherokee authenticated tribal roll of 1880 and the Cherokee census roll of 1896 as an intermarried citizen of the Cherokee Nation.

IT IS, THEREFORE, ORDERED AND ADJUDGED: That in accordance with the decision of the Supreme Court of the United States, dated November 5, 1906, in the cases of Daniel Red Bird, et al. vs. the United States, Nos. 125, 126, 127, and 128, the said applicant, Phirena Harris, is not entitled, under the provisions of Section Twenty-one of

3

the Act of Congress approved June 28, 1898 (30 Stats. 495), to enrollment as a citizen by intermarriage of the Cherokee Nation, and her application for enrollment as such is accordingly denied.

Tams Bixby

Commissioner.

Dated at Muskogee, Indian Territory,
this   FEB 27 1907

◇◇◇◇◇

REFER IN REPLY TO THE FOLLOWING:
Cherokee
2030

DEPARTMENT OF THE INTERIOR,
COMMISSIONER TO THE FIVE CIVILIZED TRIBES.

Muskogee, Indian Territory, December 24, 1906.

Pyrena Harris,
    Muskogee, Indian Territory.

Dear Madam:

November 6, 1906, the United States Supreme Court held that white persons who intermarried with Cherokee citizens according to Cherokee law prior to November 1, 1875, are entitled to enrollment and allotments of land as citizens of the Cherokee Nation.

You are advised that to properly determine your right to enrollment as a citizen by intermarriage of the Cherokee Nation, it will be necessary for you to appear before the Commissioner for the purpose of giving testimony as to the date of your marriage and whether or not your husband, by reason of your marriage to whom you claim the right to enrollment as a citizen by intermarriage of the Cherokee Nation, was a recognized Cherokee citizen at the time of your marriage to him.

You are, therefore, directed to appear before the Commissioner at Muskogee, Indian Territory, at 9 o'clock A. M., on Thursday, January 3, 1907, and give testimony as above indicated.

Respectfully,

Wm O. Beall

Acting Commissioner.

LMC

◇◇◇◇◇

Cherokee Intermarried White 1906
Volume IX

Cherokee 2030

Muskogee, Indian Territory, February 27, 1907.

W. W. Hastings,
      Attorney for the Cherokee Nation,
         Muskogee, Indian Territory.

Dear Sir:

There is enclosed herewith a copy of the decision of the Commissioner to the Five Civilized Tribes, dated February 27, 1907, rejecting the application for the enrollment of Phirena Harris as a citizen by intermarriage of the Cherokee Nation.

The decision, together with the record of proceedings had in the case, has this day been transmitted to the Secretary of the Interior for his review and decision. You will be advised of the Secretary's action as soon as this office is informed of same.

Respectfully,

SIGNED *Tams Bixby*

Enc I-57
               Commissioner.

RPI

◇◇◇◇◇

Cherokee 2030

Muskogee, Indian Territory, February 27, 1907.

Phirena Harris,
      Chaffee, Indian Territory.

Dear Madam:

There is enclosed herewith a copy of the decision of the Commissioner to the Five Civilized Tribes, dated February 27, 1907, rejecting the application for your enrollment as a citizen by intermarriage of the Cherokee Nation.

The decision, together with the record of proceedings had in the case, has this day been transmitted to the Secretary of the Interior for his review and decision. You will be advised of the Secretary's action as soon as this office is informed of same.

Respectfully,

SIGNED *Jams Bixby*

Enc I-58 1/2   Commissioner.

RPI

Register.

◇◇◇◇◇

COPY

Muskogee, Indian Territory, February 27, 1907.

The Honorable,
    The Secretary of the Interior.

Sir:

    There is transmitted herewith the record of proceedings had in the matter of the application for the enrollment of Phirena Harris as a citizen by intermarriage of the Cherokee Nation, together with the decision of the Commissioner, dated February 27, 1907, rejecting said application.

Respectfully,

SIGNED *Jams Bixby*

Enc I-59 1/2   Commissioner.

RPI

Through the Commissioner
    of Indian Affairs.

◇◇◇◇◇

Cherokee Intermarried White 1906
Volume IX

DEPARTMENT OF THE INTERIOR
OFFICE OF INDIAN AFFAIRS,
I.T.   WASHINGTON.   GAW
Reference in body
of letter.   May 11, 1907.

Subject: Motions for
review in certain Chero-
kee citizenship cases.

The Honorable,
    The Secretary of the Interior.

Sir:

There are inclosed herewith motions filed by W. W. Hastings, National Attorney for the Cherokee Nation, praying for review and rehearing of Departmental decisions authorizing the enrollment as citizens by intermarriage of the Cherokee Nation of the following persons:

42893-1907,	Jacob A. Bartles,
42895- "	Osburn J. Byrd,
42886- "	Amanda Beck,
42894- "	Sarah F. Gage,
42892- "	Phirena Harris,
42888- "	Daniel Harmon,
42891- "	Emma L. Ironsides,
42896- "	Sarah A. Jordan
42881- "	Dovie Johnson,
42882- "	Andrew H. Norwood,
42887- "	Stacy E. Perry,
42885- "	Martha Randolph, now Kernan
42893- "	John W. Smith
42884- "	John J. Smith,
42890- "	Robert H. F. Thompson,
42889- "	Hattie Wright,
42883- "	Nancy Wolfe,
42880- "	E. A. Welch.

In view of the provisions of section 2 of the act of April 26, 1906 (34 Stat. L., 137), providing that the rolls of the Five Civilized Tribes shall be fully completed on or before March 4, 1907, there appears to be no authority in law for the reconsideration of any enrollment cases at this time, and it is recommended that the office be authorized to advise Mr. Hastings that the motions for review herewith transmitted cannot be considered.

Very respectfully,

C. F. Larrabee

Acting Commissioner.

AJW-FHE.

     May 13, 1907.

Approved.

     Thos Ryan

         First Assistant Secretary.

◇◇◇◇◇

I. T. references in body of letter.	DEPARTMENT OF THE INTERIOR, OFFICE OF INDIAN AFFAIRS, WASHINGTON.	GAW

May 15, 1907.

Commissioner to the Five Civilized Tribes,
     Muskogee, Indian Territory.

Sir:

    There is inclosed copy of Office letter of May 11, 1907, approved by the Department on May 13, 1907, recommending that motions filed by W. W. Hastings, National Attorney for the Cherokee Nation, praying for a review and rehearing of Departmental decisions authorizing the enrollment of the following persons as citizens by intermarriage of the Cherokee Nation, be denied, in view of the fact that there appears to be no authority in law at this time for the reconsideration of any enrollment case.

42893-1907	Jacob A. Bartles
42895- "	Osburn J. Byrd
42886- "	Amanda Beck
42894- "	Sarah F. Gage
42892- "	Phirena Harris
42888- "	Daniel Harmon
42891- "	Emma L. Ironsides
42896- "	Sarah A. Jordan
42881- "	Dovie Johnson

42882-	"	Andrew H. Norwood
42887-	"	Stacy E. Perry
42885-	"	Martha Randolph, now Kernan
42893-	"	John W. Smith
42884-	"	John J. Smith
42890-	"	Robert H. F. Thompson
42889-	"	Hattie Wright
42883-	"	Nancy Wolfe
42880-	"	E. A. Welch

You are requested to advise the interested parties, including Mr. Hastings, of the Department's action.

Very respectfully,

C. F. Larrabee

Acting Commissioner.

AJW-FHE.

◇◇◇◇◇

Cherokee
248

Muskogee, Indian Territory, May 25, 1907.

Phirena Harris,
    Chaffee, Indian Territory.

Dear Madam:

You are hereby advised that on May 11, 1907, the Secretary of the Interior denied a motion filed by the Attorney for the Cherokee Nation, for a review of its decision authorizing your enrollment as a citizen by intermarriage of the Cherokee Nation.

For your information, there is enclosed herewith a copy of Departmental decision referred to.

Respectfully,

Commissioner.

Encl. C-5
  LMC

◇◇◇◇◇

Cherokee Intermarried White 1906
Volume IX

Cherokee
253 et al.

Muskogee, Indian Territory, May 25, 1907.

W. W. Hastings,
Attorney for the Cherokee Nation,
Muskogee, Indian Territory.

Dear Sir:

You are hereby advised that on May 13, 1907, the Secretary of the Interior denied the motion filed by you for a review of its decision authorizing the enrollment of Jacob A. Bartles, et al., as citizens by intermarriage of the Cherokee Nation.

For your information, there is enclosed herewith a copy of Departmental decision referred to.

Respectfully,

Commissioner.

Encl. C-20
LMC

Cher IW 249

◇◇◇◇◇

Department of the Interior,
Commission to the Five Civilized Tribes,
Fort Gibson, I.T., August 23, 1900.

In the matter of the application of Sarah A. Jordan for enrollment as a Cherokee by intermarriage: being sworn and examined by Commissioner Breckinridge, she testified as follows:

Q What is your full name? A Sarah A. Jordan.
Q How old are you? A I am 69 years old in November,
Q What is your post office? A McLain.
Q What is your district? A Canadian.
Q Who is it you want to have put on the roll? A Myself, and my grandson is here to put himself on the roll.
Q Just you and your grandson? A He will put himself on the roll.
Q Have you any children you want to apply for? A No, I haven't got but two children living.
Q They are of age, are they? A Yes, sir.

Cherokee Intermarried White 1906
Volume IX

Q Do you apply as a Cherokee by blood?   A I am, but then my mother never came to this country to prove her rights, she followed the Cherokees to Alabama and when she got to Alabama her and her husband stayed there.

Q Are you on any of the rolls of the Cherokee Nation?   A Yes, sir.

Q How long have you been in the Cherokee Nation?   A About 25 years I reckon.

Q How long have you been in Canadian district?   A I have been there about 20 years I suppose.

Q Are you on the roll of 1880?   A Yes, sir, if I am not I ought to be.

Q What is the name of your father?   A My father's name is Joseph Williams.

Q Is he a Cherokee or a white man?   A He was a white man.

Q Is he dead or alive?   A He is dead.

Q How long has he been dead?   A He has been dead about 5 years.

Q What is the name of your mother?   A Martha Williams.

Q She was a Cherokee or a white woman?   A She was a Cherokee.

Q Is she dead or alive?   A She is dead.

Q How long has she been dead?   A She has been dead about 35 years.

Q What was your husband's name?   A Andrew V. Jordan.

Q Is he dead? A Yes, sir.

Q Was he a Cherokee or a white man?   A He was a Cherokee.

Q When did he die?   A He died in 1861.

(On 1880 roll, page 27, No. 756, S. A. Jordan, Canadian district;

on 1896 roll, page 89, No. 138, Sarah A. Jordan, Canadian district.)

Q You have lived in the Cherokee Nation ever since you were enrolled in 1880?
A Yes, sir, I have.

Q Do you apply now as a Cherokee by blood or as an adopted Cherokee?
A Adopted, because my parents never came here.

      The applicant is identified on the rolls of 1880 and 1896 as an adopted Cherokee; she has lived in the Cherokee Nation ever since her enrollment in 1880, and she will now be listed for enrollment as a Cherokee by adoption.

--------0--------

      Bruce C. Jones, being duly sworn, says that as stenographer to the Commission to the Five Civilized Tribes he correctly recorded the proceedings and testimony in the above case, and the foregoing is a true and complete transcript of his stenographic notes thereof.

Bruce C Jones

Sworn to and subscribed before me this the 1st of September, 1900.

C R Breckinridge

Commissioner

◇◇◇◇◇

(Copy of original document from case.)
◇◇◇◇◇

DEPARTMENT OF THE INTERIOR.
Commission to the Five Civilized Tribes.
Muskogee, Indian Territory, October 14th, 1902.

In the matter of the application of Sarah A. Jordan for the enrollment of herself as a citizen by intermarriage of the Cherokee Nation.

Supplemental to #1874.

Sarah A. Jordan, being duly sworn, testified as follows:

Examination by the Commission.

Q. What is your name?   A. Sarah A. Jordan.

Q. How old are you?   A. I will be 71 the 3rd day of next month if I live to see the day.

Q. What is your post office?   A. Bartlesville.

Q. Was it McLain?   A. Yes, sir; it was McLain when I come in before.

Q. You are a white woman, are you?   A. Yes, sir.

Q. You are on the eighty roll as an intermarried white woman?   A. Yes, sir.

Q. What was the name of your husband in 1880?   A. Andrew V. Jordan.

Q. Is he still living?   A. He died in '62.

Q. Then he wasn't your husband in 1880? He was dead before 1880?
A. Yes, sir; he was.

Q. Have you married since 1880? A. No, sr[sic].

Q. Have you been living in the Cherokee Nation all the time since 1880?
A. Yes, sir; ever since 1880; I have.

Q. Never lived anywhere else?   A. No, never have been outside of the Cherokee Nation. I have lived within 15 miles of this town close to 25 years.

++

Jesse O. Carr, being duly sworn, states that as stenographer to the Commission to the Five Civilized Tribes he reported the above entitled case and that the foregoing is a true and complete transcript of his stenographic notes thereof.

Jesse O. Carr.

Subscribed and sworn to before me this 3rd day of January, 1903.

John O. Rosson
Notary Public.

◇◇◇◇◇

CHEROKEE-1874.

DEPARTMENT OF THE INTERIOR,
COMMISSIONER TO THE FIVE CIVILIZED TRIBES.
Muskogee, Indian Territory, January 4, 1907.

In the matter of making proof of the marriage of Sarah A. Jordan to her Cherokee husband, prior to November 1, 1875.

John D. Jordan, being sworn by W. W. Chappell, Notary Public, testified as follows:

Cherokee Intermarried White 1906
Volume IX

COMMISSIONER:

Q. What is your name?   A. John D. Jordan.

Q. What is your age?   A. 52.

Q. What is your post office address?   A. I live near Ramona.

Q. How long have you lived there?   A. I have lived on the place I am now on for 5 years last november[sic], I believe.

Q. In whose behalf do you appear here today?   A. My mother's, Sarah A. Jordan.

Q. Is she living at this time?   A. No sir.

Q. When did she die?   A. The 6th. of June, 1906.

Q. Did she claim citizenship in the Cherokee Nation by intermarriage? A. Yes sir.

Q. Through whom did she make that claim?   A. Through her marriage with A. V. Jordan -- Andrew Vann Jordan.

Q. When were they married?   A. I can't tell you the year they were married. I have no record of it at all.

Q. Where were they married?   A. In Rusk County, Texas, near Henderson, the county-seat.

Q. Have you a certified copy of the marriage license?   A. No sir.

Q. They were married under a license issued by the State of Texas?
    A. Yes sir that is my understanding.

Q. When did they remove to the Cherokee Nation A. We come here -- my father died in '62, and me and my mother and brothers and sisters moved here in '78 and proved up our citizenship before the Chambers' Court in '79. We have a certificate at home, if I haven't got it lost.

Q. A certified copy of the act of admission to citizenship by the Chambers' Court in '79.
    A. Yes sir.

Q. Did Sarah A. Jordan marry again?   A. She never did.

Q. Did she reside continuously in the Cherokee Nation from the time of her removal from Texas until her death?   A. Yes sir, she never was outside of the Cherokee Nation after that.

Q. You don't know how long prior to the death of her husband it was that they moved to the Cherokee Nation?   A. It was since his death. My father died in '62, and we moved here in '78 and were admitted in '79.

Q. Was she recognized on any of the Cherokee rolls?   A. Yes sir, as well as I remember, she drawed money here once -- what was called the Bread Money. Her name was taken on all of the rolls that were ever taken in the country, as an adopted citizen.

Q. Were you ever recognized on any of the rolls?   A. Yes sir, all of them.

Q. Are there any other children besides yourself?   A. Yes sir, there were three others.

Q. What were their names?   A. James Alexander Jordan, Martin Jordan and my sister was named Fannie.

Q. In what years were they born?   A. I couldn't tell you. They are all dead but me.

Q. None of them living at this time?   A. No sir.

(Commissioner -- The name of Sarah A. Jordan appears upon the 1880 Roll opposite No. 256, in Canadian District; also upon the 1896 Census Roll opposite No. 138.)

Witness excused.

Eula Jeanes Branson, being duly sworn, states that she correctly reported the proceedings had in the above and foregoing on the 4th. day of January, 1907.

Eula Jeanes Branson

Subscribed and sworn to before me, this 4th. day of January, 1907.

Edward Merrick
Notary Public.

◇◇◇◇◇

C. F. B.   Cherokee 1878.

DEPARTMENT OF THE INTERIOR,
COMMISSIONER TO THE FIVE CIVILIZED TRIBES.
Muskogee, Indian Territory, January 8, 1907.

Supplemental Proceedings in the Matter of the Application for the Enrollment of Sarah A. Jordan as a citizen by Intermarriage of the Cherokee Nation.

Sarah A. Halton being first duly sworn by John E. Tidwell, Notary Public, testified as follows:

ON BEHALF OF COMMISSIONER.

Q   What is your name?   A   Sarah A. Halton.
Q   What is your age?   A   75.
Q   What is your post office address?
A   Muskogee.
Q   You appear here for the purpose of giving testimony in the matter of the application for the enrollment of Sarah A. Jordan as a citizen by intermarriage of the Cherokee Nation?
A   Yes sir.
Q   Is Sarah A. Jordan living or dead?
A   She is dead.
Q   When did she die?
A   I don't know the time of her death.
Q   When did you first become acquainted with her?
A   In about '48 or '49.
Q   Where was she living at that time?
A   Russ County, Texas.

Q   She was not a Cherokee by blood?
A   I think not.
Q   Did you know her husband?
A   Yes sir.
Q   What was his name?
A   Andrew V. Jordan.
Q   He is dead?   A   Yes sir.
Q   Do you know when Sarah A. Jordan was married to her husband Andrew V. Jordan?
A   Not exactly; '52 or '53 I think.
Q   They were married in Texas?
A   Yes sir; Russ County.
Q   Do you know when they first came to the Cherokee Nation?
A   I do not.
Q   Can you give anywhere near the year?
A   I don't believe I can. We have been here 13 years and they had been here several years when we came here.
Q   You knew them all the time after you became acquainted with them, as man and wife?
A   Yes sir.
Q   Did you know either of them before their marriage?
A   Both of them.
Q   And you have every reason to believe that they were married according to the laws of Texas?
A   Yes sir.
Q   And you know of your own personal knowledge that from the time of their reputed marriage, they lived together as man and wife until the death of Mr. Jordan?
A   Yes sir.
Q   Do you remember when he died?
A   No sir; I do not.
Q   Since the death of Mr. Jordan, has Sarah A. Jordan re-married?
A   No sir.
Q   She has remained a widow ever since the death of her husband?
A   Yes sir.
Q   Were either of these parties ever married prior to the time they were married to each other?
A   No sir.
Q   Did you know Andrew V. Jordan's father?
A   No sir; he was dead before I went to Texas.
Q   Did you now his mother?
A   Yes sir.
Q   They hd[sic] been living in Texas had they, for a number of years prior to the marriage of Andrew V. Jordan to his wife, Sarah A. Jordan?
A   Yes sir.
Q   You had known them for 6 or 7 years, had you?
A   Yes sir; 6 or 7 years.
Q   What was the name of Andrew V. Jordan's mother?

A   Nancy Jordan. After the death of Mr. Jordan, she then married a Mr. Anderson.

Q   Her name then at the time of her death was Sarah Anderson?

A   Yes sir.

John D. Jordan being first duly sworn by John E. Tidwell, Notary Public, testified as follows:

ON BEHALF OF COMMISSIONER.

Q   What is your name?   A   John D. Jordan.

Q   What is your age?   A   52.

Q   What is your post office address?

A   Ramona, Indian Territory, Cherokee Nation.

Q   What is the name of your mother?

A   Sarah A. Jordan.

Q   Is she living or dead?   A   Dead.

Q   When did she die?   A   6th day of June, 1906.

Q   What is the name of your father?

A   Andrew V. Jordan.

Q   He is dead?   A   Yes sir.

Q   When did he die?   A   May 9, 1862.

Q   Your father was a Cherokee?   A   Yes sir.

Q   Your mother possessed no Cherokee blood?

A   None at all.

Q   She claims the right to enrollment as a citizen of the Cherokee Nation by virtue of her marriage to your father?

A   Yes sir.

Q   Where was your father living at the time he married your mother, do you know?

A   Seven miles southeast of Henderson, Russ County, Texas.

Q   You were born in Texas?   A   Yes sir.

Q   When?   A   March 7, 1854.

Q   When were your father and mother married, do you know?

A   Only from the records; 9th of December, 1851 I think.

Q   Was your father living in Texas at that time?

A   Yes sir; I suppose he was.

Q   And it is your understanding and you believe, do you not, that your father and mother were married in Texas and that from the time of their marriage, they continued to live together as husband and wife until the time of the death of your father, which occurred you say in 1862?

A   Yes sir.

Q   After the death of your father, did your mother continue to reside in the State of Texas?

A   Until '78.

Q   She removed then to the Cherokee Nation in 1878?

A   Yes sir.

Cherokee Intermarried White 1906
Volume IX

Q After coming to the Cherokee Nation, her children as descendants of her husband went before the Cherokee authorities and were admitted to citizenship in the Cherokee Nation?
A Yes sir.
Q That was in 1878?
A 1879 when we were admitted.
Q By what authority were you admitted, do you remember?
A Chambers Court.
Q Have you any information as to where your father was born?
A Only what I have been told; he was born on the road from the old Nation to the Cherokee Nation here.
Q He arrived then in the Cherokee Nation not long after his birth?
A Yes sir.
Q What was his name in full?
A Andrew Vann Jordan.
Q What was his mother's name?
A Her name was Nancy Rogers.
Q You have no knowledge of course as to the date of the removal of your father from the Cherokee Nation to the State of Texas?
A None at all.
Q You have no knowledge whatever as to how long he had been in Texas prior to his marriage to your mother?
A No sir; I don't know how long they lived in this country.
Q Did his father and mother go to Texas?
A Yes sir.
Q His father and mother then moved to Texas and he lived with them there?
A Yes.

Jim Pope being first duly sworn by John E. Tidwell, Notary Public, testified as follows:

ON BEHALF OF COMMISSIONER.
Q What is your name?   A Jim Pope.
Q What is your age?   A 56 years old.
Q What is your post office address?
A My home is in Centralia. I have been here now for two or three weeks.
Q Did you ever know a person by the name of Sarah A. Jordan?
A Yes sir.
Q Was she a white woman?
A Yes sir.
Q She was married at one time to a Cherokee by blood?
A Yes sir. That is what I always understood.
Q What was her husband's name?   A Andrew Vann Jordan.
Q Where were Andrew Vann Jordan abd[sic] Sarah A. Jordan married?
A In Texas, is what they all said.
Q You didn't witness the marriage?

A No sir.

Q But it was understood among all the people who knew them that they were man and wife?

A Yes sir.

Q They lived together as man and wife until the death of Andrew V. Jordan?

A Yes sir; a long time go though.

Q Did you know either of these parties or both of them before they were married?

A I don't remember.

Q Do you remember when Sarah A. Jordan came to the Cherokee Nation?

A Yes sir; about the time.

Q In what year?

A It has been over 25 years ago. They came before I did and I have been here about 23 years.

The undersigned being first duly sworn states that as stenographer to the Commission to the Five Civilized Tribes, she recorded the testimony taken in this case and that the foregoing is a full, true and correct transcript of her stenographic notes thereof.

Myrtle Hill

Subscribed and sworn to before me this the 12th day of January, 1907.

Chas E Webster
Notary Public.

◇◇◇◇◇

E C M   Cherokee 1874.

DEPARTMENT OF THE INTERIOR,
COMMISSIONER TO THE FIVE CIVILIZED TRIBES.

In the matter of the application for the enrollment of SARAH A. JORDAN as a citizen by intermarriage of the Cherokee Nation.

D E C I S I O N

THE RECORDS IN THIS OFFICE SHOW: That at Fort Gibson, Indian Territory, August 23, 1900 application was received by the Commission to the Five Civilized Tribes for the enrollment of Sarah A. Jordan as a citizen by intermarriage of the Cherokee Nation. Further proceedings in the matter of said application were had at Muskogee, Indian Territory, October 14, 1902 and January 4, and January 8, 1907.

THE EVIDENCE IN THIS CASE SHOWS: That the applicant herein, Sarah A. Jordan, who is identified on the Cherokee authenticated tribal roll of 1880 as an intermarried citizen of the Cherokee Nation, is a white woman and neither claims nor possesses any right to enrollment as a citizen of the Cherokee Nation other than such right as she may have acquired by virtue of her marriage in the State of Texas about the year 1858 to one Andrew V. Jordan, since deceased, a Cherokee by blood; that the said Andrew V. Jordan was not at the time of said marriage a recognized citizen by blood of the Cherokee Nation; that said Andrew V. Jordan died in the State of Texas without becoming a citizen of the Cherokee Nation; that in 1878 the said Sarah A. Jordan removed to the Cherokee Nation, and the said applicant does not claim to have been admitted to citizenship in the Cherokee Nation until the year 1879. Said applicant did not, therefore, marry a recognized citizen by blood of the Cherokee Nation prior to November 1, 1875.

IT IS, THEREFORE, ORDERED AND ADJUDGED: That in accordance with the decision of the Supreme Court of the United States dated November 5, 1906, in the cases of Daniel Red Bird, et al. vs. the United States, Nos. 125, 126, 127, and 127[sic], the said applicant, Sarah A. Jordan is not entitled, under the provisions of Section Twenty-one of the Act of Congress approved June 28, 1898 (30 Stats. 495), to enrollment as a citizen by intermarriage of the Cherokee Nation, and her application for enrollment as such is accordingly denied.

Tams Bixby
Commissioner.

Dated at Muskogee, Indian Territory,
this   FEB 25 1907

◇◇◇◇◇

Act Jan'y 29, 1887.

Roll No. *11*

ARMY VOUCHER No. ___ (B.)

8169

WIDOW.

Sarah A. Jordan

Andrew T. Jr. M.

189__

4 NOV. 1895
To
4 FEB. 1897

Return this voucher for payment to
G. W. GLICK,
U. S. Pension Agent.
TOPEKA, KANS.

STATE OF _____, COUNTY OF _____, ss:

I, _____, Clerk of the _____ Court of the County and State aforesaid, do hereby certify that _____ is _____, duly commissioned and qualified, and that he has authority to administer oaths for general purposes; that his commission was dated on the _____ day of _____, 18___, and will expire on the _____ day of _____, 189___, and that his signature within written is genuine.

GIVEN under my hand and the seal of said Court this _____ day of _____, 189___.

_____
Clerk.

INSTRUCTIONS TO MAGISTRATES.

Magistrate should compare this voucher with pension certificate, exercising the utmost care in its execution.

Vouchers may be executed before any officer authorized to administer oaths for general purposes. If he has a seal it should be affixed ; if not, a certificate of the proper officer, showing the commencement and termination of his term of office, must be filed in this Agency. Vouchers may also be executed before fourth-class postmasters.

INSTRUCTIONS TO PENSIONERS.

Give the magistrate the exact post-office address (street and number) to which you wish the check to be sent, and see that it is written in its place in the voucher.

Delay is occasioned by errors in giving post-office address.

State: _____
County: _____
Town: _____
Street: _____
Name: _____

WRITE NAME AND P. O. ADDRESS PLAINLY HERE.

(Other side of document below.)

3—281

Magistrate and pensioner before executing this voucher should read carefully the special instructions on face and back of same.

DO NOT EXECUTE BEFORE

B   **WIDOW.**   FEB 4 1897   **B**

Be it known, That I *Sarah A. Jordan* do solemnly swear that I am the identical person named in pension certificate in my possession, No. *3769*, dated *16* day of *met*, 18*8*
and whose name is inscribed on the rolls of the **Topeka** Agency at the rate of *8* dollar per month,

That I am the widow *Andrew V. Jordan*, who was a *Pt*
and that I have not remarried since his death; that my P. O. address is
in the County of
State of

(If pensioner signs by mark, two witnesses who can write.)

(Pensioner's signature.)   *Sarah A Jordan*

DEPOSITION OF TWO WITNESSES.

We, the undersigned witnesses, do solemnly swear that we are well acquainted with the above-named pensioner; that she is the identical person that she represents herself to be; and that, to our best knowledge and belief, she has not remarried since the death of her late husband, above named; and that our acquaintance with her is such that, if she had resumed marriage relations, the fact would have become known to us.

(If mark is made, one witness is sufficient in addition to magistrate's jurat.)

(Witness' signature.)

(Witness' signature.)

THE PENSION CERTIFICATE MUST BE EXHIBITED TO THE MAGISTRATE WHEN THIS VOUCHER IS EXECUTED.

State of _____, County of _____, ss:

Personally appeared before me, this _____ day of _____, 189 , the above witnesses,
of _____, and
of _____, whom I
believe to be credible persons, and the pensioner, above named, and made oath in due form of law to the truth of the foregoing statements subscribed by them; and I certify that the aforesaid pensioner has this day exhibited to me her pension certificate, above described, and signed the following duplicate receipts in my presence.

(If mark is made, one witness is sufficient in addition to jurat of magistrate, who must certify to any erasures or alterations.)

(Magistrate's signature.)

(Official character.)

THE PENSIONER WILL SIGN THESE RECEIPTS IN THE PRESENCE OF THE MAGISTRATE.

Received of **G. W. GLICK.**, U. S. Pension Agent at **TOPEKA, KAS**,
Twenty-four ____ dollars by check No. _____
dated _____, 189 , being for *3* months' and _____ days' pension due me
on pension certificate No. *3169*, from the *4* day of NOV 1896 , 189 , to
the *4* day of FEB 1897 , 189 , for which I have signed duplicate receipts.

S E Jordan   *Sarah A Jordan*

(B.)

Received of **G. W. GLICK.**, U. S. Pension Agent at **TOPEKA, KAS**
_____ dollars by check No. _____
dated _____ 189 , being for *3* months' and _____ days' pension due me
on pension certificate No. *3169*, from the *4* day of NOV 1896 , 189 , to
the *4* day of FEB 1897 , 189 , for which I have signed duplicate receipts.

S. A. Jordan   *Sarah A Jordan*

Receipts MUST NOT be dated.

(Copy of original document from case.)

◇◇◇◇◇

Cherokee
1874.

Muskogee, Indian Territory, December 24, 1906.

Sarah A. Jordan,
    Bartlesville, Indian Territory.

Dear Madam:

    November 6, 1906, the United States Supreme Court held that white persons who intermarried with Cherokee citizens according to Cherokee law prior to November 1, 1875, are entitled to enrollment and allotments of land as citizens of the Cherokee Nation.

    You are advised that to properly determine your right to enrollment as a citizen by intermarriage of the Cherokee Nation, it will be necessary for you to appear before the Commissioner for the purpose of giving testimony as to the date of your marriage and whether or not your husband, by reason of your marriage to whom you claim the right to enrollment as a citizen by intermarriage of the Cherokee Nation, was a recognized Cherokee citizen at the time of your marriage to him.

    You are, therefore, directed to appear before the Commissioner at Muskogee, Indian Territory, at 9 o'clock A. M., on Thursday, January 3, 1907, and give testimony as above indicated.

                         Respectfully,

LMC   Acting Commissioner.

◇◇◇◇◇

(The above letter given again.)

◇◇◇◇◇

Cherokee Intermarried White 1906
Volume IX

Cherokee 1874.

Muskogee, Indian Territory, February 26, 1907.

Sarah A. Jordan,
      Bartlesville, Indian Territory.

Dear Madam:

      There is enclosed herewith a copy of the decision of the Commissioner to the Five Civilized Tribes, dated February 26, 1907, rejecting the application for your enrollment as a citizen by intermarriage of the Cherokee Nation.

      The decision, together with the record of proceedings had in the case, has this day been transmitted to the Secretary of the Interior for his review and decision. You will be advised of the Secretary's action as soon as this office is informed of same.

Respectfully,

SIGNED *Tams Bixby*

Encl. H-112   Commissioner.
   JMH

Register.

◇◇◇◇◇

Cherokee 1874

Muskogee, Indian Territory, February 26, 1907.

W. W. Hastings,
      Attorney for the Cherokee Nation,
            Muskogee, Indian Territory.

Dear Sir:

      There is enclosed herewith a copy of the decision of the Commissioner to the Five Civilized Tribes, dated February 26, 1907, rejecting the application for the enrollment of Sarah A. Jordan as a citizen by intermarriage of the Cherokee Nation.

      The decision, together with the record of proceedings had in the case, has this day been transmitted to the Secretary of the Interior for his review and decision. You will be advised of the Secretary's action as soon as this office is informed of same.

Respectfully,

SIGNED *Jams Bixby*

Encl. H-113   Commissioner.
JMH

◇◇◇◇◇◇

COPY

Muskogee, Indian Territory, February 26, 1907.

The Honorable,
        The Secretary of the Interior.

Sir:

There is transmitted herewith the record of proceedings had in the matter of the application for the enrollment of Sarah A. Jordan as a citizen by intermarriage of the Cherokee Nation, together with the decision of the Commissioner, dated February 19, 1907, denying said application.

Respectfully,

SIGNED *Jams Bixby*

Encl H-114   Commissioner.
JMH

Through the Commissioner
of Indian Affairs.

◇◇◇◇◇◇

(COPY)

DEPARTMENT OF THE INTERIOR,
OFFICE OF INDIAN AFFAIRS,
LAND   WASHINGTON/[sic]

The Honorable,
        The Secretary of the Interior.

Sir:

I have the honor to invite your attention to the enclosed records of the Commissioner to the Five Civilized Tribes in certain intermarried Cherokee cases, wherein the Commissioner determined that the applicants were not entitled to enrollment:

25

21892- Mary M. Reece;
21893- Joseph A. Thompson;
21898- Joseph B. Ladd;
21884- Sarah A. Jordan.

The record in the case of Sarah Jordan shows that her name appears on the 1880 approved roll of the Cherokee Nation, as well as the 1896 census roll. Under the opinion of the Attorney General of the United States, of February 26, 1907, persons whose names appear on the Cherokee tribal roll of 1880, which was confirmed by the Act of June 28, 1898, are entitled to enrollment in the Cherokee Nation under subsequent laws. It is therefore recommended that the decision of the Commissioner be reversed and that Sarah A. Jordan be enrolled as a citizen of the Cherokee Nation.

As to the other cases, after an investigation made in the Office it has been determined that the decisions of the Commissioner are correct and it is recommended that they be approved.

Very respectfully,

C. F Larrabee,

EBH-GH.   Acting Commissioner.

◇◇◇◇◇

SPECIAL.

DEPARTMENT OF THE INTERIOR,   FHE   JRJr.

I. T. D.   WASHINGTON/[sic]
8034-1907.

LRS.   March 4, 1907

DIRECT.

Commissioner to the Five Civilized Tribes,
        Muskogee, Indian Territory.

Sir:

The Department hereby affirms your decisions adverse to the applicants in the following Intermarried Cherokee enrollment cases, received with your letters of February 28, 1907, and Indian Office letter of March 4, 1907 (Land 21892 et al.), copy inclosed, viz:

Mary M. Reese
Josephine A. Thompson
Joseph B. Ladd.

Relative to the Sarah A. Jordan case, also received with said Indian Office letter, the Department, concurring in the recommendation of the Indian Office, considers that said Jordan is entitled to enrollment as an intermarried Cherokee, in view of the opinion of the Attorney-General in the Gleason case, and that of the Assistant Attorney-General in the Bartles case. Your decision as to her, dated February 26, 1907, is accordingly reversed, and you are directed to enroll said Sarah A. Jordan as a citizen by intermarriage of the Cherokee Nation.

The papers in all the cases mentioned have been sent to the Indian Office with a copy hereof.

Respectfully,

Jesse E Wilson,
Acting Secretary.

1 inc and
__ for Ind Of. with
copy hereof.

AFMc
3-4-07.

Copy

◇◇◇◇◇

Cherokee 1874   COPY

Muskogee, Indian Territory, March 21, 1907.

Sarah A. Jordan,
        Bartlesville, Indian Territory.

Dear Madam:

You are hereby advised that the decision of the Commissioner to the Five Civilized Tribes, dated February 26, 1907, rejecting your application for enrollment as a citizen by intermarriage of the Cherokee Nation, was reversed by the Secretary of the Interior, March 4, 1907, and said application granted.

For your information, there is enclosed herewith a copy of Departmental decision referred to.

Respectfully,

Commissioner.

Encl. H-102
    JMH

◇◇◇◇◇

Cherokee MM-20,   COPY
R-3, 10091, 1874.

Muskogee, Indian Territory, March 21, 1907.

W. W. Hastings,
     Attorney for the Cherokee Nation,
        Muskogee, Indian Territory.

Dear Sir:

     You are hereby advised that the decisions of the Commissioner to the Five Civilized Tribes, dated February 28, 1907, rejecting the applications for the enrollment of Mary M. Reese, Josephine A. Thompson and Joseph B. Ladd, as citizens by intermarriage of the Cherokee Nation, were affirmed, and decision of February 26, 1907, rejecting the application for the enrollment of Sarah A. Jordan, as a citizen by intermarriage, was reversed by the Secretary of the Interior, March 4, 1907.

     For your information, there is enclosed herewith a copy of Departmental decision referred to.

                Respectfully,

                         SIGNED *Jams Bixby*
                         Commissioner.

Encl. H-103
JMH

<><><><><>

Cherokee
N B 1874

             Muskogee, Indian Territory, March 26, 1907.

John D. Jordan,
     Ramona, Indian Territory.

Dear Sir:-

     In reply to your letter of March 11, 1907, you are advised that the decision of the Commissioner to the Five Civilized Tribes refusing the application for the enrollment of Sarah A. Jordan as a citizen by intermarriage of the Cherokee Nation was, on March 4, 1907, reversed by the Secretary of the Interior. You will be duly advised when her name is placed upon a schedule of such citizens approved by the Secretary of the Interior.

     That part of your letter requesting a ticket of admission to the Cherokee Land Office will be made the subject of a separate communication.

Respectfully,

L M B

Acting Commissioner

◇◇◇◇◇

(The above letter given again.)

◇◇◇◇◇

GAW

DEPARTMENT OF THE INTERIOR
OFFICE OF INDIAN AFFAIRS,
WASHINGTON.

I.T.
References in body
of letter.

May 11, 1907.

Subject: Motions for
review in certain Chero-
kee citizenship cases.

The Honorable,
    The Secretary of the Interior.

Sir:

    There are inclosed herewith motions filed by W. W. Hastings, National Attorney for the Cherokee Nation, praying for review and rehearing of Departmental decisions authorizing the enrollment as citizens by intermarriage of the Cherokee Nation of the following persons:

42893-1907,	Jacob A. Bartles,
42895- "	Osburn J. Byrd,
42886- "	Amanda Beck,
42894- "	Sarah F. Gage,
42892- "	Phirena Harris,
42888- "	Daniel Harmon,
42891- "	Emma L. Ironsides,
42896- "	Sarah A. Jordan
42881- "	Dovie Johnson,
42882- "	Andrew H. Norwood,
42887- "	Stacy E. Perry,
42885- "	Martha Randolph, now Kernan
42893- "	John W. Smith

42884-	"	John J. Smith,
42890-	"	Robert H. F. Thompson,
42889-	"	Hattie Wright,
42883-	"	Nancy Wolfe,
42880-	"	E. A. Welch.

In view of the provisions of section 2 of the act of April 26, 1906 (34 Stat. L., 137), providing that the rolls of the Five Civilized Tribes shall be fully completed on or before March 4, 1907, there appears to be no authority in law for the reconsideration of any enrollment cases at this time, and it is recommended that the office be authorized to advise Mr. Hastings that the motions for review herewith transmitted cannot be considered.

Very respectfully,

C. F. Larrabee

Acting Commissioner.

AJW-FHE.

May 13, 1907.

Approved.

Thos Ryan

First Assistant Secretary.

◇◇◇◇◇

I. T. References
in body of letter.

DEPARTMENT OF THE INTERIOR,
OFFICE OF INDIAN AFFAIRS,
WASHINGTON.   GAW

May 15, 1907.

Commissioner to the Five Civilized Tribes,
Muskogee, Indian Territory.

Sir:

There is inclosed copy of Office letter of May 11, 1907, approved by the Department on May 13, 1907, recommending that motions filed by W. W. Hastings, National Attorney for the Cherokee Nation, praying for a review and rehearing of

Departmental decisions authorizing the enrollment of the following persons as citizens by intermarriage of the Cherokee Nation, be denied, in view of the fact that there appears to be no authority in law at this time for the reconsideration of any enrollment case.

42893-1907	Jacob A. Bartles
42895- "	Osburn J. Byrd
42886- "	Amanda Beck
42894- "	Sarah F. Gage
42892- "	Phirena Harris
42888- "	Daniel Harmon
42891- "	Emma L. Ironsides
42896- "	Sarah A. Jordan
42881- "	Dovie Johnson
42882- "	Andrew H. Norwood
42887- "	Stacy E. Perry
42885- "	Martha Randolph, now Kernan
42893- "	John W. Smith
42884- "	John J. Smith
42890- "	Robert H. F. Thompson
42889- "	Hattie Wright
42883- "	Nancy Wolfe
42880- "	E. A. Welch

You are requested to advise the interested parties, including Mr. Hastings, of the Department's action.

Very respectfully,
C. F. Larrabee
Acting Commissioner.

AJW-FHE.

◇◇◇◇◇

Cherokee
253.   et al

Muskogee, Indian Territory, May 25, 1907.

W. W. Hastings,
Attorney for the Cherokee Nation,
Muskogee, Indian Territory.

Dear Sir:

You are hereby advised that on May 13, 1907, the Secretary of the Interior denied the motion filed by you for a review of its decision authorizing the enrollment of Jacob A. Bartles, et al., as citizens by intermarriage of the Cherokee Nation.

For your information, there is enclosed herewith a copy of Departmental decision referred to.

Respectfully,

Commissioner.

Encl. C-20
LMC

◇◇◇◇◇

Cherokee
249

Muskogee, Indian Territory, May 25, 1907.

Sarah A. Jordan,
    Bartlesville, Indian Territory.

Dear Madam:

You are hereby advised that on May 13, 1907, the Secretary of the Interior denied the motion filed by the Attorney for the Cherokee Nation, for a review of its decision authorizing your enrollment as a citizen by intermarriage of the Cherokee Nation.

For your information, there is enclosed herewith a copy of Departmental decision referred to.

Respectfully,

Commissioner.

Encl. C-9
    LMC

Cher IW 250

◇◇◇◇◇

COPY

Department of the Interior.
Commission to the Five Civilized Tribes.
Tahlequah, I. T., December 13, 1900.

In the matter of the application of Rober[sic] H. F. Thompson for the enrollment of himself, wife and child as Cherokee citizens; he being sworn and examined by Commissioner C. R. Breckinridge, testified as follows:

Q Give me your full name.   A Robert H. F. Thompson.
Q How old are you?   A 60 years old.

Cherokee Intermarried White 1906
Volume IX

Q What is your postoffice?   A I have just recently moved in the last week. My former postoffice is Westville.

Q Where do you want us to address a letter to you in case we wish to write to you?
A Kansas.

Q What district are you living in?   A Delaware.

Q Who is it you want to enroll; yourself and family?   A Myself, wife and part of my children.

Q How many children have you that are under 21 years of age and not married?
A Only one.

Q Are you a Cherokee by blood?   A White man.

Q Is your wife a Cherokee by blood?   A Yes sir.

Q When were you married to your wife?   A In '72.

Q Have you lived with her ever since you were married?   A Yes sir.

Q And all the time in the Cherokee Nation?   A With the exception of four years.

Q What four years?   A I went back to the state of Georgia in the winter of '74 and came back in '78.

Q Live here ever since '78?   A Yes sir.

Q You are on the roll of 1880, are you?   A Yes sir.

Q Give me the name of your wife. A Narcissa.

Q How old is she?   A About 53.

Q You and your wife have lived together ever since you were married in '72?
A Yes sir.

Q Give the name of this child?   A Ethel.

Q How old is Ethel?   A 12 years old.

Q She's living with you now, is she?   A Yes sir.

1880 roll; page 397, #1351, R.H.F. Thompson, Flint district.
1880 roll; page 397, #1352, Narsissa[sic] "
1896 roll; page 829, #191, Robert H.   "   Goingsnake district
1896 roll; page 797, #2136, Narcissa   "
1896 roll; page 797, #2141, Ethel   "

Commissioner Breckinridge-

The applicant applies for the enrollment of himself, his wife, and one child. He is identified on the roll of 1880 and 1896 as an adopted Cherokee. He is a white man. He has lived in the Cherokee Nation and with his Cherokee wife since prior to his enrollment in 1880, and he will now be listed for enrollment as a Cherokee by intermarriage. His wife is identified on the rolls of 1880 and 1896 as a native Cherokee. she has lived in the Cherokee Nation since prior to her enrollment in 1880, and she will now be listed for enrollment as a Cherokee by blood. The child, Ethel, a minor, is identified with her parents on the roll of 1896. She is living with them now, and will be listed for enrollment as a Cherokee by blood.

———

E. G. Rothenberger, being duly sworn, states that as stenographer to the Commission to the Five Civilized Tribes, he reported in full the testimony and proceedings in the above case, and that the foregoing is a full, true and correct transcript of his stenographic notes in said case.

E.G. Rothenberger

Subscribed and sworn to before me this 14th day of December, 1900.

T. B. Needles.

Endorsement.

DEPARTMENT OF THE INTERIOR   Commissioner.
COMMISSION TO THE FIVE CIVILIZED TRIBES
                    FILED
          DEC 15 1900
               Tams Bixby, Acting Chairman

◇◇◇◇◇

R.
Cher. 6571.

Department of the Interior,
Commission to the Five Civilized Tribes.
Tahlequah, I. T., October 6, 1902.

SUPPLEMENTAL TESTIMONY AND PROCEEDINGS in the matter of the application for the enrollment of ROBERT H. F. THOMPSON as a citizen by intermarriage of the Cherokee Nation.

ROBERT H. F. THOMPSON, being first duly sworn, and being examined testified as follows:

BY COMMISSION: What is your name?   A Robert H. F. Thompson.
Q How old are you?   A I am sixty-two.
Q What is your post office address?   A Kansas, I. T.
Q Are you a white man?   A Yes sir.
Q Have you heretofore made application to this Commission for enrollment as a citizen by intermarriage of the Cherokee Nation?   A Yes sir.
Q What is the name of your wife?   A Narcissa.
Q Is she living?   A Yes sir.
Q Is she a Cherokee by blood?   A Yes sir.
Q When were you and she married?   A About thirty years ago.
Q Have you and she lived together continuously since the date of your marriage?
A We have.
Q Are you living together now?   A We are.
Q Do you claim your right to enrollment by reason of your marriage to her?   A Yes sir.
Q Were you ever married before you married her?   A Yes sir.
Q What was the name of your former wife? A Mary Cowart.

Q Is she living?   A No sir.

Q Was she a Cherokee by blood? A Yes sir.

Q Did you and she lived together until the time of her death? A Yes sir.

Q Do you know her former husband's name?   A Her husband's name was Lemuel Cowart.

Q Did she live with him until he died?   A Yes sir.

Q Was your second wife ever married before she married you?   A No sir.

Q Have you resided in the Cherokee Nation continuously since the date of your application for enrollment?   A Yes sir.

This testimony will be filed with and made a part of the record in the matter of the application for the enrollment of Robert H. F. Thompson as a citizen by intermarriage of the Cherokee Nation.

Wm. Hutchinson, being first duly sworn, states that as stenographer to the Commission to the Five Civilized Tribes he correctly recorded the testimony and proceedings in this case, and that the foregoing is a true and complete transcript of the stenographic notes thereof.

Wm Hutchinson

Subscribed and sworn to before me this 10th day of October, 1902.

Copy

John O Rosson
Notary Public.

◇◇◇◇◇

C. F. B.   Cherokee 6571.

DEPARTMENT OF THE INTERIOR,
COMMISSION TO THE FIVE CIVILIZED TRIBES.
Muskogee, Indian Territory, January 7, 1907.

In the Matter of the Application for the Enrollment of Robert H. F. Thompson as a citizen by intermarriage of the Cherokee Nation.

Applicant appears in person.

APPEARANCES:

Cherokee Nation represented by
W. W. Hastings, Attorney.

Robert H. F. Thompson being first duly sworn by John E. Tidwell, Notary Public, testified as follows:

ON BEHALF OF COMMISSIONER.

Cherokee Intermarried White 1906
Volume IX

Q   What is your name?   A   Robert H. F. Thompson.
Q   What is your age?   A   67.
Q   What is your post office address?
A   Row.
Q   You are an applicant for enrollment as a citizen by intermarriage of the Cherokee Nation?
A   Yes sir.
Q   You have no Cherokee blood?
A   No sir.
Q   Your only claim to the right to enrollment as a citizen of the Cherokee Nation is by virtue of your marriage to a citizen by blood?
A   Yes sir.
Q   What is the name of the citizen through whom you claim that right?
A   Narcissa Thompson; Brown before we married.
Q   Is she living?
A   Yes sir.
Q   When did you marry her?
A   '72.
Q   Was she a recognized citizen of the Cherokee Nation at the time you married her?
A   So far as I know, she was.
Q   Was she living in the Cherokee country?
A   Yes sir.
Q   Since you marriage to her, have you and she continuously lived in the Cherokee Nation?
A   No sir; I was absent from the Cherokee Nation nearly 4 years.
Q   Was she absent with you?
A   Yes sir.
Q   During what years?
A   I believe it was in the fall of '74 that I went to Atlanta, Georgia, and came back in '79.
Q   What was the cause of your absence?
A   Visiting my family relations.
Q   When you left the Cherokee Nation to go to Georgia, did you have a home in the nation?
A   Yes sir.
Q   Did you keep your home during your residence in Georgia?
A   No sir; I didn't keep my home but I left part of my effects here.
Q   Was it your intention to return to the Cherokee Nation?
A   Yes sir.
Q   And your presence in Georgia was in the nature of a visit?
A   Yes sir.
Q   Did you marry your wife in accordance with the laws of the Cherokee Nation?
A   I have been married twice in the Cherokee Nation. My first wife, Mary A. Thompson, I married in 1869 according to the Cherokee law; that is, I got a petition and it was signed by so many citizens as to my good character. I then went to the District Clerk, secured license, took the oath of allegiance to the Cherokee Nation,

was married and returned my license. That was in 1869. In 1970 my first wife died and in '72, I married my second wife.

Q   Was she a Cherokee by blood also?
A   Yes sir.
Q   Your first wife was a Cherokee by blood?
A   Yes sir.
Q   Was your wife Mary A. ever married prior to her marriage to you?
A   No sir.
Q   Was she your first wife?
A   Yes sir.
Q   In what district was that license issued authorizing your marriage to your first wife?
A   Flint District.
Q   Who do you remember who issued it?[sic]
A   J. Warren Adair.
Q   Who married you?
A   Reverend Duncan.
Q   You and your second wife have continuously lived together as husband and wife from the date of your marriage up to the present time?
A   Yes sir.

The applicant, Robert H. F. Thompson is identified on the Cherokee authenticated tribal roll of 1880, Flint District, No. 1351. The name of his second wife, Narcissa Thompson, appears on said roll at No. 1352 and is included in the approved partial roll of citizens of the Cherokee Nation, opposite No. 15739.

Q   What was the name of your first wife's father?
A   William Dameron.
Q   What was her mother's name?
A   Nancy.
Q   Did they live long enough for their names to appear on the 1880 roll?
A   I don't hardly believe they did.
Q   Has your first wife any relatives who reside in the Cherokee Nation?
A   I don't know that I could locate any.

ON BEHALF OF CHEROKEE NATION.

Q   Where did you live when you left the Cherokee Nation in '74 to back to Georgia?
A   I was living in Flint District, at Stilwell.
Q   Did you have a farm there then?
A   Yes sir.
Q   About what size farm?
A   It was a small place.
Q   Did you dispose of it in '74?
A   Yes sir.
Q   To whom?
A   To George Starr.

Q   Did you have any children born when you went back to Georgia?
A   Yes sir.
Q   Did you go to visit your folks or your wife's folks?
A   My folks.
Q   What did you do the four or five years you were in Georgia?
A   I run a blacksmith shop and a little country store.
Q   You went in the mercantile business did you?
A   Yes sir.
Q   And also conducted a blacksmith shop?
A   Yes sir.
Q   It was your mercantile business?
A   Yes sir.
Q   And you blacksmith shop?
A   Yes sir.
Q   In the State of Georgia?
A   Yes sir.
Q   And you continued to do that until about '79?
A   Yes sir.
Q   And then you returned to this country?
A   Yes sir.
Q   You had no home in this country during that time?
A   No; I had no place here.
Q   You spoke of leaving some effects here?
A   Yes sir.
Q   What effects?
A   Some household furniture and some bedding and some other things.
Q   With whom?
A   My father-in-law; old man Brown.
Q   You went back to Georgia by wagon?
A   No sir.
Q   Where did you take the train?
A   At Altus, Arkansas; that was the terminus of the road then.
Q   What became of this household furniture?
A   It was there when I returned from Georgia.
Q   That was such as you couldn't very conveniently take with you?
A   That was it.
Q   Did you buy you a place in Georgia?
A   No sir.
Q   Did you by a house?
A   No sir.
Q   Rent one?
A   No sir.
Q   But you bought you a mercantile store?
A   No, I just bought a small affair there to pay my expenses while I was there. The property, I rented. I rented a wagon yard and there was a blacksmith shop on the place and a store there. The man had about $150 worth of goods.

Q   You stayed there five years?

A   I went there in the fall of '74 and came back here in the fall of '79.

Q   Were you ever married prior to the time you married your wife, Mary A. Thompson?

A   No sir.

Q   What relative lived near you in Georgia?

A   My brother.

Q   Your father living?

A   No sir.

Q   When did he die?

A   He died the year I came back here from Georgia; '79.

Q   Your mother survived your father?

A   No, she's been dead for 40 odd years.

Q   Had your father been sick any length of time when he died or did he die of some disease?

A   He died suddenly.

Q   Are you on the 1880 roll?

A   I think so.

The original marriage records, Flint District, Cherokee Nation, book "B" in possession of this office, show that on April 1, 1869, a license was issued by James W. Adair, district clerk Flint District, authorizing the marriage of Robert H. F. Thompson, a citizen of the United States, and Mary Cowart, a Cherokee by birth, and that said parties were united in marriage in accordance with the terms of said license April 1, 1869, by W. A. Duncan, Minister of the Gospel.

The undersigned being first duly sworn states that as stenographer to the Commission to the Five Civilized Tribes, she correctly recorded the testimony taken in this case and that the foregoing is a full, true and correct transcript of her stenographic notes thereof.

Myrtle Hill

Subscribed and sworn to before me this the 8th day of January, 1907.

John E. Tidwell
Notary Public.

◇◇◇◇◇

C.F.B. Cherokee 6571.

DEPARTMENT OF THE INTERIOR,

COMMISSIONER TO THE FIVE CIVILIZED TRIBES.

———————————

In the matter of the application for the enrollment of ROBERT H. F. THOMPSON as a citizen by intermarriage of the Cherokee Nation.

D E C I S I O N

THE RECORDS OF THIS OFFICE SHOW: That on December 13, 1900, application was received by the Commission to the Five Civilized Tribes for the enrollment of Robert H. F. Thompson as a citizen by intermarriage of the Cherokee Nation. Further proceedings in the matter of said application were had at Tahlequah, Indian Territory, October 6, 1902, and at Muskogee, Indian Territory, January 7, 1907.

THE EVIDENCE IN THIS CASE SHOWS: That the applicant herein, Robert H. F. Thompson, a white man, was married in accordance with Cherokee law April 1, 1869, to his wife, Mary A. Thompson, nee Cowart, a recognized citizen by blood of the Cherokee Nation; that the said Mary A. Thompson died in 1870, and in 1874 the applicant herein was lawfully married to Narcissa Thompson, nee Brown, who was at the time of said marriage a recognized citizen by blood of the Cherokee Nation, and who is identified[sic] on the Cherokee authenticated tribal roll of 1880, Flint District, No. 1352, as a native Cherokee; that subsequent to said marriage the said Narcissa Thompson removed, with her said husband, to the State of Georgia, where they continuously resided for a period of about four years, and during which time they neither owned nor controlled any property in the Cherokee Nation.

Section 2, Article 1, of the Cherokee Constitution, in part provides:

"Whenever any citizen shall remove with his effects out of the limits of this Nation, and becomes a citizen of any other government, all his rights and privileges as a citizen of this Nation shall cease."

It is further shown that after their return to the Cherokee Nation, in the year 1879, the said Narcissa Thompson was readmitted to citizenship in said Nation by the duly constituted authorities thereof December 10, 1879, no mention being made in said at of readmission of the applicant, Robert H. F. Thompson.

In view of the foregoing, it is considered that the applicant herein, Robert H. F. Thompson, forfeited, under the provisions of Section 2, Article 1, of the Cherokee Constitution above noted, by reason of his removal from the Cherokee Nation and his continued residence in the State of Georgia for a period of four or five years, any right that he may have possessed to citizenship in the Cherokee Nation; and that he acquired no right to enrollment as a citizen by intermarriage of the Cherokee Nation by reason of the readmission to citizenship in the Cherokee Nation of his wife, the said Narcissa Thompson, December 10, 1879.

IT IS, THEREFORE, ORDERED AND ADJUDGED: That in accordance with the decision of the Supreme Court of the United States, dated November 5, 1906, in the cases of Daniel Red Bird, et al., vs. the United States, Nos. 125, 126, 127, and 128, the said applicant, Robert H. F. Thompson, is not entitled, under the provisions of Section 21 of the Act of Congress approved June 28, 1898 (30 Stats. 495), to enrollment as a citizen by intermarriage of the Cherokee Nation, and his application for enrollment as such is accordingly denied.

Tams Bixby
Commissioner.

Dated at Muskogee, Indian Territory,
this   Feb 22 1907

Copy

◇◇◇◇◇

C.F.B.

COPY

DEPARTMENT OF THE INTERIOR,

COMMISSIONER TO THE FIVE CIVILIZED TRIBES.

In the matter of the application for the enrollment of ROBERT H. F. THOMPSON as a citizen by intermarriage of the Cherokee Nation.

An examination of the records of the Cherokee Nation in the possession of this office of persons admitted to Cherokee citizenship by the National Council and the Supreme Court of the Cherokee Nation since the Treaty of 1866 shows that Mrs. Narcissa Thompson, Jesse, Andrew L., Robert H., Hattie E. and James C. Thompson, wife and children of the applicant herein, Robert H. F. Thompson, were admitted to citizenship in the Cherokee Nation December 10, 1879.

It is ordered that this statement be filed with and made a part of the record in the matter of the application for the enrollment of Robert H. F. Thompson as a citizen by intermarriage of the Cherokee Nation.

SIGNED   *Tams Bixby*
Commissioner.

Dated at Muskogee, Indian Territory,
this   FEB 22 1907

◇◇◇◇◇

41

COMMISSIONERS:
HENRY L. DAWES,
TAMS BIXBY,
THOMAS B. NEEDLES,
C. R. BRECKINRIDGE.

DEPARTMENT OF THE INTERIOR,
COMMISSION TO THE FIVE CIVILIZED TRIBES.

Cherokee No. 6571

ALLISON L. AYLESWORTH,
SECRETARY.

ADDRESS ONLY THE
COMMISSION TO THE FIVE CIVILIZED TRIBES.

Muskogee, Indian Territory,   **September 25th**   1902

Robert H. F. Thompson,
   Kansas, Indian Territory.

Dear Sir:

The Act of Congress, approved July 1, 1902, and entitled "An Act To provide for the enrollment of the lands of the Cherokee Nation, for the disposition of town sites therein, and for other purposes," (Public No. 241), provides that "the roll of citizens of the Cherokee Nation shall be made as of September first, nineteen-hundred and two."

In accordance with said provision, you are hereby notified that the Commission to the Five Civilized Tribes will be at its offices at Muskogee, Indian Territory, until Friday, October 31, 1902, inclusive, for the purpose of affording you an opportunity to show that you have not, between the date of the original application for your enrollment and Sept 2, 1902, forfeited your right as a citizen by intermarriage of the Cherokee Nation.

This evidence should be introduced immediately, as it is necessary in determining your right to share in the allotment of the lands of the Cherokee Nation, and until the same is furnished no further action can be taken looking toward your final enrollment as an intermarried citizen.

Yours truly,

Tams Bixby
Acting Chairman.

◇◇◇◇◇

Cherokee
6571

Muskogee, Indian Territory, December 27, 1906.

Robert H. F. Thompson,
Chance, Indian Territory.

Dear Sir:

November 6, 1906, the United States Supreme Court held that white persons who intermarried with Cherokee citizens according to Cherokee law prior to November 1, 1875, are entitled to enrollment and allotments of land as citizens of the Cherokee Nation.

You are advised that to properly determine your right to enrollment as a citizen by intermarriage of the Cherokee Nation, it will be necessary for you to appear before the Commissioner for the purpose of giving testimony as to the date of your marriage and whether or not your wife, by reason of your marriage to whom you claim the right to enrollment as a citizen of the Cherokee Nation, was a recognized citizen of the Cherokee Nation at the time of your marriage to her, and whether or not you were married to her in accordance with Cherokee laws.

You are therefore directed to appear before the Commissioner at Muskogee, Indian Territory, at 9 o'clock A. M., on Saturday, January 5, 1907, and give testimony as above indicated.

Respectfully,

S.W.   Acting Commissioner.

◇◇◇◇◇

Cherokee 6571

Muskogee, Indian Territory, February 22, 1907.

W. W. Hastings,
Attorney for the Cherokee Nation,
Muskogee, Indian Territory.

Dear Sir:

There is enclosed herewith a copy of the decision of the Commissioner to the Five Civilized Tribes, dated February 22, 1907, rejecting the application for the enrollment of Robert H. F. Thompson, as a citizen by intermarriage of the Cherokee Nation.

The decision, together with the record of proceedings had in the case, has this day been transmitted to the Secretary of the Interior for his review and decision. You will be advised of the Secretary's action as soon as this office is informed of same.

Respectfully,

Commissioner.

Encl. A-76
RA

◇◇◇◇◇

Muskogee, Indian Territory, February 22, 1907.

The Honorable,
    The Secretary of the Interior.

Sir:

There is transmitted herewith the record of proceedings had in the matter of the application for the enrollment of Robert H. F. Thompson as a citizen by intermarriage of the Cherokee Nation, together with the decision of the Commissioner, dated February 22, 1907, denying said application.

Respectfully,

Commissioner.

Encl. A-77
RA

Through the Commissioner
    of Indian Affairs.

◇◇◇◇◇

Cherokee 6571

Muskogee, Indian Territory, February 22, 1907.

Robert H. F. Thompson,
    Row, Indian Territory.

Dear Sir:

There is enclosed herewith a copy of the decision of the Commissioner to the Five Civilized Tribes, dated February 22, 1907, rejecting the application for your enrollment as a citizen by intermarriage of the Cherokee Nation.

44

The decision, together with the record of proceedings had in the case, has this day been transmitted to the Secretary of the Interior for his review and decision. The action of the Secretary will be made known to you as soon as this office is informed of the same.

Respectfully,

Commissioner.

Encl. A-75
   RA

Register.

◇◇◇◇◇

D.C. 13347-1907   J.F.

W.H.M.

DEPARTMENT OF THE INTERIOR,

WASHINGTON.

I.T.D. 7780-1907.   March 4, 1907.
    7982- "
LRS

    <u>DIRECT</u>.

Commissioner to the Five Civilized Tribes,
    Muskogee, Indian Territory.

Sir:

By letter of this date, the Department affirmed your decision in the matter of the application of Robert H. F. Thompson for enrollment as a citizen by intermarriage of the Cherokee Nation. Your decision was adverse to applicant.

It appears from your telegram of March 4, 1907, filed in the Department this day, that Thompson was denied enrollment by the because of alleged forfeiture by removal from the Cherokee Nation for four years prior to 1880.

You state that your decision in the Thompson case does not show 1880 enrollment, but records show such enrollment.

Following the opinion of the Attorney-General in the John W. Gleason case, copy of which has been sent you, and the decision of the Department in the case of Jacob H. Bartles, the decision of the Department adverse to Thompson of March 4, 1907, is rescinded and his application for enrollment is granted.

45

His name will be placed upon the proper roll by your representative here.

A copy hereof has been sent to the Indian Office.

Respectfully,

Copy hereof to Ind. Of. (Signed) Jesse E. Wilson,
AFMc   Acting Secretary.
3-4-07

◇◇◇◇◇

D.C. 13378-1907.   Y.P.

                                                          W.H.M.
                    DEPARTMENT OF THE INTERIOR,
I.T.D. 7730, 7738-1907.
    7760, 7762- "   WASHINGTON.

L.R.S.   March 4, 1907.

Direct.

Commissioner to the Five Civilized Tribes,
    Muskogee, Indian Territory.

Sir'[sic]

Your decisions in the following Cherokee citizenship cases, adverse to the applicants, are hereby affirmed. Copies of Indian Office letters, submitting your reports and recommending that the decisions be affirmed, are enclosed herewith:

Title of case.	Date of your letter of transmittal.
Christina Foster (freedman),	February 23, 1907.
Theodore R. Vann (freedman),	February 27, 1907.
Alburton Brown (intermarriage),	February 23, 1907.
James A. Nolen (intermarriage),	February 27, 1907.
Jackson Kelly (intermarriage),	February 27, 1907.
Sarah J. Harlan (intermarriage),	February 27, 1907.
Amanda M. Keys (intermarriage),	February 20, 1907.
Robert H. F. Thompson (intermarriage),	February 22, 1907.
Nancy M. Jack, et al. (citizens),	February 25, 1907.
Fannie M. Elliott, et al (by blood)	February 26, 1907.

A copy hereof and all the papers in the above mentioned cases have been sent to the Indian Office.

Copy of Indian Office letter forwarding the first two cases will be found with the Mollie Owen, Chickasaw, case.

Respectfully,

E. A. Hitchcock

Secretary.

3 enclosures, and
20 enclosures to Ind. Of.,
with copy hereof.

W C F
3/5/07.

◇◇◇◇◇

(COPY)
DEPARTMENT OF THE INTERIOR,
OFFICE OF INDIAN AFFAIRS,
LAND   WASHINGTON.
19615-1907
19619-1907.   March 5, 1907.

The Honorable,
       The Secretary of the Interior.

Sir:

There are enclosed two reports from Commissioner Bixby, one dated February 20, 1907, transmitting the record relative to the application of Amanda M. Keys for enrollment as an intermarried citizen of the Cherokee Nation, and the other transmitting the record relative to the application of Robert H. F. Thompson for enrollment as an intermarried citizen of said nation, together with the Commissioner's decisions denying the applications.

The records have been examined and the decisions of the Commissioner have been found to be correct. Their approval is recommended.

Very respectfully,

C. F. Larrabee,

GAW-GH.   Acting Commissioner.

◇◇◇◇◇

Cherokee
6571.

Muskogee, Indian Territory, March 19, 1907.

W. W. Hastings,
　　Attorney for the Cherokee Nation,
　　　　Muskogee, Indian Territory.

Dear Sir:

　　You are hereby advised that the decision of the Commissioner to the Five Civilized Tribes, dated February 22, 1907, rejecting the application for the enrollment of Robert H. F. Thompson, as a citizen by intermarriage of the Cherokee Nation, was affirmed by the Secretary of the Interior, March 4, 1907.

　　For your information, there is enclosed herewith a copy of Departmental decision referred to.

　　　　　　　　　　Respectfully,
　　　　　　　　　　　　SIGNED *Jams Bixby*
　　　　　　　　　　　　Commissioner.

Encl. C-200
　LMC

◇◇◇◇◇

Cherokee 6571

Muskogee, Indian Territory, March 19, 1907.

Robert H. F. Thompson,
　　Chance, Indian Territory.

Dear Sir:

　　You are hereby advised that the decision of the Commissioner to the Five Civilized Tribes, dated February 22, 1907, rejecting your application for enrollment as a citizen by intermarriage of the Cherokee Nation, was affirmed by the Secretary of the Interior, March 4, 1907.

　　For your information, there is enclosed herewith a copy of Departmental decision referred to.

　　　　　　　　　　Respectfully,
　　　　　　　　　　　　SIGNED *Jams Bixby*
　　　　　　　　　　　　Commissioner.

Encl. H-38
　JMH

◇◇◇◇◇

GAW

DEPARTMENT OF THE INTERIOR
OFFICE OF INDIAN AFFAIRS,
WASHINGTON.

I.T.   May 11, 1907.
References in body
of letter.

Subject: Motions for
review in certain Chero-
kee citizenship cases.

The Honorable,
    The Secretary of the Interior.

Sir:

There are inclosed herewith motions filed by W. W. Hastings, National Attorney for the Cherokee Nation, praying for review and rehearing of Departmental decisions authorizing the enrollment as citizens by intermarriage of the Cherokee Nation of the following persons:

42893-1907,	Jacob A. Bartles,
42895- "	Osburn J. Byrd,
42886- "	Amanda Beck,
42894- "	Sarah F. Gage,
42892- "	Phirena Harris,
42888- "	Daniel Harmon,
42891- "	Emma L. Ironsides,
42896- "	Sarah A. Jordan
42881- "	Dovie Johnson,
42882- "	Andrew H. Norwood,
42887- "	Stacy E. Perry,
42885- "	Martha Randolph, now Kernan
42893- "	John W. Smith
42884- "	John J. Smith,
42890- "	Robert H. F. Thompson,
42889- "	Hattie Wright,
42883- "	Nancy Wolfe,
42880- "	E. A. Welch.

In view of the provisions of section 2 of the act of April 26, 1906 (34 Stat. L., 137), providing that the rolls of the Five Civilized Tribes shall be fully completed on or before March 4, 1907, there appears to be no authority in law for the reconsideration of any enrollment cases at this time, and it is recommended that the office be authorized to advise Mr. Hastings that the motions for review herewith transmitted cannot be considered.

Very respectfully,

C. F. Larrabee

Acting Commissioner.

AJW-FHE.

May 13, 1907.

Approved.

Thos Ryan

First Assistant Secretary.

◇◇◇◇◇

DEPARTMENT OF THE INTERIOR,

I. T. References   OFFICE OF INDIAN AFFAIRS,   GAW
in body of letter.   WASHINGTON.

May 15, 1907.

Commissioner to the Five Civilized Tribes,
      Muskogee, Indian Territory.

Sir:

There is inclosed copy of Office letter of May 11, 1907, approved by the Department on May 13, 1907, recommending that motions filed by W. W. Hastings, National Attorney for the Cherokee Nation, praying for a review and rehearing of Departmental decisions authorizing the enrollment of the following persons as citizens by intermarriage of the Cherokee Nation, be denied, in view of the fact that there appears to be no authority in law at this time for the reconsideration of any enrollment case.

42893-1907	Jacob A. Bartles
42895- "	Osburn J. Byrd
42886- "	Amanda Beck
42894- "	Sarah F. Gage

42892-	"	Phirena Harris
42888-	"	Daniel Harmon
42891-	"	Emma L. Ironsides
42896-	"	Sarah A. Jordan
42881-	"	Dovie Johnson
42882-	"	Andrew H. Norwood
42887-	"	Stacy E. Perry
42885-	"	Martha Randolph, now Kernan
42893-	"	John W. Smith
42884-	"	John J. Smith
42890-	"	Robert H. F. Thompson
42889-	"	Hattie Wright
42883-	"	Nancy Wolfe
42880-	"	E. A. Welch

You are requested to advise the interested parties, including Mr. Hastings, of the Department's action.

Very respectfully,
C. F. Larrabee
Acting Commissioner.

AJW-FHE.

◇◇◇◇◇

Cherokee
I.W. 250

Muskogee, Indian Territory, May 25, 1907.

Robert H. F. Thompson,
Chance, Indian Territory.

Dear Sir:

You are hereby advised that on May 13, 1907, the Secretary of the Interior denied a motion filed by the Attorney for the Cherokee Nation, for a review of its decision authorizing your enrollment as a citizen by intermarriage of the Cherokee Nation.

For your information, there is enclosed herewith a copy of Departmental decision referred to.

Respectfully,

Commissioner.

Encl. C-16
LMC

◇◇◇◇◇

Cherokee
   253 et al.

Muskogee, Indian Territory, May 25, 1907.

W. W. Hastings,
      Attorney for the Cherokee Nation,
         Muskogee, Indian Territory.

Dear Sir:

      You are hereby advised that on May 13, 1907, the Secretary of the Interior denied the motion filed by you for a review of its decision authorizing the enrollment of Jacob A. Bartles, et al., as citizens by intermarriage of the Cherokee Nation.

      For your information, there is enclosed herewith a copy of Departmental decision referred to.

Respectfully,

Commissioner.

Encl. C-20
   LMC

Cher IW 251

◇◇◇◇◇

R
Cher   **D 1786**

Department of the Interior,
Commission to the Five Civilized Tribes,
Muskogee, I. T., June 30, 1902.

      In the matter of the application of JAMES BULLETT, ET AL., for enrollment as citizens of the Cherokee Nation.

      EMMET STARR, being duly sworn and examined by the Commission, testified as follows:

Q   What is your name ?   A   Emmet Starr.
Q   What is your age ?   A   Thirty one years.
Q   What is your post office address ?   A   Claremore, I. T.
Q   You are a citizen by blood of the Cherokee Nation ?
A   Yes sir, I am.

Q   For whom do you desire to make application for enrollment   ?

A   For the following names persons on the 1896 Cherokee roll, their families and descendants:

Q   Are there any other persons for whom you desire to make application for enrollment?

A   I desire to apply for the following named persons on the 1880 Cherokee roll, their families and their descendants:

E. A. Welch, page 309, #1405, Flint District; Ad. White.
Note: "Non citizen, does not apply. P. O. Rose. Married
a man named Wright".

E. C. Bagwell, on oath states that, as stenographer to the Commission to the Five Civilized Tribes, he correctly recorded the testimony and proceedings had in the above entitled cause, and that the foregoing is an accurate transcript of his stenographic notes thereof.

E.C. Bagwell

Subscribed and sworn to before me this 2 day of August, 1902.

PG Reuter
Notary Public.

◇◇◇◇◇

E C M   Cherokee D-1786.

DEPARTMENT OF THE INTERIOR,

COMMISSIONER TO THE FIVE CIVILIZED TRIBES.

In the matter of the application for the enrollment of E. A. Welch as a citizen by intermarriage of the Cherokee Nation.

D E C I S I O N

THE RECORDS OF THIS OFFICE SHOW: That at Muskogee, Indian Territory, June 30, 1902 application was received by the Commission to the Five Civilized Tribes for the enrollment of E. A. Welch as a citizen by intermarriage of the Cherokee Nation.

THE EVIDENCE IN THIS CASE SHOWS: That the applicant herein, E. A. Welch, is a white woman and neither claims nor possesses any right to enrollment as a citizen of the Cherokee Nation other than such right as she may have acquired by virtue of her marriage to one John E. Welch, who was at the time of said marriage a recognized citizen by blood of the Cherokee Nation, who is identified on the Cherokee authenticated tribal roll of 1880, Flint District opposite No. 1405, as an adopted white. It is further shown that the said E. A. Welch and John E. welch thereafter separated, and that since said separation the said E. A. Welch has married a non-citizen of the Cherokee Nation.

In view of the foregoing it is considered that said applicant, by reason of her marriage to a non-citizen of the Cherokee Nation, forfeited whatever right she may have acquired to enrollment as a citizen by intermarriage of the Cherokee [sic] by reason of her marriage to John E. Welch.

IT IS, THEREFORE, ORDERED AND ADJUDGED: That in accordance with the decision of the Supreme Court of the United States, dated November 5, 1906, in the cases of Daniel Red Bird, et al. vs. the United States, Nos. 125, 126, 127, and 128, the said applicant, E. A. Welch, is not entitled, under the provisions of Section Twenty-one of the Act of Congress approved June 28, 1898, (30 Stats. 495), to enrollment as a citizen by intermarriage of the Cherokee Nation, and her application for enrollment as such is accordingly denied.

Tams Bixby

Commissioner.

Dated at Muskogee, Indian Territory,
this   FEB 19 1907

<><><><><>

Cherokee D-1786.

Muskogee, Indian Territory, December 4, 1902.

John E. Welch,
Edna, Kansas.

Dear Sir:

There appears upon the 1880 authenticated roll of citizens of the Cherokee Nation the name of one E. A. Welch, aged at that time twenty-six years, enrolled with you.

You are requested to advise the Commission whether or not the said E. A. Welch is living, and , if so, to furnish her present name and post office address.

Respectfully,

Signed Tams Bixby
Acting Chairman.

Env.

◇◇◇◇◇

(The letter below was originally handwritten on the microfilm.)

Coffeyville Kansas

Dec 23rd 1902

Hon L.B. Bell

Muskogee.

I thought I would write you a few lines this morning, The Commission wanted to know where the address of E. A. Welch, who was enrolled on the Rolls of 1880, was. This woman was then my wife - in 81 (I think) She was divorced from me, in Flint District. Hon Steve Tehee was the presding[sic] Judge at that time.

Soon after this woman was divorced from me she married William Wright who run a Black Smith shop on the Old George Starr farm, in Flint District, and now living at the Saline Court House. Rose is their Post office.

I called your attention to this fact thinking perhaps you might know something in regard to the matter, yourself.

Sould[sic] there be any thing else needed in regard to my wife and children being enrolled please inform me, and I will take it as a great favor.

Respectfully,

Your friend

J E Welch

Hudson

I.T.

◇◇◇◇◇

Cherokee D-1786.

Vinita, Indian Territory, January 3, 1903.

John E. Welch,
Edna, Kansas.

Dear Sir:-

When you appear before the Cherokee Land Office of this Commission at Vinita, Indian Territory, for the purpose of selecting your allotment as a citizen of the Cherokee Nation, you are requested to present yourself before the Enrollment Division of said office for the purpose of giving testimony as to the present status as a citizen of the Cherokee Nation of your former wife, E. A. Welch, whose name appears with yours on the 1880 authenticated roll of citizens of the Cherokee Nation.

Respectfully,

Acting Chairman.

R.P.

◇◇◇◇◇

COPY   Cher. D-1786.

Tahlequah, Indian Territory, November 4, 1903.

Mrs. E. A. Wright,
Rose, Indian Territory.

Dear Madam:-

Application has been made to this Commission for the enrollment as a citizen by intermarriage of the Cherokee Nation, of one E. A. Welch, who appear on the tribal roll of 1880 in Flint District as an adopted white.

The Commission has information that you are the person whose name appears on that roll and that you separated from your Indian husband and married one William Wright, a white man. Please advise the Commission whether this information is correct.

56

If you desire to introduce any testimony in support of the application which has been made for your enrollment, you may do so at the offices of the Commission at Tahlequah, Indian Territory, at any time within the next sixty days.

Unless we hear from you within that time the Commission will be at liverty[sic] to assume that you have forfeited your citizenship under the Cherokee lease by marriage to a white man, and that you do not intend to apply for enrollment.

Respectfully,

C. R. Breckenridge[sic]
Commissioner in Charge
JOC.   Cherokee Land Office.

◇◇◇◇◇

(The letter below was originally handwritten on the microfilm and typed as given.)

D. 1786.

Rose I.T.
Nov=14=03

To the Commission of the Five Civilized Tribs in answer to your question I am the person whos names appers on the roll of 1880 and that I seperated from John E. Welch and that I married a white man and forfeited my citizenship I havent made any application for enrolement what ever now I would be glad the Commison would inform me who made the application.

Yours resp.

E.A. Wright

◇◇◇◇◇

INDEXED.

COMMISSION TO FIVE TRIBES.
No. 301 Received ANSWERED
1904

Cherokee Land Office,
Tahlequah, I.T.
Jan. 4, 1904.

Transmits, for appropriate action, record in application of E.A. Welch for enrollment as an inter-married Cherokee.

(Copy of original document from case.)

◇◇◇◇◇

COMMISSIONERS:

HENRY L. DAWES,
TAMS BIXBY,
THOMAS B. NEEDLES,
C. R. BRECKINRIDGE.

ALLISON L. AYLESWORTH,   SECRETARY.
. BCJ

ADDRESS ONLY THE
COMMISSION TO THE FIVE CIVILIZED TRIBES.

DEPARTMENT OF THE INTERIOR,
COMMISSION TO THE FIVE CIVILIZED TRIBES.

REFER IN REPLY TO THE FOLLOWING:

Cherokee D 1786.

◇◇◇◇◇

Tahlequah, Indian Territory, January 4, 1904.

Commission to the Five Civilized Tribes,
   (Cherokee Division)
      Muskogee, Indian Territory.

Gentlemen:

     There is transmitted herewith for your consideration and appropriate action the record, together with the original card, in the matter of the application for the enrollment of E. A. Welch as a citizen by intermarriage of the Cherokee Nation, Cherokee D 1786.

     This applicant admits in her letter of November 4, 1903, that she has married a white man since the separation between her and her husband, John E Welch, and that she thereby forfeited her citizenship.

                  Respectfully,
                       C. R. Breckinridge
                           Commissioner in Charge
                           Cherokee Land Office.

EGR.

Enc. 7.

◇◇◇◇◇

COPY

                           Cherokee-D-1786-
                              1787.

          Muskogee, Indian Territory, January 28, 1903.

John E. Welch,
      Edna, Kansas.

Dear Sir:

     Applications have been made to this Commission for the enrollment, as citizens of the Cherokee Nation, of E. A. Welch and Loo Welch, who, if living, are about 50 and 37 years of age, respectively. Their names appear upon the 1880 Cherokee Tribal Roll, Flint District. Perhaps they are members of your family.

If you know whether they are living, please inform the Commission of their present whereabouts, giving their post office address and such other information as you may have, in order that proper steps may be taken to determine their right to enrollment.

As this matter is very important, please give it your immediate attention.

Respectfully,

SIGNED *Tams Bixby*
Chairman.

<><><><><>

Cherokee
D 1786

Muskogee, Indian Territory, February 19, 1907.

W. W. Hastings,
Attorney for the Cherokee Nation,
Muskogee, Indian Territory.

Dear Sir:

There is enclosed herewith a copy of the decision of the Commissioner to the Five Civilized Tribes, dated February 19, 1907, rejecting the application for the enrollment of E. A. Welch as a citizen by intermarriage of the Cherokee Nation.

The decision, together with the record of proceedings had in the case, has this day been transmitted to the Secretary of the Interior for his review and decision. You will be advised of the Secretary's action as soon as this office is informed of same.

Respectfully,

Commissioner.

Encl. A-87

RA

<><><><><>

Cherokee Intermarried White 1906
Volume IX

Muskogee, Indian Territory, February 19, 1907.

The Honorable,
The Secretary of the Interior.

Sir:

There is transmitted herewith the record of proceedings had in the matter of the application for the enrollment of E. A. Welch as a citizen by intermarriage of the Cherokee Nation, together with the decision of the Commissioner, dated February 19, 1907, denying the application.

Respectfully,

Commissioner.

Encl. A-88
RA

Through the Commissioner
of Indian Affairs.

◇◇◇◇◇

REFER IN REPLY TO THE FOLLOWING: Cherokee D 1786	DEPARTMENT OF THE INTERIOR, **COMMISSIONER TO THE FIVE CIVILIZED TRIBES.**

Muskogee, Indian Territory, February 19, 1907.

E. A. Welch,
Rose, Indian Territory.

Dear Madam:

There is enclosed herewith a copy of the decision of the Commissioner to the Five Civilized Tribes, dated February 19, 1907, rejecting the application for your enrollment as a citizen by intermarriage of the Cherokee Nation.

The decision, together with the record of proceedings had in the case, has this day been transmitted to the Secretary of the Interior for his review and decision. You will be advised of the Secretary's action as soon as this office is informed of same.

Respectfully,
Tams Bixby
Commissioner.

Encl. A-86
RA
Register.

◇◇◇◇◇

Refer in reply to the following: Copy.
   Land.
18386-1907.

DEPARTMENT OF THE INTERIOR,

OFFICE OF INDIAN AFFAIRS,

WASHINGTON.   February 27, 1907.

The Honorable,
   The Secretary of the Interior.

Sir:

I have the honor to transmit herewith a communication from the Commissioner to the Five Civilized Tribes, dated February 19, 1907, enclosing the record in the matter of the application of E. A. Welch for enrollment as a citizen by intermarriage of the Cherokee Nation, including his decision of the same date denying the application.

The record shows that the applicant is a white woman who at one time was married to John E. Welch, a Cherokee by blood, but that she was separated from him and later married a non-citizen white man. The record further shows that she admits forfeiting her right to citizenship, and says that she made no application for enrollment. It is shown that the application was made by Emmet Starr, apparently without her knowledge or authority. The Office concurs in the Commissioner's decision denying the application and recommendation that it be affirmed.

Very respectfully,

C. F. Larrabee,

EWE.   Acting Commissioner.

◇◇◇◇◇

DEPARTMENT OF THE INTERIOR,

WASHINGTON.

Y.P.

O.K.

LRS.
D.C. 12638-1907.
ITD. 5702, 5864, 6070, 6082,
6088, 6090, 6100, 6102,
6106, 6122, 6156, 6172,
6248, 6524--1907.

March 2, 1907.

DIRECT.

Commissioner to the Five Civilized Tribes,
    Muskogee, Indian Territory.

Sir:

    Your decisions in the following Cherokee citizenship cases adverse to the applicants are hereby affirmed. Copies of Indian Office letters submitting your reports and recommending that the decisions be affirmed are enclosed:

Title of Case.	Date of Your Letter of Transmittal
E. A. Welch,	February 19, 1907.
Belle Harlin,	February 9, 1907.
Claud L., and Martha M. Washbourne,	February 16, 1907.
George W. Evans et al.	February 12, 1907.
Joe Iney Bell (Freedman),	February 19, 1907.
Clara Ross (Freedman),	February 18, 1907.
Russel[sic] and Herman Hill (Freedmen),	February 18, 1907.
George Brown (Freedman),	February 18, 1907.
James and Mary L. Huston (Freedmen),	February 19, 1907.
Addie E. Rogers (Freedman),	February 14, 1907.
Liddy S. Thompson,	February 8, 1907.
Mary Ann Divers et al. (Freedmen),	February 11, 1907.
Beau and Johnie Ross (Freedmen),	February 15, 1907.
Ralph Elliott,	February 13, 1907.

    A copy hereof and all the papers in the above mentioned cases have been sent to the Indian Office.

Respectfully,

14 inc. and 28 inc.
for Indian Office.

Jesse E. Wilson
Assistant Secretary.

A. F. Mc.
3-2-07.

◇◇◇◇◇

D.C. 13343-1907

J.F.

DEPARTMENT OF THE INTERIOR, RJH

WASHINGTON.

I.T.D. 7982-1907. March 4, 1907.

LRS

DIRECT.

Commissioner to the Five Civilized Tribes,
    Muskogee, Indian Territory.

Sir:

It appears from your telegram of March 2, 1907, filed in the Department March 4, 1907, that E. A. Welch, applicant for enrollment as a citizen by intermarriage of the Cherokee Nation, is upon the 1880 roll. You state that in your decision of February 19, 1907, "married out date not given in decision but eighteen hundred and eighty enrollment and records show second marriage subsequent to eighteen hundred and eighty." You express the opinion that possibly this applicant may be entitled to enrollment under the John W. Gleason case.

The record has been returned to the Indian Office, and that is closed at this hour. Apparently the party is entitled to enrollment under the opinion of the Attorney General in the John W. Gleason case, and the decision of the Department in the Jacob Bartles case. The decision of the Department, adverse to the applicant, is rescinded, and his[sic] enrollment will be made by your representative here.

Respectfully,

(Signed) Jesse E. Wilson,
Acting Secretary.

Carbon copy
to Indian Office.

AFMc
3-4-07

◇◇◇◇◇

Cherokee D-1786

Muskogee, Indian Territory, March 12, 1907.

W. W. Hastings,
    Attorney for the Cherokee Nation,
        Muskogee, Indian Territory.

Dear Sir:

    You are hereby advised that the decision of the Commissioner to the Five Civilized Tribes, dated February 19, 1907, rejecting the application for the enrollment of E. A. Welch as a citizen by intermarriage of the Cherokee Nation, was affirmed by the Secretary of the Interior, March 2, 1907.

    For your information, there is enclosed herewith a copy of Departmental decision referred to.

        Respectfully,

           SIGNED *Tams Bixby*
           Commissioner.

Encl. H-108
JMH

◇◇◇◇◇

Cherokee D-1786

DEPARTMENT OF THE INTERIOR,
COMMISSIONER TO THE FIVE CIVILIZED TRIBES.

Muskogee, Indian Territory, March 12, 1907.

E. A. Welch,
    Rose, Indian Territory.

Dear Madam:

    You are hereby advised that the decision of the Commissioner to the Five Civilized Tribes, dated February 19, 1907, rejecting the application for your enrollment as a citizen by intermarriage of the Cherokee Nation, was affirmed by the Secretary of the Interior, March 2, 1907.

    For your information, there is enclosed herewith a copy of Departmental decision referred to.

        Respectfully,
           Tams Bixby
           Commissioner.

Encl. H-107
JMH

◇◇◇◇◇

Cherokee D1786   COPY

Muskogee, Indian Territory, March 21, 1907.

W. W. Hastings,
     Attorney for the Cherokee Nation,
        Muskogee, Indian Territory.

Dear Sir:

     You are hereby advised that the application for the enrollment of E. A. welch as a citizen by intermarriage of the Cherokee Nation, was granted by the Secretary of the Interior, March 4, 1907.

     For your information, there is enclosed herewith a copy of Departmental decision referred to.

                      Respectfully,

                           SIGNED *Jams Bixby*
                           Commissioner.

Enc I-604

RPI

◇◇◇◇◇

                                            CFB

REFER IN REPLY TO THE FOLLOWING:	**DEPARTMENT OF THE INTERIOR,**
Cherokee D1786	**COMMISSIONER TO THE FIVE CIVILIZED TRIBES.**

Muskogee, Indian Territory, March 21, 1907.

E. A. Welch,
     Rose, Indian Territory.

Dear Madam:

     You are hereby advised that the application for your enrollment as a citizen by intermarriage of the Cherokee Nation, was granted by the Secretary of the Interior, March 4, 1907.

     For your information, there is enclosed herewith a copy of Departmental decision referred to.

Respectfully,

Tams Bixby
Commissioner.

Enc I-605

RPI

<><><><><>

GAW

DEPARTMENT OF THE INTERIOR
OFFICE OF INDIAN AFFAIRS,
WASHINGTON.

I.T.   May 11, 1907.
Reference in body
of letter.

Subject: Motions for
review in certain Chero-
kee citizenship cases.

The Honorable,
    The Secretary of the Interior.

Sir:

    There are inclosed herewith motions filed by W. W. Hastings, National
Attorney for the Cherokee Nation, praying for review and rehearing of Departmental
decisions authorizing the enrollment as citizens by intermarriage of the Cherokee Nation
of the following persons:

42893-1907,	Jacob A. Bartles,
42895- "	Osburn J. Byrd,
42886- "	Amanda Beck,
42894- "	Sarah F. Gage,
42892- "	Phirena Harris,
42888- "	Daniel Harmon,
42891- "	Emma L. Ironsides,
42896- "	Sarah A. Jordan
42881- "	Dovie Johnson,
42882- "	Andrew H. Norwood,
42887- "	Stacy E. Perry,
42885- "	Martha Randolph, now Kernan
42893- "	John W. Smith
42884- "	John J. Smith,

42890-	"	Robert H. F. Thompson,
42889-	"	Hattie Wright,
42883-	"	Nancy Wolfe,
42880-	"	E. A. Welch.

In view of the provisions of section 2 of the act of April 26, 1906 (34 Stat. L., 137), providing that the rolls of the Five Civilized Tribes shall be fully completed on or before March 4, 1907, there appears to be no authority in law for the reconsideration of any enrollment cases at this time, and it is recommended that the office be authorized to advise Mr. Hastings that the motions for review herewith transmitted cannot be considered.

Very respectfully,

C. F. Larrabee

Acting Commissioner.

AJW-FHE.

May 13, 1907.

Approved.

Thos Ryan

First Assistant Secretary.

◇◇◇◇◇

I. T. references in   GAW
body of letter.

DEPARTMENT OF THE INTERIOR,
OFFICE OF INDIAN AFFAIRS,
WASHINGTON.

May 15, 1907.

Commissioner to the Five Civilized Tribes,
Muskogee, Indian Territory.

Sir:

There is inclosed copy of Office letter of May 11, 1907, approved by the Department on May 13, 1907, recommending that motions filed by W. W. Hastings, National Attorney for the Cherokee Nation, praying for a review and rehearing of Departmental decisions authorizing the enrollment of the following persons as citizens by intermarriage of the Cherokee Nation, be denied, in view of the fact that there appears to be no authority in law at this time for the reconsideration of any enrollment case.

42893-1907	Jacob A. Bartles
42895- "	Osburn J. Byrd
42886- "	Amanda Beck
42894- "	Sarah F. Gage
42892- "	Phirena Harris
42888- "	Daniel Harmon
42891- "	Emma L. Ironsides
42896- "	Sarah A. Jordan
42881- "	Dovie Johnson
42882- "	Andrew H. Norwood
42887- "	Stacy E. Perry
42885- "	Martha Randolph, now Kernan
42893- "	John W. Smith
42884- "	John J. Smith
42890- "	Robert H. F. Thompson
42889- "	Hattie Wright
42883- "	Nancy Wolfe
42880- "	E. A. Welch

You are requested to advise the interested parties, including Mr. Hastings, of the Department's action.

Very respectfully,
C. F. Larrabee
Acting Commissioner.

AJW-FHE.

◇◇◇◇◇

Cherokee
253 et al.

Muskogee, Indian Territory, May 25, 1907.

W. W. Hastings,
Attorney for the Cherokee Nation,
Muskogee, Indian Territory.

Dear Sir:

You are hereby advised that on May 13, 1907, the Secretary of the Interior denied the motion filed by you for a review of its decision authorizing the enrollment of Jacob A. Bartles, et al., as citizens by intermarriage of the Cherokee Nation.

For your information, there is enclosed herewith a copy of Departmental decision referred to.

Respectfully,

Commissioner.

Encl. C-20
LMC

◇◇◇◇◇

<table>
<tr><td>REFER IN REPLY TO THE FOLLOWING:</td><td>DEPARTMENT OF THE INTERIOR,</td></tr>
<tr><td>Cherokee</td><td>COMMISSIONER TO THE FIVE CIVILIZED TRIBES.</td></tr>
<tr><td>I.W.   251</td><td></td></tr>
</table>

Muskogee, Indian Territory, May 25, 1907.

E. A. Welch,
Rose, Indian Territory.

Dear Madam:

You are hereby advised that on May 13, 1907, the Secretary of the Interior denied a motion filed by the Attorney for the Cherokee Nation, for a review of its decision authorizing your enrollment as a citizen by intermarriage of the Cherokee Nation.

For your information, there is enclosed herewith a copy of Departmental decision referred to.

Respectfully,

Tams Bixby
Commissioner.

Encl. C-19
LMC

◇◇◇◇◇

Muskogee, Oklahoma, January 7, 1909.

Subject:
Correction of Cherokee
roll as to sex of E. A.
Welch.

The Honorable,
The Secretary of the Interior.

Sir:

E. A. Welch appears upon the approved roll of citizens by intermarriage of the Cherokee Nation opposite No. 251 as a male, whereas the record in her case shows that she is a female.

69

Cherokee Intermarried White 1906
Volume IX

The enrollment of E. A. welch was directed by the Department on the day the Cherokee roll was closed, March 4, 1907, and the schedule containing her name was prepared by an employe[sic] of this office then assigned to duty in your office, and this error is doubtless due to the rush of work incident to the closing of the tribal rolls on that day.

It is respectfully recommended that the sex of E. A. Welch as it appears upon the approved roll of citizens by intermarriage of the Cherokee Nation be corrected by changing opposite her name at No. 251, in the column marked "Sex" the letter "M" to the letter "F", and that the Office of Indian Affairs and this office be authorized to make such correction upon the copies of said roll in their possession.

Respectfully,

JOR (LS)   Acting Commissioner.

Through the

    Commissioner of Indian Affairs.

◇◇◇◇◇

1-7539   J.F.Jr.

Land   C.D.
2563-1909.
G R

    Subject:
Correction of desig-
nation of sex of E.A.
Welch.   January 22, 1909.

The Honorable,
    The Secretary of the Interior.

Sir:

I have the honor to transmit a communication from the Acting Commissioner to the Five Civilized Tribes, dated January 7, 1909, requesting that authority be granted to correct the designation of sex from "M" to "F" as appears opposite the name of E. A. Welch, No. 251 on the approved final roll of Citizens by Intermarriage of the Cherokee Nation. The erroneous enrollment of E. A. Welch as to her sex, was due to the rush of work incident to the closing of the Cherokee tribal rolls on March 4, 1907.

In view of the authority of the Secretary to make such corrections as expressed in Indian Office letter of August 15, 1908, Land 24218, approved by the Department on

August 17, 1908, this Office concurs in the request of the Acting Commissioner that the above correction of the designation of the sex of E. A. Welch be made as requested upon the copy of the roll of intermarried Cherokees in the possession of the Secretary of the Interior, the Indian Office and the Commissioner to the Five Civilized Tribes.

Very respectfully,

(Signed) R. W. Valentine

MOC-16.   Acting Commissioner.

January 22, 1909.

APPROVED:

(Signed) Jesse E. Wilson
Assistant Secretary.

◇◇◇◇◇

83-1909.

Land
2563-09   1 inclosure.
G R

EBH

DEPARTMENT OF THE INTERIOR,
OFFICE OF INDIAN AFFAIRS,
WASHINGTON, D.C., Jan 25, 1909.

Respectfully referred to the Commissioner
to the Five Civilized Tribes, for
appropriate action.

(Signed John Fennis Jr.

Acting Chief Land Division.

◇◇◇◇◇

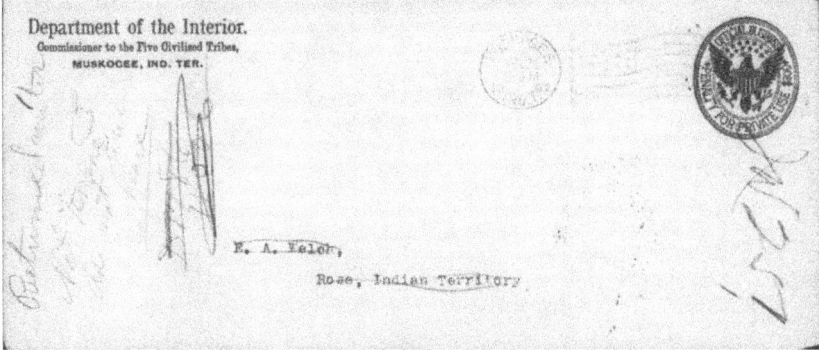

Department of the Interior.
Commissioner to the Five Civilized Tribes,
MUSKOGEE, IND. TER.

E. A. Welch,
Rose, Indian Territory

Department of the Interior.
Commissioner to the Five Civilized Tribes,
MUSKOGEE, IND. TER.

E. A. Welch,
Rose, Indian Territory

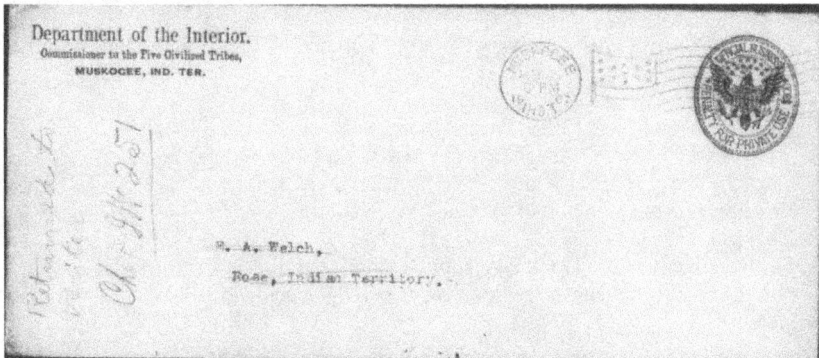

Department of the Interior.
Commissioner to the Five Civilized Tribes,
MUSKOGEE, IND. TER.

E. A. Welch,
Rose, Indian Territory.

Cherokee Intermarried White 1906
Volume IX

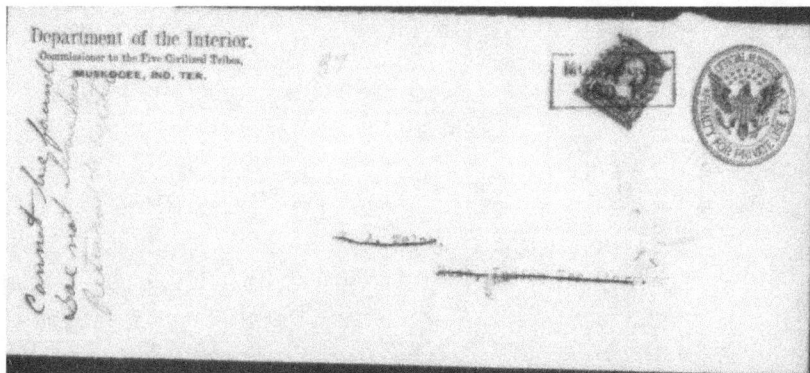

(The above are four copies of original documents from case.)

Cher IW 252

◇◇◇◇◇◇

R
Cher   **D 1786**

Department of the Interior,
Commission to the Five Civilized Tribes,
Muskogee, I. T., June 30, 1902.

In the matter of the application of JAMES BULLETT, ET AL., for enrollment as citizens of the Cherokee Nation.

EMMET STARR, being duly sworn and examined by the Commission, testified as follows:

Q   What is your name ?   A   Emmet Starr.
Q   What is your age ?   A   Thirty one years.
Q   What is your post office address ?   A   Claremore, I. T.
Q   You are a citizen by blood of the Cherokee Nation ?
A   Yes sir, I am.
Q   For whom do you desire to make application for enrollment ?
A   For the following names persons on the 1896 Cherokee roll, their families and descendants:

Q   Are there any other persons for whom you desire to make application for enrollment?

A   I desire to apply for the following named persons on the 1880 Cherokee roll, their families and their descendants:

E. A. Welch, page 309, #1405, Flint District; Ad. White.
Note: "Non citizen, does not apply. P. O. Rose. Married
a man named Wright".

E. C. Bagwell, on oath states that, as stenographer to the Commission to the Five Civilized Tribes, he correctly recorded the testimony and proceedings had in the above entitled cause, and that the foregoing is an accurate transcript of his stenographic notes thereof.

E.C. Bagwell

Subscribed and sworn to before me this 2 day of August, 1902.

PG Reuter
Notary Public.

◇◇◇◇◇

R
Cher   **D 1854**

Department of the Interior,
Commission to the Five Civilized Tribes,
Muskogee, I. T., June 30, 1902.

In the matter of the application of JAMES BULLETT, ET AL., for enrollment as citizens of the Cherokee Nation.

EMMET STARR, being duly sworn and examined by the Commission, testified as follows:

Q   What is your name ?   A   Emmet Starr.
Q   What is your age ?   A   Thirty one years.
Q   What is your post office address ?   A Claremore, I. T.
Q   You are a citizen by blood of the Cherokee Nation ?
A   Yes sir, I am.

Q   For whom do you desire to make application for enrollment   ?

A   For the following names persons on the 1896 Cherokee roll, their families and descendants:

Q   Are there any other persons for whom you desire to make application for enrollment?

A   I desire to apply for the following named persons on the 1880 Cherokee roll, their families and their descendants:

Martha Randolph, page 466, # 1377, Goingsnake District;
Ad. White;
   Note: "Married out; P. G. Foyil".

E. C. Bagwell, on oath states that, as stenographer to the Commission to the Five Civilized Tribes, he correctly recorded the testimony and proceedings had in the above entitled cause, and that the foregoing is an accurate transcript of his stenographic notes thereof.

E.C. Bagwell

Subscribed and sworn to before me this 2 day of August, 1902.

PG Reuter
Notary Public.

◇◇◇◇◇

Cherokee Intermarried White 1906
Volume IX

R.
Cher. D-1854.

Department of the Interior,
Commission to the Five Civilized Tribes.
Tahlequah, I. T., August 18, 1902.

SUPPLEMENTAL TESTIMONY AND PROCEEDINGS in the matter of the enrollment of MARTHA RANDOLPH as a citizen by intermarriage of the Cherokee Nation.

JOHNSON SPADE, being first duly sworn, and being examined, testified as follows, through official interpreter S. R. Walkingstick:

BY COMMISSION: What is your name?   A Johnson Spade.
Q   How old are you?   A Sixty-nine.
Q   What is your post office address?   A Stilwell.
Q   You are a recognized citizen by blood of the Cherokee Nation?
A   Yes sir.
Q   Do you know Martha Randolph, a white woman?   A Yes sir.
Q   She is a woman now about fifty-eight years of age?   A Yes sir.
Q   Do you know her post office address?   A No, I don't.
Q   Do you know her whereabouts?   A Could nlt[sic] state exactly. They left the district, and then went to Delaware District, where her son lives.
Q   Was Martha Randolph at one time married to a citizen by blood of the Cherokee Nation?   A Yes sir.
Q   What was the name of her Cherokee husband?   A She came from Flint District, near Evansville. I knew her husband, but can't recall his name just now. After she moved over into Goingsnake District, that was after the death of her Cherokee husband, after the death of her Cherokee husband, she married again.
Q   Did she marry a Cherokee by blood?   A No sir.
Q   She married a non -citizen?   A Yes sir.
Q   Do you know the name of her last husband?   A Kernan.
Q   About when was it that she married Kernan?   A It must have been prior to 1890. I don't know just when exactly.
Q   Have she and her husband Kernan lived together since their marriage? A Yes sir, they lived together until he died. He was killed.
Q   Do you know whether Martha Kernan has married since the death of her husband Kernan?
A   No, I don't know as to that.

1880 authenticated roll of citizens of the Cherokee Nation, examined, and applicatn[sic] identified thereon as follows:

Page 466, #1377, Martha Randolph, Goingsnake District, age 36.
Note: Married out
Witness: Post office is Foyil.

Wm. Hutchinson, being first duly sworn, states that as stenographer to the Commission to the Five Civilized Tribes he correctly recorded the testimony and proceedings in this case, and that the foregoing is a true and complete transcript of the stenographic notes thereof.

Wm Hutchinson

Subscribed and sworn to before me this 2d day of September, 1902.

John O Rosson
Notary Public.

Copy

◇◇◇◇◇

E C M   Cherokee D-1854.

DEPARTMENT OF THE INTERIOR.
COMMISSIONER TO THE FIVE CIVILIZED TRIBES.

In the matter of the application for the enrollment of MARTHA RANDOLPH, now KERNAN, as a citizen by intermarriage of the Cherokee Nation.

D E C I S I O N

THE RECORDS OF THIS OFFICE SHOW: That at Tahlequah, Indian Territory, August 18, 1902, application was received by the Commission to the Five Civilized Tribes for the enrollment of Martha Randolph as a citizen by intermarriage of the Cherokee Nation.

THE EVIDENCE IN THIS CASE SHOWS: That the applicant herein, Martha Kernan, is a white woman and neither claims nor possesses any right to enrollment as a citizen of the Cherokee Nation other than such right as she may have acquired by virtue of her marriage to a recognized citizen by blood of the Cherokee Nation; that the name of said Cherokee husband cannot be identified on any of the rolls of this office, but the said applicant is identified on the Cherokee authenticated tribal roll of 1880, Going Snake District, No. 1377 as "Martha Randolph", an adopted white. I is further shown that after the death of her said Cherokee husband and prior to September 1, 1902 the said Martha Randolph was married to a non-citizen of the Cherokee Nation.

In view of the foregoing it is considered that the said Martha Randolph, by reason of her marriage to a non-citizen of the Cherokee Nation, forfeited whatever right she may have acquired to enrollment as a citizen by intermarriage of the Cherokee Nation by reason of her marriage to a recognized citizen by blood of the Cherokee Nation.

Tams Bixby
Commissioner.

Dated at Muskogee, Indian Territory,
this   FEB 26 1907

Cherokee Intermarried White 1906
Volume IX

◇◇◇◇◇

COMMISSIONERS:
TAMS BIXBY,
THOMAS B. NEEDLES,
C. R. BRECKINRIDGE.

WM. G. BEALL,
SECRETARY.

DEPARTMENT OF THE INTERIOR,
COMMISSION TO THE FIVE CIVILIZED TRIBES.

REFER IN REPLY TO THE FOLLOWING:

Cherokee-D-1854.

ADDRESS ONLY THE
COMMISSION TO THE FIVE CIVILIZED TRIBES.

Muskogee, Indian Territory, January 28, 1905.

Martha Kerman[sic],
      Foyil, Indian Territory.

Dear Madam:

In the matter of the application which has been made to this Commission for your enrollment as a citizen of the Cherokee Nation, you are advised that, before the Commission can render its decision in the matter of said application, it will be necessary that you appear in person before the Commission, at Muskogee, Indian Territory, and testify relative to your Cherokee citizenship.

As this matter is very important, you should give it your immediate attention.

Respectfully,
      Tams Bixby
          Chairman.

◇◇◇◇◇

Cherokee
D-1854

COPY

Muskogee, Indian Territory, February 26, 1907.

Martha Kernan,
      Foyil, Indian Territory.

Dear Madam:

There is enclosed herewith a copy of the decision of the Commissioner to the Five Civilized Tribes, dated February 26, 1907, rejecting the application for your enrollment as a citizen by intermarriage of the Cherokee Nation.

The decision, together with the record of proceedings had in the matter, has this day been transmitted to the Secretary of the Interior for his review and decision. You will be advised of the Secretary's action as soon as this office is informed of the same.

Respectfully,

SIGNED *Jams Bixby*

Encl. H-118   Commissioner.
JMH

Register.

◇◇◇◇◇◇

Cherokee D-1854

COPY

Muskogee, Indian Territory, February 26, 1907.

W. W. Hastings,
    Attorney for the Cherokee Nation,
        Muskogee, Indian Territory.

Dear Sir:

There is enclosed herewith a copy of the decision of the Commissioner to the Five Civilized Tribes, dated February 26, 1907, rejecting the application for the enrollment of Martha Randolph, now Kernan, as a citizen by intermarriage of the Cherokee Nation.

The decision, together with the record of proceedings had in the case, has this day been transmitted to the Secretary of the Interior for his review and decision. You will be advised of the Secretary's action as soon as this office is informed of same.

Respectfully,

SIGNED *Jams Bixby*

Encl H-119   Commissioner.
JMH

◇◇◇◇◇◇

Cherokee Intermarried White 1906
Volume IX

COPY

Muskogee, Indian Territory, February 26, 1907.

The Honorable,
The Secretary of the Interior.

Sir:

There is transmitted herewith the record of proceedings had in the matter of the application for the enrollment of Martha Randolph, now Kernan, as a citizen by intermarriage of the Cherokee Nation, together with the decision of the Commissioner, dated February 26, 1907, denying of said application.

Respectfully,

SIGNED *Tams Bixby*

Encl. H-20   Commissioner.
JMH

◇◇◇◇◇

D.C. 13138-1907.   J.P.

DEPARTMENT OF THE INTERIOR,   RJH

WASHINGTON.

I.T.D.7982-1907.   March 4, 1907.

DIRECT.

LRS

Commissioner to the Five Civilized Tribes,
     Muskogee, Indian Territory.

Sir:

It appears from your telegram of the 2nd instant, received on the 4th instant, that Martha Randolph, now Kernan, applicant for enrollment as an intermarried citizen of the Cherokee Nation, is on the 1880 roll. You inform the Department that in your decision of February 26th "married out date not stated but eighteen hundred and eighty enrollment indicates that second marriage must have been subsequent to eighteen hundred and eighty. You consider that possibly this applicant is entitled to enrollment.

The record in her case is not before the Department, it having been returned to the Indian Office, and that office is closed at this hour. It would seem that the party is entitled to enrollment under the opinion of the Attorney-General in the John W. Gleason case, and also the decision of the Department in the case of Jacob Bartles.

The decision of the Department, adverse to her, is rescinded, and she will be enrolled as a citizen by intermarriage of the Cherokee Nation by your representative here.

Respectfully,
(Signed) Jesse E. Wilson,
Acting Secretary.

Carbon copy hereof to
Indian Office.

WCF
3/5/07

◇◇◇◇◇

Cherokee D1854   COPY

Muskogee, Indian Territory, March 21, 1907.

Martha Kernan,
Foyil, Indian Territory.

Dear Madam:

You are hereby advised that the application for your enrollment as a citizen by intermarriage of the Cherokee Nation, was granted by the Secretary of the Interior, March 4, 1907.

For your information, there is enclosed herewith a copy of Departmental decision referred to.

Respectfully,

SIGNED *Tams Bixby*
Commissioner.

Enc I-609

RPI

◇◇◇◇◇

Cherokee D1854   COPY

Muskogee, Indian Territory, March 21, 1907.

W. W. Hastings,
    Attorney for the Cherokee Nation,
        Muskogee, Indian Territory.

Dear Sir:

You are hereby advised that the application for the enrollment of Martha Randolph, now Kernan, as a citizen by intermarriage of the Cherokee Nation, was granted by the Secretary of the Interior, March 4, 1907.

For your information, there is enclosed herewith a copy of Departmental decision referred to.

Respectfully,

SIGNED *Jams Bixby*
Commissioner.

Enc I-608

RPI

◇◇◇◇◇

GAW

DEPARTMENT OF THE INTERIOR
OFFICE OF INDIAN AFFAIRS,
WASHINGTON.

I.T.   May 11, 1907.
References in body
of letter.

Subject: Motions for
review in certain Chero-
kee citizenship cases.

The Honorable,
    The Secretary of the Interior.

Sir:

There are inclosed herewith motions filed by W. W. Hastings, National Attorney for the Cherokee Nation, praying for review and rehearing of Departmental decisions authorizing the enrollment as citizens by intermarriage of the Cherokee Nation of the following persons:

42893-1907,	Jacob A. Bartles,
42895- "	Osburn J. Byrd,
42886- "	Amanda Beck,
42894- "	Sarah F. Gage,
42892- "	Phirena Harris,
42888- "	Daniel Harmon,
42891- "	Emma L. Ironsides,
42896- "	Sarah A. Jordan
42881- "	Dovie Johnson,
42882- "	Andrew H. Norwood,
42887- "	Stacy E. Perry,
42885- "	Martha Randolph, now Kernan
42893- "	John W. Smith
42884- "	John J. Smith,
42890- "	Robert H. F. Thompson,
42889- "	Hattie Wright,
42883- "	Nancy Wolfe,
42880- "	E. A. Welch.

In view of the provisions of section 2 of the act of April 26, 1906 (34 Stat. L., 137), providing that the rolls of the Five Civilized Tribes shall be fully completed on or before March 4, 1907, there appears to be no authority in law for the reconsideration of any enrollment cases at this time, and it is recommended that the office be authorized to advise Mr. Hastings that the motions for review herewith transmitted cannot be considered.

Very respectfully,

C. F. Larrabee

Acting Commissioner.

AJW-FHE.

May 13, 1907.

Approved.

Thos Ryan

First Assistant Secretary.

◇◇◇◇◇◇

DEPARTMENT OF THE INTERIOR,
OFFICE OF INDIAN AFFAIRS,   GAW
WASHINGTON.

I. T. References
in body of letter.

May 15, 1907.

Commissioner to the Five Civilized Tribes,
      Muskogee, Indian Territory.

Sir:

There is inclosed copy of Office letter of May 11, 1907, approved by the Department on May 13, 1907, recommending that motions filed by W. W. Hastings, National Attorney for the Cherokee Nation, praying for a review and rehearing of Departmental decisions authorizing the enrollment of the following persons as citizens by intermarriage of the Cherokee Nation, be denied, in view of the fact that there appears to be no authority in law at this time for the reconsideration of any enrollment case.

42893-1907	Jacob A. Bartles
42895- "	Osburn J. Byrd
42886- "	Amanda Beck
42894- "	Sarah F. Gage
42892- "	Phirena Harris
42888- "	Daniel Harmon
42891- "	Emma L. Ironsides
42896- "	Sarah A. Jordan
42881- "	Dovie Johnson
42882- "	Andrew H. Norwood
42887- "	Stacy E. Perry
42885- "	Martha Randolph, now Kernan
42893- "	John W. Smith
42884- "	John J. Smith
42890- "	Robert H. F. Thompson
42889- "	Hattie Wright
42883- "	Nancy Wolfe
42880- "	E. A. Welch

You are requested to advise the interested parties, including Mr. Hastings, of the Department's action.

Very respectfully,
C. F. Larrabee
Acting Commissioner.

AJW-FHE.

◇◇◇◇◇

Cherokee
I.W. 252.

Muskogee, Indian Territory, May 25, 1907.

Martha Kernan,
Foyil, Indian Territory.

Dear Madam:

You are hereby advised that on May 13, 1907, the Secretary of the Interior denied a motion filed by the Attorney for the Cherokee Nation, for a review of its decision authorizing your enrollment as a citizen by intermarriage of the Cherokee Nation.

For your information, there is enclosed herewith a copy of Departmental decision referred to.

Respectfully,

Commissioner.

Encl. C-13
LMC

◇◇◇◇◇

Cherokee
253 et al.

Muskogee, Indian Territory, May 25, 1907.

W. W. Hastings,
Attorney for the Cherokee Nation,
Muskogee, Indian Territory.

Dear Sir:

You are hereby advised that on May 13, 1907, the Secretary of the Interior denied the motion filed by you for a review of its decision authorizing the enrollment of Jacob A. Bartles, et al., as citizens by intermarriage of the Cherokee Nation.

For your information, there is enclosed herewith a copy of Departmental decision referred to.

Respectfully,

Commissioner.

Encl. C-20
LMC

◇◇◇◇◇

(Copy of original document from case.)

Cher IW 253

◇◇◇◇◇

(jacket missing)

Cher IW 254

◇◇◇◇◇

Department of the Interior,
Commission to the Five Civilized Tribes,
Pryor Creek, I.T., September 11, 1900.

In the matter of the application of John A. Raper for the enrollment of himself as a Cherokee by blood and his wife as a Cherokee by intermarriage: being sworn and examined by Commissioner Needles, he testified as follows:

Q   What is your name?   A John A. Raper.
Q   How old are you?   A 64 years of age.
Q   What is your post office?   A Chouteau.
Q   What district do you live in?   A Cooweescoowee district.
Q   Are you a recognized citizen of the Cherokee Nation?   A Yes, sir.
Q   By blood?   A Yes, sir.
Q   What degree of blood?   A Well, sir, I can't tell you just exactly what it is, about 1/16 I guess.
Q   For whom do you apply, who do you want to enroll?   A Myself and wife.
Q   No children?   A I haven't got any minor children.

Q   What is the name of your wife?   A Mary Ann.
Q   She a citizen by blood?   A No, sir.
Q   When did you marry her?   A In 1868.
Q   She now living?   A Yes, sir.
Q   How old is she?   A She is 55 years old.
Q   You have got no children under 21 years of age at home?   A No, sir.

(On 1880 roll, page 166, No. 2459, John A. Raper, Cooweescoowee district. Mary Ann Raper on 1880 roll, page 166, No. 2460, M. A. Raper, Cooweescoowee district. On 1896 roll, page 236, No. 2852, John A. Raper, Cooweescoowee district. Mary Ann Raper on 1896 roll, page 321, No. 821, Mary A. Raper, Cooweescoowee dist.)

The name of John A. Raper appears upon the authenticated roll of 1880, and also upon the census roll of 1896, and the name of his wife, Mary Ann, appears upon the authenticated roll of 1880, as M. A. Raper, and on the census roll of 1896, and they being both duly identified according to page and number of said roll as indicated in the testimony, and satisfactory proof having been made as to their residence, said John A. Raper and his wife, Mary Ann, will be duly listed for enrollment by this Commission as Cherokee citizens by blood.

--------o--------

Bruce C. Jones, being duly sworn, says that as stenographer to the Commission to the Five Civilized Tribes he correctly recorded the proceedings and testimony in the above case, and the foregoing is a true and complete transcript of his stenographic notes thereof.

Bruce C. Jones

Sworn to and subscribed before me this the 12th of September, 1900.

C R Breckinridge
Commissioner.

Copy

◇◇◇◇◇

Statement of Applicant Taken Under Oath.

CHEROKEES BY BLOOD AND ADOPTION.

Date _____ SEP 11 1900 _____ 1900.

Name _John A. Raper_ _Choutau_

District _COOWEESCOOWEE._ Year _1880_ Page _166_ No. _2459_

Citizen by blood _Yes_ 1/16 Mother's citizenship _____

Intermarried citizen _____

Married under what law _____ Date of marriage _____

License _____ Certificate _____

Wife's name _Mary A. Raper_

District _COOWEESCOOWEE._ Year _1880_ Page _166_ No. _2460_

Citizen by blood _____ Mother's citizenship _____

Intermarried citizen _Yes_

Married under what law _____ Date of marriage _____

License _____ Certificate _____

Names of Children:

	Dist.		Year	Page	No.	Age
	Dist.		Year	Page	No.	Age
	Dist.		Year	Page	No.	Age
	Dist.		Year	Page	No.	Age
	Dist.		Year	Page	No.	Age
	Dist.		Year	Page	No.	Age
	Dist.		Year	Page	No.	Age
	Dist.		Year	Page	No.	Age
	Dist.		Year	Page	No.	Age
	Dist.		Year	Page	No.	Age

I on 1880 roll as W. A. Raper

#2579

(Copy of original document from case.)

◇◇◇◇◇

Cherokee 2529.

Department of the Interior,
Commission to the Five Civilized Tribes,
Muskogee, I. T., October 7, 1902.

In the matter of the application of John A. Raper for he enrollment of himself as a citizen by blood, and for the enrollment of his wife, Mary A. Raper, as a citizen by intermarriage of the Cherokee Nation; Mary A. Raper, being sworn and examined by the Commission, testified as follows:

Q What is your name? A Mary A. Raper.
Q What is your age at this time? A Fifty-six as near as I can guess at it.
Q What is your postoffice? A Chouteau.
Q Are you the same Mary A. Raper for whom application was made to this Commission for enrollment as an intermarried citizen on September 11, 1900?
A Yes sir.
Q What is your husband's name? A John A. Raper.
Q Is he a Cherokee by blood? A Yes sir.
Q When were you and John A. Raper married? A We were married in '68.
Q Were you ever married prior to your marriage to John A. Raper? A No sir.
Q Was he ever married before you and he were married? A No sir.
Q Have you and John A. Raper lived together all the time as husband and wife from 1880 up to the present time? A Yes sir.
Q Never been separated during that time? A No sir.
Q And you never have been married to any other man since you married John A. Raper? A No sir.
Q Were you and John A. Raper living together as husband and wife on the first day of September, 1902? A Yes sir.
Q Have you and your husband, John A. Raper, both lived in the Cherokee Nation all the time since 1880 up until the present time? A Yes sir.
Q Neither you nor John A. Raper have lived outside of the Cherokee Nation since 1880, have you? A No sir.

The undersigned, being duly sworn, states as stenographer to the Commission to the Five Civilized Tribes he correctly recorded the testimony and proceedings in this case, and that the foregoing is a true and correct transcript of his stenographic notes thereof.

E.G. Rothenberger

Subscribed and sworn to before me this 31st day of October, 1902.

BC Jones
Notary Public.

Cherokee Intermarried White 1906
Volume IX

◇◇◇◇◇

Cherokee No. 2529.

DEPARTMENT OF THE INTERIOR.
COMMISSIONER TO THE FIVE CIVILIZED TRIBES.

Muskogee, Indian Territory, January 3, 1907.

In the matter of the application for the enrollment of Mary A. Raper as a citizen by intermarriage of the Cherokee Nation.

Mary A. Raper, being first duly sworn and examined, testifies as follows:

BY THE COMMISSIONER:

Q What is your name.[sic]   A. Mary A. Raper.
Q. How old are you?   A I am some wheres in 60.
Q What is your Post Office address?   A Choutau[sic].
Q Do you claim rights by intermarriage to the Cherokee Nation.   A Yes, sir.
Q Through whom do you claim your intermarriage rights?   A John A Raper.
Q When were you married to him?   A 1869.
Q What date in 1869?   A I don't know.
Q Were you ever married before you married John A. Raper?   A No, sir.
Q Was he ever married before he married you?   A No, sir.
Q Have you lived together continuously since the time of your marriage in 1869 up to the present time?   A Yes, sir.
Q Where were you married?   A North Carolina.
Q Have you any documentary proof of your marriage in 1869?   A No, sir, we haven't got any cirtificate[sic].
Q Who married you?   A A may[sic] by the name of Walker. A Baptist preacher.
Q How long did you live in North Carolina after your marriage?   A About three years, and then we come here.
Q When was your husband first admitted to a citizenship in the Cherokee Nation?
A. I couldn't tell you.

The applicant is identified on the 1880 Cherokee Roll opposite No. 2460. Her husband through whom she claims her rights as an intermarriage[sic] citizen is identified on said roll opposite No. 2459. He is also identified on the final roll of the citizens by blood of the Cherokee Nation opposite No. 23383.

WITNESS EXCUSED

90

John A. Raper, being first duly sworn and examined, testified as follows:

BY THE COMMISSIONER:

Q What is your name?   [sic]   John A. Raper.
Q. How old are you?   A 70 years old.
Q What is your Post Office address?   A Choutau.
Q Are you acquainted with Mary A. Raper?   A Yes, sir.
Q What relation of you bear to her?   A Man and wife.
Q When were you married?   A In 1869.
Q Where were you married?   A In North Carolina.
Q How long did you live in North Carolina after your marriage?
A I come west here in '70.
Q When were you admitted to citizenship in Cherokee Nation?
A I think it was in '71, I won't be sure.
Q How were your admitted?   A I went before a man by the name of Vann - Judge Vann.
Q Have you got a decree of the Court admitting you?   A No, sir, never did give me none.
Q When did you first vote in the Cherokee election?   A I don't remember when I did vote first.   Been voting ever since I've been here.   My first vote was cast for Chief Ross.
Q Did you make an application for citizenship immediately after you came here in 1870?
A Yes, sir, just before the new year, or right after it.
Q Was it immediately granted?   A Yes, sir.
Q Were you ever married before you married Mary A. Raper?   A No, sir.
Q Have you lived together continuously as husband and wife since your marriage in 1869?   A Yes, sir.
Q Were you ever placed on any of the Cherokee rolls prior to 1880?   A I have been on the rolls ever since I have been here.   Every roll that has ever been taken.
Q Is there any body here to-day that knows you?   A Mr. Hayden.

WITNESS EXCUSED.

Clement Hayden, being first duly sworn and examined, testifies as follows:

BY THE COMMISSIONER:

Q. What is your name?   A Clement Hayden.
Q How old are you?   A 60 years old.
Q What is your Post Office address?   A Chouteau.
Q Are you a citizen or non-citizen of the Cherokee Nation?
A I am an adopted citizen.
Q Do you know John Raper?   A Yes, sir.
Q How long have you known him?   A 20 or 25 years.
Q Did you know him when he first came out here from North Carolina?
A Yes, sir.

Q Do you know when he was admitted to citizenship in the Cherokee Nation?
A No, sir.

WITNESS EXCUSED.

F. Elma Lane, upon oath, states that she reported the proceedings in the above entitled cause and that the foregoing is a true and correct transcript of her stenographic notes taken therein.

F. Elma Lane

Subscribed and sworn to before me this 3rd day of January, 1907.

Chas E Webster
Notary Public.

Copy

◇◇◇◇◇

(The below typed as given.)

An act for taking a census of the Cherokee Nation in the year 1870,and conferring power upon the Supreme Court, to try and determin cases of doubtful citizenship,at an extra term.

Sec,I,

Be it enacted by the National Council;

That two expert responsible persons to be appointed by the Principal Chief,(in each district)and who shall be residents of the district from which they are appointed,, be, and they are hereby directed and authorized,to take the census of their respective districts,between the first day of March and the first day of September 1870;and make a full and certified returns thereof to the Principal Chief on or before the first day of October of said year. The said census takers, before entering upon the duties hereby assigned them, shall take an oath for the full, impartial, and correct performance of the same, as hereinafter defined.

2d. That it shall be the duty of said census takers, to take a full and complete return of all persons found residing or sojourning within the limits of their respective Districts as the time of making the enumeration, as required by the foregoing section. And said returns, shall show the names of all heads of families; the names of all males above the age of eighteen; the names of all females above the age of eighteen years; the names a of all males under eighteen years; the names, sex, and ages of all orphans under sixteen years of age; names of all whites entitled by law to citizenship within the ages above specified; the names of whites not so entitled; the name s of all colored persons entitled by law to citizenship, within said ages; and the names of all such persons not so entitled, and the names of all Indians not so entitled.

s. 3. That is shall be the duty of the Principal Chief, to cause ruled blanks to be prepared of a suitable and convenient form, and to furnish to said census takers for the purpose of making the enumeration herein provided for; and said census takers shall be allowed $3.00 per day while engaged in the performance of the duties hereinbefore imposed upon them.

S. 4. That is shall be the duly of the Princiapl Chief, to cause a summary of the returns of said census to be prepared and laid before the Nation Council together with the full returns of same, at the beginning of the annual session thereof in 1870.

And which returns, shall serve as the basis for apportioning the representation of the several Districts in the Cherokee Nation, in the National Council, in accordance with the amendment of the Constitution dated November 28, 1866.

S. % 5. That all persons whose rights to citizenship in the Cherokee Nation, shall be called in question and who shall be reported by the persons authorized by this act to take the census of the Cherokee people, on the list of doubtful persons, shall be required to appear before the Supreme Court of the Cherokee Nation, at Tahlequah, on the first Monday in December, 1870, then and there to establish their rights to citizenship in the Cherokee Nation. And the said Supreme Court, is hereby specially impowered to act as a court of commission on behalf of the Nation for the hearing and determining nation of all cases of doubtful citizenship which shall be reported to them by the census takers, or by the Solicitors of the several Districts. And the decision of said court shall be deemed final and conclusive in the premises, as to the rights of said persons to citizenship in the Cherokee Nation. And the said court, shall cause a correct list of the names and ages of all persons whose rights they may confirm; and one of all those whose rights they may reject; to be placed on record in their office, and a copy of the same to be furnished the Principal Chief for the use of the Executive Department.

Tahlequah, C. N., Nov. 26, 1869.

Approved 3d Dec. 1869, the date of presentation.

Lewis Downing,
Principal Chief.

EXECUTIVE DEPARTMENT, CHEROKEE NATION,
TAHLEQUAH? IND. TER.

I, A. B. Cunningham, Executive Secretary of the Cherokee Nation, do hereby certify that the above and foregoing is a true and correct copy of an Act of the National Council entitled "An Act for taking a Census of the Cherokee Nation in the year 1870. And conferring power upon the Supreme Court to try and determine cases of doubtful citizenship, at an extra term.", as of record in this office.

A. B. Cunningham
Feby 16 - 1907   Executive Secretary,
Cherokee Nation.

No.8.--John A.Raper, a man aged thirty four years, born and raised in the State of North Carolina, and came into the Cherokee Nation about the 20th, day of December last,who has a wife named Mary Ann and two children, named as follows, William Penn Raper and Henry Marshall Raper, who claims to be Cherokees by blood, and wishes to establish his rights and that of his children as such, introducing R.W.Walker and James Hollan to prove his rights, with his children to Cherokee Citizenship.

Cherokee Nation, ()
   Tahlequah,   ()
       ()   Personally came before me,R.B.Daniel,Chief Justice of the Supreme Court of the Cherokee Nation,R.W.Walker and James Hollan, and being duly sworn,deposeth and sayeth,that they know that John A.Raper the above claimant is a Cherokee by blood,by his mother Polly Raper,and that it would naturally follow that his children,to wit:William Penn Raper and Henry Marshall Raper, are Cherokees.

R.W.Walker,
James Hollan.
Sworn to and subscribed before me this 4th,day of Jany,1871.
R.B.Daniel,
C.J.S.Ct,."

Cherokee Intermarried White 1906
Volume IX

Executive Department,
Cherokee Nation,
Tahlequah, Indian Territory.

I,A.B.Cunningham, Executive Secretary of the Cherokee Nation, do hereby, Certify that the above and foregoing is a true and correct transcript of the record in the matter of the application of John A.Raper, and Children

for citizenship in the Cherokee Nation, before the Honorable R.B.Daniel, Chief Justice of the Supreme Court of the Cherokee Nation, sitting as a Court of Commission, to hear and determin citizenship cases as provided by an act of the Cherokee National Council, approved by the Principal Chief of the Cherokee Nation, December 3rd, 1869.

Said transcript taken from page 13, of the "Record of applications and affadavits in citizenship cases before the Supreme Court of the Cherokee Nation,in 1870 and 1871."

In testimony whereof, I hereunto set my hand and affix the seal of the Cherokee Nation, this the 16th, day of February, 1907.

A B Cunningham
Executive Secretary
Cherokee Nation.

Copy

◇◇◇◇◇

(The Affidavit below originally handwritten on microfilm and typed as given.)

Affidavit:
Chouteau, Ind. Tery.
March 1st 1907

I John A. Raper wish the Commissioner Tams Bixby to allow this statement of mine filed, to correct some errors in the Protest received yesterday in the case of my wife Mary A Raper. I was here in the Cherokee Nation, I.T., in person in 1870 and appeared before Judge John T. Vann Judge of the Supreme Court of the Cherokee Nation at Tahlequah, I.T. with my two witnesses Wesley Walker and James Hollan and the evidence was taken then on the 4" of January 1871 and the prosecuting attorney for the Cherokee Nation then, made a long statement to the court in my favor, as he had known ~~me~~ the family for years before, father & mother all their lives, his name was Johnson Foreman (and not as stated in the protest in 1872) as to legal marriage, living together as man and wife for 38 years is a living witness to establish same if nothing more was addressed.

2<u>d</u>   I have always been a recognized Cherokee citizen by blood here since 1870 (my coming here).

3d My admission dates from the time of taking the evidence in my case, Jany 4"/71, as I did all that was required of any one else and was never required to furnish any thing more but on the contrary have execised all the functions of any other Cherokee citizen, this is also clearly shown and proven by the statement of Cale Wright an old and reliable Cherokee Indian whose statement is herewith submitted as regard the statement of the Cherokee attorney that I wa not admitted until enrolled upon the 1880 roll which is wrong, as I have always been a full fledged ~~Cher~~ citizen of the Cherokee Nation here since the evidence was taken before Judge John Vann in my case in 1870 or 71, when me and my family appeared before him.

John A. Raper

Northern District

Indian Territory

    Subscribed and sworn to before me this 1st day of March 1907

Will A Crockett

My com expires Dec 7th 1910

I. P. Bledsoe representative of Mary Ann Raper

◇◇◇◇◇

(The Affidavit below originally handwritten on microfilm and typed as given.)

<u>Affidavit</u>   Tahlequah I.T. - 2/16/07

    Personally appeared before me Cale Wright who after being duly sworn states -
My name is Cale Wright - I am 61 years old. I live in Tahlequah - I am a Cherokee by blood. I have known Catherine Johnson and Eliza Brown and Nancy Harlin ever since 1868 in the Cherokee Nation, Flint Dist and I saw John A Raper (or Powell) in 1870 in Flint Dist. C. N. and I know that he had a family at that time and I know that he is a brother of the above named women and I know that John A (or Powell) Raper moved from Flint Dist about 1876 to Cooiscoowee Dist C.N. and that he & his family have lived there ever since and that they have always been since 1870 recognized Cherokee citizens. The record of the Executive Office show of April 3d 1875 that these people Catherine Johnson - Eliza Brown appeared before the Supreme Court by (Hon. J. L. Adair) at Tahlequah I.T. and made the second application for admission to citizenship. Stating therein that their former application in /70 or /71 had been lost or misplaced. These people are all recognized as good Cherokee citizens.

Cale Wright

Subscribed and sworn to before me on
this Feby. 16" 1907
Tahlequah I.T.

Wm F Rasmus
Notary Public

MY COMMISSION EXPIRES APRIL 12 -1909.

Copy

◇◇◇◇◇

The Department of the Interior.

Commissioner to the Five Civilized Tribes.

In the matter of the application for the enrollment of Mary Ann Raper as A citizen by intermarriage of the Cherokee Nation.

The evidence and records show that said Mary Ann Raper, a white woman, married John A. Raper in 1868[sic] in South[sic] Carolina and moved West into the Cherokee Nation in 1870 and were admitted by the Supreme Court and their names and two of their children, William Penn and H. Marshall Raper were enrolled on the Senate Journal of said Nation, and that they have continuously resided in said Nation and lived together as man and wife and their names appear upon the rolls of 1880 (authenticated) and also upon the approved roll of the Dawes Commission. And under the act of June 28, 1898, Sec. 21 of an act of Congress, the said Mary Ann Raper is entitled to enrollment.

Choteau I.T.

Feby 26"/07

Respectfully submitted,
I. P. Bledsoe

◇◇◇◇◇

E C M

Cherokee 2529.

DEPARTMENT OF THE INTERIOR,
COMMISSIONER TO THE FIVE CIVILIZED TRIBES.

In the matter of the application for the enrollment of MARY A. RAPER as a citizen by intermarriage of the Cherokee Nation.

D E C I S I O N

THE RECORDS OF THIS OFFICE SHOW: That at Pryor Creek, Indian Territory, September 11, 1900 application was received by the Commission to the Five Civilized Tribes for the enrollment of Mary A. Raper as a citizen by intermarriage of the Cherokee Nation. Further proceedings in the matter of said application were had at Muskogee, Indian Territory, October 7, 1902 and January 3, 1907.

THE EVIDENCE IN THIS CASE SHOWS: That the applicant herein, Mary A. Raper, a white woman, was married in the State of North Carolina in the year 1869 to one John A. Raper; that in 1872 the said John A. Raper and Mary A. Raper removed to the Cherokee Nation where they have since continuously resided as husband and wife; that on January 4, 1871 application was made to the Supreme Court of the Cherokee Nation for the admission to citizenship in the Cherokee Nation of John A. Raper. The records of said case are incomplete, but the Cherokee Nation, after ample opportunity having been allowed, has failed to show that said applicants were refused admission to citizenship therein. The said John A. Raper is identified on the Cherokee authenticated tribal roll of 1880, Cooweescoowee District No. 2459 as a native Cherokee. It is further shown that from the time of said removal to the Cherokee Nation the said John A. Raper and Mary A. Raper resided together as husband and wife and continuously lived in the Cherokee Nation up to and including September 1, 1902. Said applicant is identified on the Cherokee authenticated tribal roll of 1880 and the Cherokee census roll of 1896 as an intermarried citizen of the Cherokee Nation.

IT IS, THEREFORE, ORDERED AND ADJUDGED: That in accordance with the decision of the Supreme Court of the United States, dated November 5, 1906, in the cases of Daniel Red Bird, et al. vs. the United States, Nos. 125, 126, 127, and 128, the said applicant, Mary A. Raper is entitled, under the provisions of Section Twenty-one of the Act of Congress approved June 28, 1898 (30 Stats. 495), to enrollment as a citizen by intermarriage of the Cherokee Nation, and her application for enrollment as such is accordingly granted.

Tams Bixby
Commissioner.

Dated at Muskogee, Indian Territory,
this   FEB 28 1907

◇◇◇◇◇

DEPARTMENT OF THE INTERIOR,
COMMISSIONER TO THE FIVE CIVILIZED TRIBES.

In the matter of the application of Mary A. Raper to be enrolled as a citizen by intermarriage of the Cherokee Nation.

Protest of the Cherokee Nation.

The representative of the Cherokee Nation cannot agree with the decision of the Commissioner to the Five Civilized Tribes ordering the applicant in the above case to be enrolled, for the reason that the record shows that the applicant and her husband were married in the State of North Carolina; that in 1872 they came to the Cherokee Nation; that previous to that time, namely, on January 4, 1871, application was made to the Supreme Court of the Cherokee Nation for their admission to citizenship in the Cherokee Nation, but evidently the record being incomplete no action was taken thereon, and they were not admitted to citizenship in the Cherokee Nation, although subsequent to that time it appears that John A. Raper succeeded in getting his name placed upon the authenticated roll of 1880, and therefore he and his descendants are entitled to be enrolled, but we contend that Mary A. Raper is not entitled because at the time of her marriage to John A. Raper in 1869 he was not a recognized citizen of the Cherokee Nation, but a resident of North Carolina, and there is no evidence which tends to show that he was recognized as a citizen of the Cherokee Nation until his name as placed upon the roll of 1880.

Second, we desire to most vigorously protest against the doctrine embodied in the decision of the Commissioner, wherein it is held, "But the Cherokee Nation, after ample opportunity having been allowed, has failed to show that said applicants were refused admission to citizenship therein." Such doctrine has never been held in a prior decision. The burden is upon the applicant to show:

First, a legal marriage to her husband.

Second, that her husband at the time of that marriage was a recognized Cherokee citizen by blood, or,

Third, that he was admitted to citizenship in the Cherokee Nation prior to November 1, 1875.

It has been satisfactorily shown that she was married to her husband in 1869, and, second, it is admitted that at that time John A. Raper was not a recognized citizen by blood of the Cherokee Nation, but it is contended that they were subsequently admitted prior to November 1, 1875, but the burden is upon the applicant to show this. It is shown that they made application and some testimony was taken before the Supreme Court of the Cherokee Nation to be readmitted, and we submit that the records so far as the admission to citizenship in the Cherokee Nation is concerned are complete, and this the Commissioner to the Five Civilized Tribes and the Secretary of the Interior is aware of, and we submit that the only reasonable theory is that the record shows that these applicants did not come to the Cherokee Nation until 1872; that they had had application made for them prior to that time, namely, on January 4, 1871, but evidently the record was incomplete and that no action was taken thereon, and that it remained in abeyance until perhaps John A. Raper, the husband, went before the Council Committee in 1880 and succeeded in getting his name placed upon the 1880 roll, which was confirmed and authenticated and our contention is that his citizenship dates from that date, and that he was readmitted by the authentication of the 1880 roll, and if so, and our contention in this respect is correct, he was not a citizen of the Cherokee Nation prior to November 1, 1875, and therefore his wife is not entitled to be enrolled as a citizen by intermarriage of the Cherokee Nation.

Cherokee Intermarried White 1906
Volume IX

Respectfully submitted,

W. W. Hastings

Attorney for the Cherokee Nation.

◇◇◇◇◇

Cherokee
2529

Muskogee, Indian Territory, December 24, 1906.

Mary A. Raper,
    Choteau, Indian Territory.

Dear Madam:

November 6, 1906, the United States Supreme Court held that white persons who intermarried with Cherokee citizens according to Cherokee law prior to November 1, 1875, are entitled to enrollment and allotments of land as citizens of the Cherokee Nation.

You are advised that to properly determine your right to enrollment as a citizen by intermarriage of the Cherokee Nation, it will be necessary for you to appear before the Commissioner for the purpose of giving testimony as to the date of your marriage and whether or not your husband, by reason of your marriage to whom you claim the right to enrollment as a citizen by intermarriage of the Cherokee Nation, was a recognized Cherokee citizen at the time of your marriage to him.

You are, therefore, directed to appear before the Commissioner at Muskogee, Indian Territory, at 9 o'clock A. M., on Thursday, January 3, 1907, and give testimony as above indicated.

Respectfully,

JMH

Acting Commissioner.

◇◇◇◇◇

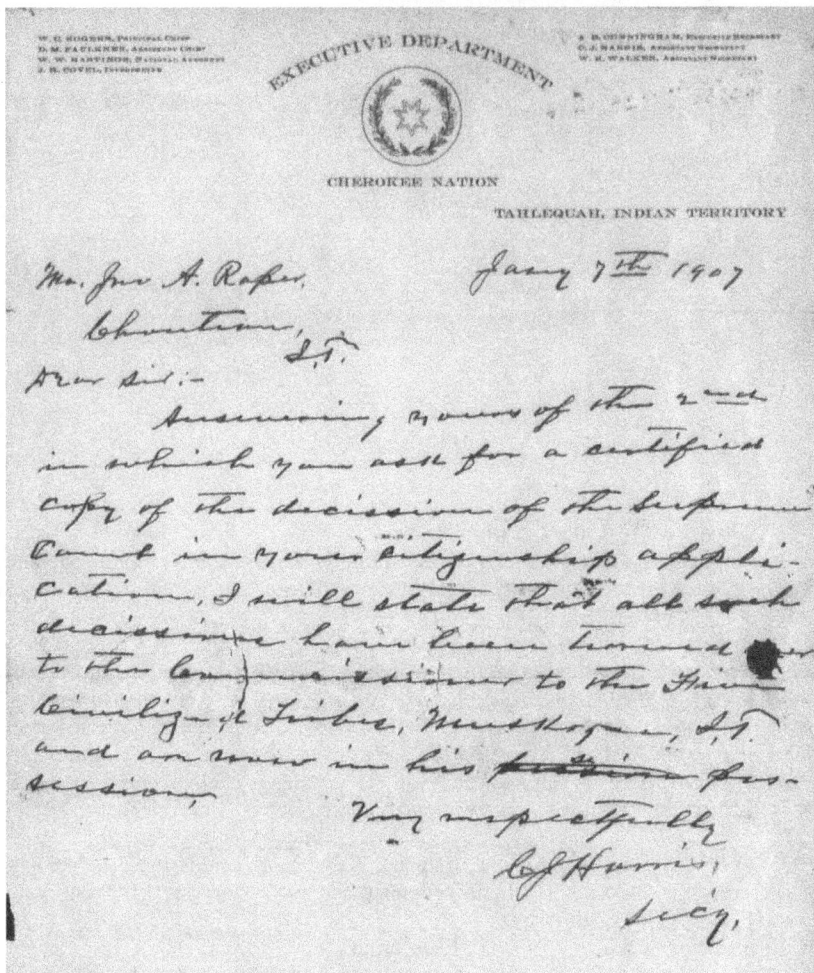

(Copy of original document from case.)

(The transcription of the above letter is below and typed as given.)

EXECUTIVE DEPARTMENT
CHEROKEE NATION.

TAHLEQUAH, INDIAN TERRITORY.
Jany 7th 1907

Mr. Jno. A. Raper,
Chouteau, I.T.

Dear Sir:-

Answering yours of the 2nd. in which you ask for a certified copy of the decission of the Supreme Court in your citizenship application, I will state that all such decisions have been turned over to the Commissioner to the Five Civilized Tribes, Muskogee, I.T. and are now in his possession.

Very respectfully,

C J Harris

Secy.

◇◇◇◇◇

EXECUTIVE DEPARTMENT
CHEROKEE NATION.

TAHLEQUAH, INDIAN TERRITORY.
January 21, 1907.

Tams Bixby, Commissioner,
Muskogee, Indian Territory.

Sir:

Referring to your letter of the 19, inst, Cherokee 2529, requesting that a certified copy of the decision of Judge Vann, admitting John A. Raper to cherokee[sic] Citizenship. I enclose herewith certified copy of the record in the above matter. It appears that the record was never completed as I find no decision of the Court.

Respectfully,

Signed,   A.B. Cunningham

Executive Secretary.

INDEXED
COMMISSIONER to Five Tribes
No. 4035   Received Jan 23 1907

Cunningham, A
    Tahlequah, I.T., Cherokee Nation, Jan. 21, 1907.

                    Transmits certified copy of record, admitting
John A. Raper to citizenship of the Cherokee Nation.
                Cherokee Enrollment.

◇◇◇◇◇

                    Choteau, I.T.
                    Feby 4th 1907.

To The Com'r to the Five Civilized Tribes.
    Sir-

          I herewith return to you the letter of C.J. Harris assistant Executive Secy. of the Cherokee Nation- together with my Affidavit this day sworn to before a Notary Public.

    I am confident that if the Records are carefully examined you will find a record of my admission, which by my affidavit show that I was admitted in 1870 or 1871.
                Very respectfully,
                    John. A. Raper

INDEXED

Commissioner to Five Tribes
No. 6695   Received Feb-5-1907

    Raper, John A.,
          Choteau, I.T. Cherokee Nation, Feb. 4, 1907.

Transmit affidavit and letter from C.J. Harris relative to his Cherokee citizenship.

              Cherokee Enrollment.

◇◇◇◇◇

Cherokee 2529

COPY

Muskogee, Indian Territory, February 28, 1907.

Mary A. Raper,
Choteau, Indian Territory.

Dear Madam:

There is enclosed herewith a copy of the decision of the Commissioner to the Five Civilized Tribes, dated February 28, 1907, granting your application for enrollment as a citizen by intermarriage of the Cherokee Nation.

You are advised that the Attorney for the Cherokee Nation protests against your enrollment as a citizen by intermarriage of the Cherokee Nation. Said protest, together with the record of proceedings had in your case, and the Commissioner's decision, has this day been transmitted to the Secretary of the Interior for his review and decision. You will be advised of the Secretary's action as soon as this office is informed of the same.

Respectfully,

SIGNED *Jams Bixby*

Encl. GL-L[sic]   Commissioner.
 GHL

<><><><><>

Cherokee 2529   COPY

Muskogee, Indian Territory, February 28, 1907.

I. P. Bledsoe,
    Attorney for Mary A. Raper,
        Choteau, Indian Territory.

Dear Sir:

There is enclosed herewith a copy of the decision of the Commissioner to the Five Civilized Tribes, dated February 28, 1907, granting the application for the enrollment of Mary A. Raper as a citizen by intermarriage of the Cherokee Nation.

You are advised that the Attorney for the Cherokee Nation protests against the enrollment of Mary A. Raper as a citizen by intermarriage of the Cherokee Nation. Said protest, together with the record of proceedings had in said case, and the Commissioner's decision, has this day been transmitted to the Secretary of the Interior for his decision.

Respectfully,

SIGNED *Tams Bixby*
Commissioner.

Encl. H-GL-2
GHL

◇◇◇◇◇

COPY

D.C. 13025-1907.   SPECIAL   J. P.
                                                                              FHE.

DEPARTMENT OF THE INTERIOR,

I.T.D. 7904-1907.   WASHINGTON.

                                                                    March 4, 1907.
LRS.

<u>DIRECT</u>.

Commissioner to the Five Civilized Tribes,
        Muskogee, Indian Territory.

Sir:

In accordance with the recommendation contained in your letter of February 21, 1907, your decision adverse to Mattie Mackey for her enrollment as a Cherokee freedman, is reversed; the decision of the Department affirming your decision is accordingly rescinded. Her application for enrollment is granted and the schedule submitted with your letter, bearing her name, has been approved this day and will be disposed of in the usual manner.

The Indian Office submitted your said report with its letter of March 2, 1907 (Land 21810 et al), copy inclosed, and also the records in the cases of Amanda Hill, et al., Cherokee Freedman, Martha Pheasant and Mary A. Raper, applicants for enrollment as intermarried Cherokees. It recommended the approval of your decisions in all these cases in favor of the applicants, and also of the schedules submitted therewith bearing their names.

In accordance with your recommendation and that of the Indian Office, your decisions in favor of the applicants in said cases are hereby approved, also said schedules, which will be disposed of in the usual manner. The papers in the cases have been sent to the Indian Office.

Respectfully,
                (Signed) E. A. Hitchcock,
                                Secretary.

9 inc. and
18 for Ind. Of. with
copy hereof.

A.F.Mc   3-4-07

◇◇◇◇◇

Cherokee IW-254.
629-1908.

Muskogee, Oklahoma, January 16, 1908.

Mrs. Mary A. Raper,
    Choteau, Oklahoma.

Madam:

In reply to your recent letter without date, you are advised a careful examination of the records of this office fails to show that a certificate showing the marriage of yourself and John A. Raper was filed in connection with your claim for enrollment as a citizen by intermarriage of the Cherokee Nation.

Respectfully,

JOR (LS)   Commissioner.

Cher IW 255

◇◇◇◇◇

Cher   **D 1850**

Department of the Interior,
Commission to the Five Civilized Tribes,
Muskogee, I. T., June 30, 1902.

In the matter of the application of JAMES BULLETT, ET AL., for enrollment as citizens of the Cherokee Nation.

EMMET STARR, being duly sworn and examined by the Commission, testified as follows:

Q   What is your name ?   A   Emmet Starr.
Q   What is your age ?   A   Thirty one years.
Q   What is your post office address ?   A   Claremore, I. T.

Q   You are a citizen by blood of the Cherokee Nation ?

A   Yes sir, I am.

Q   For whom do you desire to make application for enrollment ?

A   For the following names persons on the 1896 Cherokee roll, their families and descendants:

Q   Are there any other persons for whom you desire to make application for enrollment?

A   I desire to apply for the following named persons on the 1880 Cherokee roll, their families and their descendants:

Martha Pheasant, page 462, # 1310, Goingsnake District;
Adopted White;
    Note: "Cincinnatti[sic], Ark."

E. C. Bagwell, on oath states that, as stenographer to the Commission to the Five Civilized Tribes, he correctly recorded the testimony and proceedings had in the above entitled cause, and that the foregoing is an accurate transcript of his stenographic notes thereof.

E.C. Bagwell

Subscribed and sworn to before me this 2 day of August, 1902.

PG Reuter
Notary Public.

◇◇◇◇◇

Cherokee D-1850.

DEPARTMENT OF THE INTERIOR,
COMMISSION TO THE FIVE CIVILIZED TRIBES.

---o---

In the matter of the application for the enrollment of Martha Pheasant as a citizen by intermarriage of the Cherokee Nation.

-- -- -- -- -- -- -- --

DECISION.

The record in this case shows that on June 30, 1902, Emmet Starr appeared before the Commission at Muskogee, Indian Territory, and made application for the enrollment of Martha Pheasant as a citizen by intermarriage of the Cherokee Nation. Further proceedings in the matter of said application were had at Tahlequah, Indian Territory, on August 23, 1902.

The evidence in this case shows that Martha Pheasant is a white woman and is identified on the Cherokee Authenticated Roll of 1880 as an intermarried white person. It is further shown that, subsequent to the death of her husband, she removed to the State of Arkansas, and has resided therein continuously for nine years next preceeding[sic] the date of this application.

Paragraph nine, Section twenty-one, of the Act of Congress approved June 28, 1898, (30 Stats., 495), provides:

"No person shall be enrolled who has not heretofore removed to
and in good faith settled in the nation in which he claims citizenship".

It is, therefore, the opinion of this Commission that the application for the enrollment of Martha Pheasant as a citizen by intermarriage of the Cherokee Nation should be denied, and it is so ordered.

COMMISSION TO THE FIVE CIVILIZED TRIBES.

_____
Acting Chairman.

_____
Commissioner.

_____
Commissioner.

Dated at Muskogee, Indian Territory,
this _____

◇◇◇◇◇

POWER OF ATTORNEY.

Know all men by these presents:

That I, Martha Pheasant Of Chance Indian Territory have made constituted and appointed and by these presents do make constitute and appoint for me in my name place and stead John Scott of Chance Indian Territory my true and lawful attorney for the purposes of representing me as my agent before the Daws[sic] Commission to the Five Civilized Tribes in prosecuting my rights to enrollment as a citizen by intermarriage of the Cherokee Indian Nation and also to attend to the renting and leasing of my allotment of Cherokee Indian lands, with full power and authority to collect rents from the same and to do any and all other lawful acts and things pertaining to the same where in his judgement[sic] it will inure to my benefit, he being the sole judge, and with full power and authority to sign any vouchers for any moneys that are due me or that may become due me from the distribution of any funds arizing[sic] from the distribution of the funds of the Cherokke[sic] Nation by the United States Government, or from any persons or corporation concerning my said allotment of Cherokke Indian lands.

And I do by this recind[sic] any all former powers of attorney that I may have made, and the powers herein granted shall be irrevocable until all my rights to citizenship in the Cherokee Indian Nation as an intermarried citizen of the Cherokee Nation the same are finally settled and a complete settlement of my interests in same are made.

Witness my hand and seal this the 10th day of March A.D. 1905.

Signed and executed in the presence of

G. C. Morris

Henry Scott

Martha x Pheasant
her
mark

United States of America.

Northern District.

Indian Territory.

Be it known, that on this the 10th day of March 1905, personally appeared before me R.H. Couch a Notary Public within and for the Northern District Indian Territory duly commissioned and acting, Martha Pheasant   Personally known to me as the person who signed and executed the above and foregoing Power of attorney and being duly sworn in the absence of her said attorney deposes that she had signed and executed the same for the purposes therein mentioned and set forth as her own free voluntary act and deed without any undue influence of her said attorney, and I do hereby so certify.

Witness my hand and seal as such Notary Public the day and year last above written.

RH Couch
Notary Public

Cherokee Intermarried White 1906
Volume IX

My commission expires Jan. 28th, 1907.

◇◇◇◇◇

POWER OF ATTORNEY.

KNOW ALL MEN BY THESE PRESENTS:

That I, Martha Pheasant of Chance Indian Territory, have made constituted and appointed, and by these presents do hereby make constitute and appoint John Scott of Chance I.T. my true and lawful attorney for me in my name place and stead to file for me on my allotment of Cherokee Indian ~~allotment~~ Land and to designate my homestead of the same before the Tahlequah Land Office of the Daws[sic] Commission, and I do hereby delegate to my said attorney full and complete power and authority to do and perform all and every lawful act deed and thing requisite and necessary to perfect my said filing and the designation of my homestead of the same as fully to all intents and purposes as I could do it I were present, with full power of substitution and revocation.

And I assign my reasons for this that the said John Scott is my son and a citizen of the Cherokee Indian Nation by intermarriage, and that I am not physically able to make the trip to Tahlequah to attend to this, that I cannot leave my room to do anything and am not likely to be able to ever attend to it.

Witness my hand and seal this the 10th day of March A.D. 1905.

Henry Scott ⎱ Witness
(Name Illegible) ⎰ to mark

her
Martha x Pheasant
mark

United States of America.
Northern District.
Indian Territory.

Be it known that on this the 10th, day of March 1905, personally appeared before me the undersigned Notary Public within and for the Northern District Indian Territory duly commissioned and acting, Martha Pheasant Personally well known to me to be the party who has signed and executed the above and foregoing Power of attorney and in the absence of her attorney acknowledged that she had signed and executed the same for the purposes therein mentioned and set forth, and I do hereby so certify.

This the 10th day of March 1905.

My commission expires January 28th 1907.

RH Couch
Notary Public

◇◇◇◇◇

110

Cherokee Intermarried White 1906
Volume IX

Cherokee D-1850.

DEPARTMENT OF THE INTERIOR,
COMMISSION TO THE FIVE CIVILIZED TRIBES.
CHEROKEE ENROLLMENT FIELD PARTY.
WESTVILLE, I. T., MARCH 23, 1905.

SUPPLEMENTAL PROCEEDINGS had in the matter of the application for the enrollment of MARTHA PHEASANT as a citizen by blood[sic] of the Cherokee Nation.

GEORGE CRITTENDEN, being first duly sworn, testified as follows:

BY THE COMMISSION:
Q What is your name?   A George Crittenden.
Q What is your age?   A 59.
Q What is your post office address?   A Westville, I. T.
Q Are you a citizen by blood of the Cherokee Nation?   A Yes sir.
Q How long have you lived in Goingsnake District?   A All my life.
Q Were you once acquainted with a white woman an adopted citizen of the Cherokee Nation by the name of Martha Pheasant?   A Yes sir.
Q Were you personally acquainted with her?   A Yes sir.
Q Was she at one time married to a citizen by blood of the Cherokee Nation? A Yes sir
Q What was his name?   A James Pheasant.
Q Is he living or dead?   A He is dead.
Q How long has he been dead?   A 15 years I guess about that long.
Q Did Martha Pheasant once live in your community?   A Yes sir, she lived down here at Goingsnake Court House.
Q Has she married since the death of her Cherokee husband?   A Not that I know of.
Q Do you remember about the year that she and James Pheasant were married?   A Just immediately after peace was declared, married about '65 or '66.
Q Do you know whether or not they were married in accordance with Cherokee laws?
A No sir I don't.
Q Do you know whether or not Martha Pheasant is living or not?   A She was the last account that has been avout[sic] a couple or three months ago, her son-in-law stayed all night with me and said she was in the Creek Nation.
Q Where is she living at present?   A The last account I heard of her she was living with her son-in-law in the Creek Nation.
Q Has she ever lived outside of the Cherokee Nation with the exception of her present residence in the Creek Nation? A She stayed over in Arkansas.
Q How long?   A I don't know but some time.
Q When was it she was over there?   A It has been since 1894, couldn't just tell what year.
Q You don't know how long she stayed in Arkansas? A No sir.
Q But with the exception of her stay in Arkansas and her residence in the Creek Nation she has lived since your first acquaintance with her in the Cherokee Nation?   A Yes sir, about 4 miles west of here.

Q You don't know her present post office address? A No sir.

--------------------------oOo--------------------------

George H. Lessley, being first duly sworn, states that as stenographer to the Commission to the Five Civilized Tribes, he reported the proceedings had in the above entitled cause, and that the above and foregoing is a true and correct transcript of his stenographic notes thereof.

George H Lessley

Subscribed and sworn to before me this April 18, 1905.

Myron White
Notary Public.

◇◇◇◇◇

Cherokee D-1850.

DEPARTMENT OF THE INTERIOR,
COMMISSIONER TO THE FIVE CIVILIZED TRIBES.
MUSKOGEE, I. T., NOVEMBER 20, 1905.

SUPPLEMENTAL PROCEEDINGS had in the matter of the application for the enrollment of MARTHA PHEASANT as a citizen by intermarriage of the Cherokee Nation.

MARTHA PHEASANT, being first duly sworn, testified as follows:

ON BEHALF OF THE COMMISSIONER:

Q What is your name? A Martha Pheasant.
Q How old are you? A 72, will be the 16th of next December.
Q What is your post office? A Okmulgee.
Q What is the name of your father? A His name was Johnson.
Q His full name? A William Johnson, he is dead long ago.
Q Your father was a white man? A Yes sir.
Q What is the name of your mother? A Before she was married.
Q Her married name either? A Elizabeth Johnson.
Q She is dead? A Yes sir.
Q Was she a white woman? A Yes sir.
Q Were you at one time married to a citizen by blood of the Cherokee Nation?
A Yes sir.
Q What was his name? A I don't remember now.
Q Your husband? A Jim Pheasant.
Q He was a Cherokee by blood? A Yes sir.
Q Is he living? A No sir, he is dead.
Q How long has he been dead? A 16 years.
Q When were you and he married? A Well I can't remember how long it has been. It has been a good long time, about 26 years I reckon.

Q Before or after the war? A Since the war.

Q Do you know about how long after the war? A About two years I reckon.

Q Did you and he live together until he died? A Yes sir.

Q Have you married since he died? A No sir.

Q Where did he die? A He died in Goingsnake close to the Court house.

Q Cherokee Nation? A Yes sir.

Q Were you and he living together when he died? A Yes sir.

Q Did you and he live together continuously from the time of your marriage until his death? A Yes sir.

Q Where did he make his home all of his life? A Ever since I knew him right there in Goingsnake.

Q Did he ever live out of the Cherokee Nation? A Not that I know of he never did.

Q Did you live with him in the Cherokee Nation during his life time? A Yes sir.

Q Where have you lived since he died? A I have been in the Cherokee Nation part of the time. I just stayed around amongst my children. I have got not[sic] home, not able to keep house, sometime I am in the Cherokee Nation and sometimes I am down here at Okmulgee.

Q Now after his death where did you go? A I went to my daughter's.

Q Where is that? A Cincinnati.

Q That is in Arkansas? A Yes sir.

Q How long did you live with her then? A Just a short while, not very long. I went back to my son's down in the Cherokee Nation.

Q Did you ever stay with your daughter as much as a year? A No sir.

Q Just a short time? A Yes sir.

Q Then how long did you live with your son in the Cherokee Nation?

A I couldn't tell you, I stayed there a good long time.

Q Several years? A Yes sir.

Q Then where did you go next? A I just visited around and stayed among the children.

Q Have you any children besides your daughter's[sic] who lived outside of the Cherokee Nation? A I have three living.

Q Any besides your daughter live outside of the Cherokee Nation or Indian Territory?

A Not that I know of.

Q Where have you lived for the last 6 or 8 years? A For the last 4 years I have been living here at Okmulgee with my son.

Q Then just prior to that where did you live? A I lived with my sons.

Q Does your name appear on the roll of 1880? A I reckon that is the time, I don't remember what time it was put on.

Q Does your name appear on the roll of 1896 or any other roll besides the 1880 roll?

A That is all I reckon, the time they put our names on the roll, the last time, I was in bed paralyzed and wasn't able to get up and go.

WITNESS EXCUSED.

Cherokee Intermarried White 1906
Volume IX

WILLIAM SCOTT, being first duly sworn, testified as follows:

ON BEHALF OF THE COMMISSIONER:

Q What is your name? A William Scott.

Q How old are you? A I can't tell you just exactly but I am somewhere in 40, my age got burnt up.

Q What is your post office? A Okmulgee.

Q Are you a citizen of the Cherokee Nation? A No sir.

Q Do you know the applicant here, Martha Pheasant? A I know her, yes sir.

Q Is she any relation of yours? A She is my mother.

Q Where has your mother lived since 1880? A She lived at Fayetteville, Arkansas, in the Cherokee Nation, and at Okmulgee.

Q Now for the past 8 years where has she lived? A Part of the time she has been in the Cherokee Nation and part of the time in the Creek Nation and two years she lived in Arkansas.

Q Do you know what two years they were? A No sir, I don't but it was 6 years ago that she lived in Arkansas. We have been here four years last August.

Q Now for the past four years has she lived in the Indian Territory? A Yes sir.

Q in the Creek Nation? A Creek and Cherokee, she went up to my brother's and stayed pretty near a year.

Q What is his name? A John Scott.

Q Whereabouts does he live in the Cherokee Nation? A He lives out about 16 miles south of Cincinnati.

Q He lives in the Cherokee Nation does he? A Yes sir.

Q Was that the year just prior to the four years she lived with you in the Creek Nation?

A Yes sir, she lived with me in the Creek Nation four years and with me at Fayettville two years before that.

Q She must have lived with your brother before she lived with you in Arkansas, that was in 1900? A Yes sir, it must have been.

Q For the past several years she has just lived with her children? A Yes sir.

Q Has she ever had any property interest outside of the Cherokee Nation? A No sir.

Q When was it she lived with you first, do you know? A No sir, I couldn't tell you when.

Q Do you know the greatest length of time she lived outside of the Cherokee Nation?

A Two years.

Q Was that when she lived with her daughter at Cinnatti[sic]? A Two years at a time is as long as she ever lived out that I know of. That is when she lived with me.

Q Where was that? A At Fayettville.

Q Fayettville, Arkansas? A Yes sir.

Q Do you know what two years that was? A It was 6 years ago, you can count it back.

Q Six years ago? A Yes sir, we have been here four years and we just come from Fayettville down her.

Q And she has lived with you for the last six years? A Yes sir, all but the exception of last winter, she went up to my brothers[sic] in the Cherokee Nation.

Q   And with the exception of nearly a year she lived with your brother in the Cherokee Nation she has lived with you?   A Yes sir.

Q   And for the last four years she has lived in the Creek Nation?   A Yes sir, out of the four years she lived nearly a year in the Cherokee Nation.

Q   And two years prior to the time you moved to the Creek Nation you lived at Fayettville, Arkansas?   A Yes sir.

Q   And she lived with you those two years?   A Yes sir.

Q   Where did she live just before then, just prior to that time?   A She was at John's in the Cherokee Nation.

Q   Was that with your brother?   A Yes sir.

Q   How long did she live with him then?   A I couldn't tell you. I come from the Chickasaw country up there and took care of her.

WITNESS EXCUSED.

MARTHA PHEASANT RECALLED:

ON BEHALF OF THE COMMISSIONER:

Q   Before you began living with your son here present, where did you live?

A   I lived with my other son.

Q   Where was that?   A Cherokee Nation.

Q   How long did you live with him that time?   A I lived there two years I know, but sometimes I would come and visit my daughter's in the State, but I wouldn't stay long.

Q   Just a short visit?   A Yes sir.

Q   And did you live with her up to the time you lived that two years with your brother[sic] in the Cherokee Nation?   A It was my son.

Q   I mean your son, yes?   A I lived with him and his wife.

Q   Whereabouts?   A Lived in Goingsnake I guess, I think it is out northwest of Goingsnake Court House about six miles.

Q   How long has it been since you lived with your daughter at Cincinnati?

A   I aint[sic] lived with her to say live with her, in a long time.

Q   You think it has been more than eight years?   A No sir, I was up there this last summer.

Q   I mean to live with her?   A It has been eight years I know.

Q   Have you for the last 6 or 8 years had any property interest in the Cherokee Nation?

A   I haven't any property at all.

Q   Have you always identified yourself with the Cherokee Nation?   A Yes sir.

WITNESS EXCUSED.

------------------------------oOo------------------------------

Cherokee Intermarried White 1906
Volume IX

George H. Lessley, being first duly sworn, states that as stenographer to the Commissioner to the Five Civilized Tribes, he reported the proceedings had in the above entitled cause, and that the above and foregoing is a true and correct transcript of his stenographic notes thereof.

George H Lessley

Subscribed and sworn to before me this 27th day of November, 1905.

Myron White
Notary Public.

◇◇◇◇◇

DEPARTMENT OF THE INTERIOR
COMMISSIONER TO THE FIVE CIVILIZED TRIBES
MUSKOGEE, IND. TER.
JAN. 3, 1907

CHEROKEE D. 1850

IN THE MATTER OF THE APPLICATION FOR THE ENROLL-
MENT OF MARTHA PHEASANT AS A CITIZEN BY INTER-
MARRIAGE OF THE CHEROKEE NATION.

JOHN WESLEY SCOTT BEING FIRST DULY SWORN BY B.P. RASMUS A NOTARY PUBLIC TESTIFIED AS FOLLOWS:

EXAMINATION BY THE COMMISSION. COMMISSIONER:

Q. What is your name.[sic] A John Wesley Scott.
Q   What is your age? A Fifty four.
Q   What is your post office address? A Chance, I.T.
Q   You appear here for the purpose of giving testimony relative to the right to enrollment of Martha Pheasant as a citizen by intermarriage of the Cherokee Nation do you? A Yes.
Q   Are you related in any way to this Martha Pheasant?
A   She's my mother.
Q   Your mother Martha Pheasant is a white woman is she?
A   Yes sir.
Q   She has no Cherokee blood. A No sir, not that I know of.
Q   The only claim that she makes to the right to enrollment as a citizen of the Cherokee Nation is by virtue of her marriage to a citizen by blood of the Cherokee Nation is it? A Yes sir.
Q   What is the name of the Cherokee citizen thru whom she claims the right to enrollment.[sic] A James Pheasant.
Q   Is he living or dead. A He's dead.
Q   When did he die. A He died about fifteen or sixteen years ago.

116

Q   You are his son are you. A I'm his step-son.

Q   He was not your father? A No sir.

Q   Do you know when your mother married him?   A She married him in about sixty-six or sixty-seven, somewhere along about that time if I remember right.

Q   Was he recognized as a citizen by blood of the Cherokee Nation prior to his death?

A   Yes sir he was a full blood Cherokee.

Q   Was your mother ever married prior to her marriage to him?   A She was married in the states.

Q   Was she ever married before she married this man James Pheasant?   A She was married once before that, before the war, and my father went off to the army and he never came back and then along in '66 or '67 somewhere about that time we come to the Territory and she married here in the Territory.

Q   Her former husband then was dead at the time she married this James Pheasant a Cherokee by blood. A I couldn't tell you.

Q   How long had he been absent from home?   A Well he had be[sic] been in the beginning of the war, the civil war.

Q   Had he been absent for a period of five years or more.

A   Yes sir just about five years or more.

Q   Then your mother Martha Pheasant had no knowledge of the whereabouts of her former husband for at least five years prior to her marriage to James Pheasant.

A   No not any knowledge of him.

Q   Where did she marry James Pheasant. A At that time there was no law for lawful marrying; they never was lawfully married; they just took up together and they lived together twenty or twenty five years.

Q   There was no marriage ceremony performed.

A   No sir she lived with him up to the time of his death

Q   When did he die. A He died, well it's been about fifteen or sixteen years ago.

Q   Has she married since his death?   A No sir.

Q   But she's living at the present time is she not, living in the Cherokee Nation. A She's with my brother in Okmulgee now; she's part of the time with me and part of the time with my brother; there's two of us brothers.

Q   What does she consider her home.

A   Well she makes her home mostly with my brother; he has no family.

Q   How long has she been over there living with him?

A   She's been there two years.

Q   From the time of the marriage of your mother Martha Pheasant to her deceased husband James Pheasant did she continuously reside with her husband as his wife until the time of his death?   A Yes sir.

Q   And they lived in the Cherokee Nation did they.

A   Lived in the Cherokee Nation.

Q   After his death did she continue to reside in the Cherokee Nation up to and including September 1, 1902.

A   Well, no sir, she went right across the line to my sisters[sic] and stayed there a while for a couple of years, and then she come back and stayed with me three or four years and then she went to Fayetteville with my brother and stayed with him a while and then she come back to me and stayed a while; then she went to my sisters and stayed a while and then two years ago she went to Okmulgee and I haven't seen her since; I got a letter from her two or three weeks ago; she's in very bad health; I don't look for her to be here on the 5th; I taken out them papers; she wasn't able to get out of the house; she's very old.

Q   Her feeble condition is the cause of her not appearing today is it. A I expect so; she was to be here on the 5th; she was notified to be here on the 5th and I'm to lay over and see whether she gets here or not.

Q   Since the death of her husband has she owned any property in the Cherokee Nation.

A   No sir, she sold out what little she had.

Q   When did he die, this man James Pheasant. A About fifteen years ago or sixteen; I think it was sixteen years ago.

Q   He died then about the year 1890. A Yes sir.

Q   Up until that time your mother Martha Pheasant had continuously resided in the Cherokee Nation since her marriage to her husband James Pheasant. A Yes; she had kept her house plunder, part of it at my house all the time; some of her things. Her bedding and her clothing she takes that back and forth wherever she goes.

Q   Since the death of her husband she has been living at various places with her children? A Yes sir.

Q   Where has she considered her home since then. A She considered her home at my place for a good while and my brother got at her to come with him and try to keep house for him; he has no family; and he wanted her to come with him and she went and stayed with him but she made her home generally at my house until she went with him to try to keep house.

Q   Did she leave any of her personal effects at you place when she left. A Yes sir.

Q   Has she any property with you now, any personal effects or anything like that.

A   She has nothing but some cooking vessels now; she left a large table that she had; she used to run a boarding house and she had a large table; she left that with me; it's been destroyed.

EXAMINATION BY MR. VANCE.

Q   Did she leave anything with you other than this table you speak of; what else did she leave with you besides the table you speak of. A She left some cooking vessels with me and she left some chairs with me a while and she come and got her chairs, and the table and he cooking vessels is about all that I could say she left there.

Q   What became of the table and what became of the cooking vessels. A I've got the cooking vessels, some of them there yet and the table it was set out until the legs rotted off of it and I tore it up.

Q   Do you know what year your father went to the war.

A   No sir; I dont[sic]; I was quiet small.

Q   Do you know about what year. A No I cant[sic] say; I expect I was about twenty years old.

Q   Do you remember when your mother and this man James Pheasant married or took up together. A Yes sir I remember well.

Q   You just give the date from your recollection. A Yes sir

Q   You have no record or evidence of it. A No sir.

Cherokee Intermarried White 1906
Volume IX

THE COMMISSIONER:

Q How much of the time since 1890 has your mother Martha Pheasant lived in the Cherokee Nation. A She hasn't been with me a great deal in that time; she wintered with me, was there last winter was a year ago and went back in the spring and has been gone ever since; she would come and stay a few weeks and go back.

Q Those visits she made were in the nature of visits were they. A Yes sir; she made her home just as much at other places or a little more I expect than she did at my house but then she considered either place her home.

Q She has no permanent home? A No sir.

MR VANCE:

Q Why wasn't application made for your mother's enrollment in 1901 or two when the Commission was receiving applications for enrollment. A She had went to my brother's at Fayetteville at that time and she was lying there under the doctor a good while, under the doctor at Fayetteville.

Q Did she claim at that time to be a citizen by intermarriage of the Cherokee Nation?

A I dont[sic] know whether she did or not at that time because she didn't know but very little at that time; she was suffering; she had the worst rising I ever say; lay a month with it.

Q She didn't make any effort to have application made for her. A No sir she hadn't any idea of getting well at that time.

The applicant Martha Pheasant is identified on the Cherokee Authenticated Tribal Roll of 1880, Goingsnake District No. 1310.

ooOoo

Clara Mitchell Wood being first duly sworn upon her oath states that as stenographer to the Commissioner to the Five Civilized Tribes she reported the above and foregoing proceedings and that this is a correct transcript of her stenographic notes.

Clara Mitchell Wood

Subscribed and sworn to before me this 3rd day of January 1907

B.P. Rasmus
Notary Public.

◇◇◇◇◇

C.F.B.   Cherokee D 1850.

DEPARTMENT OF THE INTERIOR,

COMMISSIONER TO THE FIVE CIVILIZED TRIBES.

In the matter of the application for the enrollment of Martha Phesant[sic] as a citizen by intermarriage of the Cherokee Nation.

D E C I S I O N.

THE RECORDS OF THIS OFFICE SHOW: That at Muskogee, Indian Territory, June 30, 1902, application was received by the Commission to the Five Civilized Tribes for the enrollment of Martha Pheasant, as a citizen by intermarriage of the Cherokee Nation. Further proceedings in the matter of said application were had at Tahlequah, Indian Territory, August 23, 1902, at Westville, Indian Territory, March 23, 1905, and at Muskogee, Indian Territory, November 20, 1905, and January 3, 1907.

THE EVIDENCE IN THIS CASE SHOWS: That the applicant herein, Martha Pheasant, a white woman, married about the year 1866, one James Pheasant, since deceased, who was, at the time of said marriage, a recognized citizen by blood of the Cherokee Nation, and who is identified on the Cherokee authenticated tribal roll of 1880, Going Snake District, No. 1309, as a native Cherokee; that from the time of said marriage until the death of said James Pheasant, which occurred about the year 1892, the said James and Martha Pheasant resided together as husband and wife and continuously lived in the Cherokee Nation. It is further shown that since the death of her said husband, the said Martha Pheasant has resided at various places outside and within the domain of the Five Civilized Tribes, but it is considered by this office that her residence outside the Cherokee Nation has not been of such a character as would forfeit her right to Cherokee citizenship. Said applicant is duly identified on the Cherokee authenticated tribal roll of 1880.

IT IS, THEREFORE, ORDERED AND ADJUDGED: That in accordance with the decision of the Supreme Court of the United States, dated November 5, 1906, in the cases of Daniel Red Bird, et al., vs. the United States, Nos. 125, 126, 127, and 128, the said applicant, Martha Pheasant is entitled under the provisions of Section twenty-one of the Act of Congress approved June 28, 1898 (30 Stats., 495), to enrollment as a citizen by intermarriage of the Cherokee Nation, and her application for enrollment as such is accordingly granted.

Tams Bixby
Commissioner.

Dated at Muskogee, Indian Territory,
this   FEB 27 1907

◇◇◇◇◇

COPY

C D 1815.

DEPARTMENT OF THE INTERIOR,
COMMISSIONER TO THE FIVE CIVILIZED TRIBES.

In the matter of the application for the enrollment of Martha Phesant[sic] as a citizen by intermarriage of the Cherokee Nation.

Protest of the Cherokee Nation.

The Cherokee Nation cannot consent to the enrollment of this applicant as a citizen by intermarriage of the Cherokee Nation, for the reason that the testimony conclusively and clearly shows that the applicant Martha Phesant was never lawfully married to James Phesant, through whom she claims citizenship, and reference is made to the testimony of her son, John Wesley Scott, given before the Commissioner on January 3, 1907, wherein it was asked:

"Q. Where did she (referring to Martha Phesant) marry James Phesant?
A. At that time there was no law for lawfully marrying; they never was lawfully married; they just took up together and they lived together 20 or 25 years."
"Q. There was no marriage ceremony performed?   A No sir, she lived with him up until the time of his death."

There is some testimony tending to show that her first husband was not dead, and there is also some testimony tending to show that she has not retained her residence in the Cherokee Nation since 1890, but we think that the testimony is conclusive that there was no lawful marriage, and for that reason the applicant should not be enrolled as a citizen by intermarriage of the Cherokee Nation.

Respectfully, submitted,

Attorney for the Cherokee Nation.

Endorsement:
DEPARTMENT OF THE INTERIOR
Commissioner to the Five Civilized Tribes.
RECEIVED
FEB 28, 1907.

◇◇◇◇◇

Blank 731.

Cherokee Roll Citizens By Intermarriage

No.	Name				Card No.
255	Pheasant, Martha	67	F		11009

(Copies of original documents from case.)

Cherokee Intermarried White 1906
Volume IX

◇◇◇◇◇

DEPARTMENT OF THE INTERIOR   Black 744.

United States Indian Service

Five Civilized Tribes

Muskogee, Oklahoma.

This is to certify that I am the officer having the custody of the records pertaining to the enrollment of the members of the Choctaw, Chickasaw, Cherokee, Creek, and Seminole tribes of Indians, and the disposition of the land of said tribes, and the following described papers, attached hereto, are true and correct copies of the entire enrollment record on file in this office in connection with the application of

Roll No. ___255___, for enrollment as a citizen by intermarriage of the _Cherokee_ Nation:

Cherokee Indian Census Cards No. 255 and 11009, Testimony dated June 30, 1902, March 23, 1905, November 20, 1905, January 3, 1907;
Letters dated September 15, 1905, September 18, 1905, December 28, 1906, two dated February 28, 1907; March 2, 1907, March 4, 1907, March 18, 1907; Decision no date; Decision dated February 27, 1907
Two Powers of Attorney; Protest dated February 28, 1907.

C.L. Ellis
Dist. Supt. in Charge.

BY   P.L. Snyder   CLERK
IN CHARGE   Cherokee   RECORDS
DATE   Dec. 29, 1926.

◇◇◇◇◇

Cherokee Intermarried White 1906
Volume IX

(The letter below typed as given.)

-COPY-

Beggs Ind. Ter.

Sepet 15 1905

Tams BixBy

Commissioner To the five Civilized Tribes

Muskogee I. T.

I new those persons By the name of Martha Peasant age about 80 years old She is living in going Snake Dist. I. T. her P. O. Westville I. T. That I find here name upon 80 roll and her Husband name James Pheasant whent By the name of Kerin Pheasant his Cherokee name, she is Entitled to enrollment, and also Martha Spade She left Ter about 10 years ago went back To little Rock of fort Smith Ark. her Husband name Jack Spade, I Saw the list of persons names That you had in the possession who have not been accounted for, I have not heared from Martha Spade Sence She left The Ter.

This is all for This Time

Yours Respectfully,

(Signed)   Tillmon England

◇◇◇◇◇

Cherokee D 1850.

COPY.

Muskogee, Indian Territory, September 18, 1905.

James Oates,

Cincinnati, Arkansas.

Dear Sir:

This office is in receipt of your letter of September 9, in reference to one Martha Pheasant, who you state is visiting her daughter at Cincinnati, and whose name you claim appears in the advertised list of persons whose names are on the Cherokee tribal roll of 1880 not accounted for. You ask to be advised if it will be necessary for her to appear in person before this office, stating that she is seventy-two years of age.

In reply you are advised that the name of Martha Pheasant to which you refer, appears upon the 1880 authenticated roll of citizens of the Cherokee Nation, Going-Snake district, as an adopted white, forty-five years of age at that time; her name follows that of James Pheasant, a native Cherokee, forty years of age at that time, marked "Dead", and precedes that of Walker Pheasant, a native Cherokee, twenty years of age, also marked "Dead".

124

If the Martha Pheasant to whom you refer is the person whose name is above referred to, it will be necessary that further testimony be introduced in her case before her right to enrollment as a citizen of the Cherokee Nation can be definitely determined.

Respectfully,

SIGNED

LS   Wm O. Beall

◇◇◇◇◇

Cherokee
D-1850

Muskogee, Indian Territory, December 28, 1906.

Martha Pheasant,
   c/o W. A. Scott,
      Okmulgee, Indian Territory.

Dear Madam:

November 6, 1906, the United States Supreme Court held that white persons who intermarried with Cherokee citizens according to Cherokee law prior to November 1, 1875, are entitled to enrollment and allotments of land as citizens of the Cherokee Nation.

You are advised that to properly determine your right to enrollment as a citizen by intermarriage of the Cherokee Nation, it will be necessary for you to appear before the Commissioner for the purpose of giving testimony as to the date of your marriage and whether or not your wife[sic], by reason of your marriage to whom you claim the right to enrollment as a citizen of the Cherokee Nation, was a recognized citizen of the Cherokee Nation at the time of your marriage to her[sic], and whether or not you were married to her[sic] in accordance with Cherokee laws.

You are, therefore, directed to appear before the Commissioner at Muskogee, Indian Territory, at 9 o'clock A. M., on Saturday, January 5, 1907, and give testimony as above indicated.

Respectfully,

JMH   Acting Commissioner.

◇◇◇◇◇

COPY

Cherokee
D 1850

Muskogee, Indian Territory, February 28, 1907.

Martha Pheasant,
    c/o W. A. Scott,
        Okmulgee, Indian Territory.

Dear Madam:

There is inclosed herewith a copy of the decision of the Commissioner to the Five Civilized Tribes, dated February 27, 1907, granting the application for your enrollment as a citizen by intermarriage of the Cherokee Nation.

You are advised that the Attorney For the Cherokee Nation protests against your enrollment as a citizen by intermarriage of the Cherokee Nation. Said protest, together with the record of proceedings in your case, and the Commissioner's decision has this day been transmitted to the Secretary of the Interior for his decision.

Respectfully,

SIGNED *Jams Bixby*

Incl. GL-4.
GHL

Commissioner.

◇◇◇◇◇

Muskogee, Indian Territory, February 28, 1907

The Honorable,
    The Secretary of the Interior.

Sir:

There is enclosed the record of proceedings had in the matter of the application for the enrollment of Martha Pheasant as a citizen by intermarriage of the Cherokee Nation, together with the decision of the Commissioner dated February 27, 1907, granting her application.

You are advised the Attorney for the Cherokee Nation protests against her enrollment, and his protest, filed this day, is enclosed.

There is also enclosed a schedule containing the name of Martha Pheasant, and in the event of the approval of the Commissioner's decision in this case, the approval of the schedule is also recommended.

126

It will be noted that no roll number has been given the person whose name appears upon the schedule herewith transmitted. This action is taken in accordance with procedure reported by me to the Department on January 28, 1907, and approved by the Department's telegram of February 9, 1907. It is recommended that a number be placed upon this schedule by Mr. McGarr, the employe[sic] of my office now in Washington.

Respectfully,

Commissioner

Through the Commissioner of
Indian Affairs.

Encl. B-71

◇◇◇◇◇

(COPY)

Land Reference in
body of letter.

DEPARTMENT OF THE INTERIOR,
OFFICE OF INDIAN AFFAIRS,
WASHINGTON.

March 2, 1907.

The Honorable,
The Secretary of the Interior.

Sir:

There are forwarded herewith several reports from Commissioner Bixby, transmitting the records in certain citizenship cases, together with the decision of the Commissioner, granting the application for the enrollment of the persons involved in the following cases:

CHEROKEE FREEDMEN.

21810.   Mattie Mackey.

21811.   Amanda Hill, et al.

CHEROKEE BY INTERMARRIAGE.

21806.   Martha Pheasant.

21807.   Mary A. Raper.

The Office examined the record in each of the above cases and recommends that the decision of the Commissioner granting the applications of the persons therein involved, be approved.

There is also inclosed with each case a schedule containing the names of the persons involved therein. The approval of these schedules is also recommended.

It will be noted that no roll numbers have been placed on these schedules opposite the names of the persons appearing thereon, and the Commissioner suggests that this be done by Mr. McGarr, an employe[sic] of his Office now in washington[sic].

Respectfully,

C. F. Larrabee,

AJW:LM   Acting Commissioner.

◇◇◇◇◇

D.C.13025-1907.   SPECIAL   J.P.

DEPARTMENT OF THE INTERIOR,   FHE.

WASHINGTON.

I.T.D. 7904-1907.   March 4, 1907.

LRS

DIRECT.

Commissioner to the Five Civilized Tribes,
    Muskogee, Indian Territory.

Sir:

In accordance with the recommendation contained in your letter of February 28, 1907, your decision adverse to Mattie Mackey for her enrollment as a Cherokee freedman, is reversed; the decision of the Department affirming your decision is accordingly rescinded. Her application for enrollment is granted and the schedule submitted with your letter, bearing her name, has been approved this day and will be disposed of in the usual manner.

The Indian Office submitted your said report with its letter of March 2, 1907 (Land 21810 et al), copy inclosed, and also the records in the cases of Amanda Hill, et al., Cherokee Freedmen, Martha Pheasant and Mary A. Raper, applicants for enrollment as intermarried Cherokees. It recommended the approval of your decisions in all these cases in favor of the applicants, and also of the schedules submitted therewith bearing their names.

In accordance with your recommendation and that of the Indian Office, your decisions in favor of the applicants in said cases are hereby approved, also said schedules, which will be disposed of in the usual manner. The papers in the cases have been sent to the Indian Office.

Respectfully,

(Signed) E. A. Hitchcock,
Secretary.

9 inc. and
18 for Ind. Of. with
copy hereof.

AFMc
3-4-07

◇◇◇◇◇

COPY

Cherokee D1850

Muskogee, Indian Territory, March 18, 1907.

Martha Pheasant,
      Care of W. A. Scott,
            Okmulgee, Indian Territory.

Dear Madam:

You are hereby advised that the decision of the Commissioner to the Five Civilized Tribes, dated February 27, 1907, granting the application for your enrollment as a citizen by intermarriage of the Cherokee Nation, was affirmed by the Secretary of the Interior, March 4, 1907.

For your information, there is enclosed herewith a copy of Departmental decision referred to.

Respectfully,

SIGNED *Tams Bixby*
Commissioner.

Enc I-11

RPI

◇◇◇◇◇

Cherokee D1850

COPY

Muskogee, Indian Territory, March 18, 1907.

W. W. Hastings,
　　Attorney for the Cherokee Nation,
　　　　Muskogee, Indian Territory.

Dear Sir:

　　You are hereby advised that the decision of the Commissioner to the Five Civilized Tribes, dated February 27, 1907, granting the application for the enrollment of Martha Pheasant, as a citizen by intermarriage of the Cherokee Nation, was affirmed by the Secretary of the Interior, March 4, 1907.

　　For your information, there is enclosed herewith a copy of Departmental decision referred to.

　　　　　　　　　　　　Respectfully,
　　　　　　　　　　　　SIGNED *Tams Bixby*
　　　　　　　　　　　　Commissioner.

Enc I-10

RPI

Cher IW 256

◇◇◇◇◇

Department of the Interior.
Commission to the Five Civilized Tribes.
Muskogee, I. T., February 16, 1901.

　　In the matter of the application of Woods B. Rogers for enrollment as a Cherokee citizen; he being sworn and examined by Commissioner C. R. Breckinridge, testified as follows:

Q Give me your full name. A Woods B. Rogers.
Q How old are you? A 64.
Q What is your postoffice? A Checotah.
Q In what district do you live? A I am living in the Creek Nation at present.
Q Do you claim citizenship in the Cherokee Nation? A Yes sir.
Q In what district do you claim citizenship? A I was married in Canadian district.
Q So you would consider yourself a citizen of Canadian? A I have not lived there.
Q You were married in Canadian district, but you are not very definite as to where your citizenship would be at this time? A No sir.

Cherokee Intermarried White 1906
Volume IX

Q Who, is it you want to enroll, yourself and family?   A Just myself.

Q Do you apply for enrollment as a Cherokee by blood?   A No sir.

Q As a white man?   A Yes sir.

Q Intermarried citizen?   A Yes sir.

Q Have you your Cherokee license and certificate of marriage?   A No sir, I suppose they were destroyed; I never got them.

Q You never got the license and certificate of marriage?   A I never got the certificate. I got my regular license.

Q In what district did you get out a license?   A In Canadian.

Q When were you married?   A In '69.

Q To whom were you married?   A Kate D. Drew.

Q Is she dead?   A No sir, she's alive.

Q Is she a Cherokee by blood?   A Yes sir.

Q How long did you and she live together?   A We lived together, and are still living together.

Q Why don't you apply for her enrollment?   A She enrolled in the Creek Nation.

Q You say she enrolled in the Creek Nation, and you expect to apply through her as a Cherokee?   A Yes sir.

Q How long did you and your wife live in the Cherokee Nation after your marriage?

A We lived right on the edge of the Cherokee Nation for about a year.

Q But not inside?   A Part of the place was in the Cherokee Nation, and part in the Creek Nation.

Q Where was the house?   A In the Creek Nation.

Q So you and your wife never lived in the Cherokee Nation after you married?

A No sir.

Q You never had your house or actual residence inside of the Cherokee Nation since you were married in 1869?   A No sir.

Q Have you lived all the time since your marriage in 1869 in this way in the Creek Nation?   A Yes, in the Creek Nation.

Q Are you on any of the rolls of the Cherokee Nation?   A I think my name is on the roll as an adopted citizen. The roll that was made for the Cherokee strip payment.

Q They didn't pay adopted citizens - you didn't get any Cherokee strip money, did you?

A No sir.

Q You are not on the roll of 1880?   A No sir.

Q And not on the census roll of 1896?   A No sir.

Q And never drew any strip money?   A No sir, my family drew strip money.

Q Do you say that your wife claims to be a Creek citizen at this time?   A She is part Creek and part Cherokee.

Q Under which does she claim?   A She is allotted in the Creek Nation.

Q And has secured her land?   A Yes sir.

Q Now, you are not upon any of the rolls of the Cherokee Nation, and you have no marriage license from the Cherokee Nation, nor a certificate of marriage, on what do you base your claim?   A I have affidavits.

Q Have you ever been admitted to citizenship by the Cherokee Commission or Council?

A They recognized my rights.

Q Have they ever given you a certificate of admission?   A No sir.

(Copy of original document from case.)

Q Did you ever apply to the Dawes Commission for admission to citizenship?
A Yes sir.
Q When in '96? A Yes sir, my application went in in 1896.
Q It does not appear from the search that has been made from the records of the Commission that any application was ever submitted by you to the Dawes Commission - did you ever hear from the application?   A Yes sir.

132

Q What did the Commission do with your case?   A Rejected it.

Q What did you do then?   A I applied to the United States Court.

Q And what did the Court do?   A They recognized my rights.

Q What evidence have you of that?   A I tried to get it from here, but they said it was filed with the Commission here.

Q Who were your attorneys?   A I had none.

Q You just filed your own case.[sic] A Yes sir, I made my affidavits before Judge Ross.

Upon further examination of the records of the Commission, it is found in Docket "B", page 216, case 4255, that W. B. Rogers applied for admission to Cherokee citizenship before the Dawes Commission; petition filed September 9, 1896, and the application was denied by the Commission; appeal was taken to the United States Court, and the decision of the Commission was reversed by the Court in Court Case No. 132, and the applicant was admitted.

Q How old is your wife now?   A 54.

(The authenticated roll of 1880 examined, and the name of the applicant, nor any of his family, are found of record thereon).

(The census roll of 1896 examined, and the name of the applicant, nor any of his family, are found of record thereon).

Q Did you wife draw Cherokee strip money?   A Yes sir.

By J. L. Baugh, representative of the Cherokee Nation-

Q Where was your wife born at, in which Nation?   A In the Cherokee Nation.

Q How long did she live in the Cherokee Nation before she moved to the Creek Nation?
A She moved from the Cherokee Nation when she was quite young; she moved to Texas.

Q You know how long she lived in Texas?   A No sir, I do not. She was about 21 years old when she came back from Texas. She came back after the war.

Q You know whether or not she and her folks ever went back and were readmitted to citizenship in the Cherokee Nation?   A They made application to Council and were recognized.

Q Did the Council admit them?   A Admitted them, yes sir. I forget what year; it was during William P. Adair's life time.

Q You said awhile ago that your place was right on the line - did you continue to have any improvements in the Cherokee Nation after your marriage?   A No sir.

Q Have you any now? A No sir.

Commissioner-

Q Have you any evidence of your wife's readmission to citizenship after her return from Texas?   A I think it is on the books or act of Council in the Cherokee Nation.

Q You have no copy of the act of readmission?   A No sir, I have a certificate too; I don't know whether it is on file with the takers that I made application to or not. I don't know whether it is or whether I have it at home. I got a certificate from the Clerk at Tahlequah there.

Commissioner Breckinridge-

The applicant is shown to have been admitted to citizenship by decision of the United States Court, Judge Springer, Indian Territory presiding, in case No. 132, on appeal from his application in 1896 to the Dawes Commission. He states that he and his wife were married in 1869, and have lived together ever since. He does not present a Cherokee license and certificate of marriage, and he is not found upon any roll of the Cherokee Nation, and neither he, or his wife, have lived in the Cherokee Nation since their marriage in 1869, but have lived continuously in the Creek Nation, nor has the applicant possessed any improvement in the Cherokee Nation since 1869. His wife is identified on the roll of 1894, but upon no other roll, and the applicant states that she has been enrolled as a Creek citizen with their children, and that she had been allotted land as a Creek. He further states that his wife moved to the State of Texas when she was very young, and returned to the Cherokee Nation (he now says Creek Nation) when she was 21 years of age. He claims that she was readmitted to Cherokee citizenship, and thinks that the certificate of her readmission in on file with his Court papers or at home. The applicant has not lived in the Cherokee Nation since his admission by the United states Court. For the further consideration of this case under the conditions stated, he will now be listed for enrollment as a Cherokee by intermarriage upon a doubtful card and the Cherokee representative protests against his enrollment under the conditions already given and because, as they allege that evidence before the United States Court was an unreliable character.

(Statement by applicant:- I want to say that I merchandised in Tahlequah in the Cherokee Nation about a year after the strip payment.

E. G. Rothenberger, being duly sworn, states that as stenographer to the Commission to the Five Civilized Tribes, he reported in full the testimony and proceedings in the above case, and that the foregoing is a full, true and correct transcript of his stenographic notes in said case.

E.G. Rothenberger

Subscribed and sworn to before me this 18th day of February, 1901.

T B Needles
Commissioner.
Copy

◇◇◇◇◇

Cherokee D 1108

Department of the Interior,
Commission to the Five Civilized Tribes,
Muskogee, I. T., March 19, 1902.

In the matter of the application of W. B. Rogers for the enrollment of himself as a Cherokee citizen.

Appearances:
N.A. Gibson, Muskogee, I.T., attorney for applicant;
W.W. Hastings, attorney for the Cherokee Nation.

BY COMMISSION: The applicant was notified by registered letter February 28th, 1902, that his application for the enrollment of himself as a citizen of the Cherokee Nation would be taken up for final consideration by the Commission at its offices in Muskogee, Indian Territory on the 19th day of March, 1902. Applicant this day appears by his attorney, N. A. Gibson.

BY MR. GIBSON: We close the case.

W. B. ROGERS, being first duly sworn and being examined on behalf of the Cherokee Nation testified as follows:
BY MR. HASTINGS:
Q   What is your name?   A Woods B. Rogers.
Q   What is your age?   A 65.
Q   You are a white man?   A Yes sir.
Q   What is your wife's name?   A Kate D. Rogers.
Q   How long have you been living with her?   A 33 years.
Q   Where did she take her allotment?   A In the Creek Nation.
Q   In the Creek Nation?   A Yes sir.
Q   She is a Creek is she?   A Yes sir.
BY MR. HASTINGS: Comes now the representatives of the Cherokee Nation and refer the Commission to the Five Civilized Tribes Will E. Linton case, versus the Cherokee Nation, same being Court No. 253, as a decision which should govern in this case.

BY COMMISSION: The attorney for the applicant and the representative of the Cherokee Nation present submit the case; same is deemed completed, and will be reported to the Commission for final decision based upon the evidence now of record.

The attorney for the applicant requests and will be granted 15 days in which to file a brief in this case, one copy with the Commission an one copy with the representative of the Cherokee Nation.

Cherokee Intermarried White 1906
Volume IX

I, M. D. Green, do hereby certify that as stenographer to the Commission to the Five Civilized Tribes I correctly recorded the testimony and proceedings in this case and that the foregoing is a true and complete transcript of my stenographic notes thereof.

MD Green

<><><><><>

Cherokee D-1108.

Department of the Interior,
Commission to the Five Civilized Tribes,
Muskogee, I. T., September 29, 1902.

In the matter of the application of Woods B. Rogers for the enrollment of himself as a citizen by intermarriage of the Cherokee Nation: he being sworn and examined by the Commission, testified as follows:

Q What is your name?   A Woods B. Rogers.
Q How old are you at this time?   A 66.
Q What is your postoffice address?   A Checotah, I.T.
Q You claim as an intermarried citizen of the Cherokee Nation?   A Yes sir.
Q Are you the same Woods B. Rogers for whom application was made to this Commission on February 18, 1901?   A Yes sir.
Q What is your wife's name?   A Kate D. Rogers.
Q Is she a Cherokee citizen?   A She is a Cherokee by blood.
Q When were you and she married?   A On the fourth day of March, '69.
Q Is she living?   A Yes sir.
Q Were you ever married prior to your marriage to her?   A No sir.
Q Was she ever married before she and you were married?   A No sir.
Q Have you and she lived together continuously as husband and wife since the date of your marriage up until the present time?   A Yes sir.
Q And you are living together now as husband and wife?   A Yes sir.
Q You never have been separated?   A No sir.
Q You have never been married to any other woman?   A No sir.
Q How lon have you been living in the Cherokee Nation?   A I am not living in the Cherokee Nation, I am living in the Creek Nation.
Q How long have you lived in the Indian Territory?   A Since 1861.
Q Never made your home anywhere else except in the Indian Territory?   A No sir.
Q Has your wife lived in the Indian territory ever since you were married?   A Yes sir.
Q Have you got any children under 21 years old?   A They are all married.

The undersigned, being duly sworn, states that as stenographer to the Commission to the Five Civilized Tribes he correctly recorded the testimony and proceedings in this case, and that the foregoing is a true and correct transcript of his stenographic notes thereof.

E.G. Rothenberger

Subscribed and sworn to before me this 16th day of October, 1902.

BC Jones
Notary Public.

◇◇◇◇◇

Cherokee D-1108.

DEPARTMENT OF THE INTERIOR,   AAD
COMMISSION TO THE FIVE CIVILIZED TRIBES.

In the matter of the application of Woods B. Rogers for enrollment as a citizen by intermarriage of the Cherokee Nation.

D E C I S I O N

The records in this case shows that on February 16, 1901, Woods B. Rogers appeared before the Commission at Muskogee, Indian Territory, and made application for enrollment as such is accordingly granted. a citizen by intermarriage of the Cherokee Nation. Further proceedings in the matter of said application were had at Muskogee, Indian Territory, on March 19, and September 29, 1902.

The evidence shows that the said Woods B. Rogers filed his application with the Commission to the Five Civilized Tribes, under the act of June 10, 1896 (29 Stats., 321), to be admitted to citizenship in the Cherokee Nation; that his said application was denied by the Commission and that on appeal to the United States Court in Indian Territory for the Northern District, the decision of the Commission was reversed and the said Woods B. Rogers was admitted by the judgment of said Court, as a citizen by intermarriage of the Cherokee Nation.

The evidence further shows that Kate D. Rogers, the applicants[sic] wife, has made her election to be enrolled as a citizen of the Creek Nation and to take her allotment of lands in said Nation.

The evidence further shows that the said Woods B. Rogers has resided in the Indian Territory ever since his admission to citizenship.

It is the opinion of this Commission that, inasmuch as the applicant was admitted to citizenship in the Cherokee Nation by a judgment of the United States Court, his wife's election to be enrolled as a citizen of the Creek Nation is not considered to affect the applicant's rights as an intermarried Cherokee citizen and that he should therefore be enrolled as a citizen by intermarriage of the Cherokee Nation, in accordance with the provisions of Section twenty-one of the Act of Congress approved June 28, 1898, (30 Stats., 495), and it is so ordered.

COMMISSION TO THE FIVE CIVILIZED TRIBES.

Tams Bixby
> Chairman.

TB Needles
> Commissioner.

C. R. Breckinridge
> Commissioner.

Dated at Muskogee, Indian Territory,
this   NOV 20 1902

Copy

◇◇◇◇◇

DEPARTMENT OF THE INTERIOR.
Commission to the Five Civilized Tribes ,
Muskogee I. T. December 9th 1902.
In the matter of the application of Woods B. Rogers for enrollment as a citizen by intermarriage of the Cherokee Nation.
Cherokee D 1108.

Protest of the Cherokee Nation.

Comes now the Cherokee Nation and protests against the decision rendered by the Commission on November 20th 1902 in this case and asks that the same be forwarded to the Honorable Secretary of the Interior for Review. Attention is called to the brief filed by the Cherokee Nation in this case.

The record shows that this mans[sic] wife has elected to take her allotment in the Creek Nation and the case is exactly similar to the Will E. Linton case decided by the United States Court for the Northern District upon appeal from the Commission to the Five Civilized Tribes in 1896. It is true the applicant was admitted in 1896 as a citizen by intermarriage but it was on the theory that his wife was a Cherokee only. The Curtis bill provides that those of part Cherokee and part Creek blood must elect to take in one or the other nation but can not take in both. Awhile prior to 1896 they were in a habit of being married upon both rolls where payments were made in either nation. We contend that since his wife has elected to take in the Creek Nation and renounces her Cherokee Citizenship that in as much as the Applicant claims through his wife that under the decision of the United States Court in the Will E Linton case he is not entitled to be enrolled as a citizen of the Cherokee Nation by intermarriage.   Copy

Respectfully submitted,

W W Hastings   JCS
Attorney for the Cherokee Nation.

◇◇◇◇◇

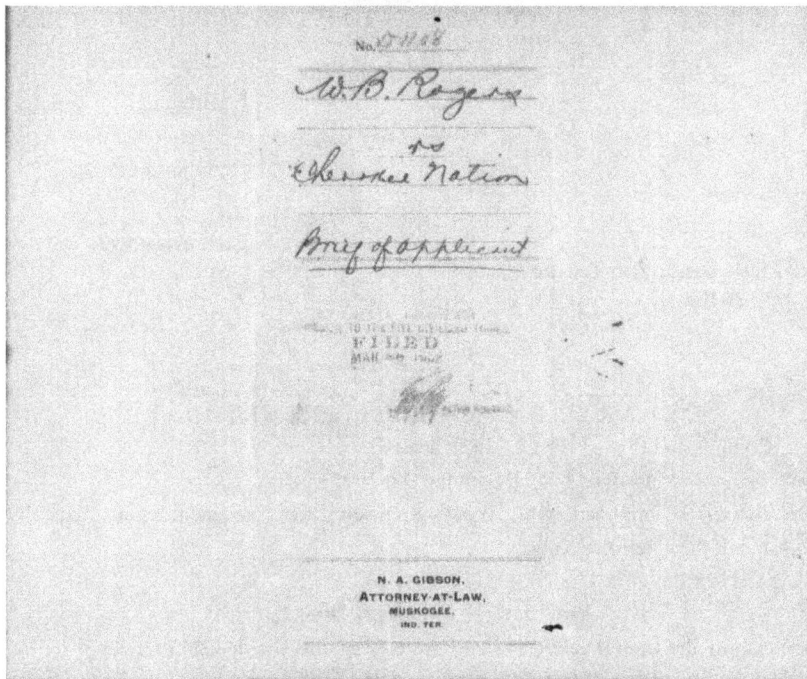

(Copy of original document from case.)

◇◇◇◇◇◇

DEPARTMENT OF THE INTERIOR
COMMISSIONER TO THE FIVE CIVILIZED TRIBES

On Page 18 of "A Record of Persons Admitted to Cherokee Citizenship by the National Council and Supreme Court since the Treaty of 1866" appears among other things, the following:

Rogers---W.B.   Dec. 16 '70   Admitted <u>White</u> must marry lawfully
  "   Kate D   "   "   "   "   "   "   "

Cherokee Intermarried White 1906
Volume IX

It is hereby ordered that this supplemental statement be filed with and made a part of the record in the matter of the application of Woods B. Rogers, for enrollment as a citizen by intermarriage of the Cherokee Nation.

SIGNED *Jams Bixby*
Commissioner.

Dated this 15th day of February, 1907.

◇◇◇◇◇

T.W.L.   Cherokee D 1108

DEPARTMENT OF THE INTERIOR

COMMISSIONER TO THE FIVE CIVILIZED TRIBES

In the matter of the application for the enrollment of Woods B. Rogers as a citizen by intermarriage of the Cherokee Nation.

D E C I S I O N

THE RECORDS OF THIS OFFICE SHOW: That at Muskogee, Indian Territory, February 16, 1901, application was received by the Commission to the Five Civilized Tribes for the enrollment of Woods B. Rogers, as a citizen by intermarriage of the Cherokee Nation. Further proceedings in the matter of said application were had at Muskogee, Indian Territory, March 19, 1902 and September 29, 1902.   That on November 20, 1902, it appearing that the said Woods B. Rogers had, in a decision reversing the decision of the Commission to the Five Civilized Tribes, been admitted to citizenship as a citizen by intermarriage of the Cherokee Nation by a decree of the United States Court in Indian Territory for the Northern District, and that the said Woods B. Rogers had resided in Indian Territory since his admission to citizenship, the Commission to the Five Civilized Tribes rendered its decision herein, granting the application of the said Woods B. Rogers for enrollment as a citizen of the Cherokee Nation by intermarriage; that thereafter, the Cherokee Nation filed a protest herein, protesting against the enrollment of said applicant, as heretofore stated, for the reason that the applicant's wife, Kate D. Rogers, through whom he claims his right to enrollment, had elected to take her allotment in the Creek Nation; that on December 13, 1902, the record in the matter of this application was forwarded to the Department; that on November 30, 1906 (I.T.D. 1552-1903) the First Assistant Secretary of the Interior stated that the said election of the said Kate D. Rogers, to be enrolled as a citizen of the Creek Nation, did not affect the right of this applicant to enrollment as an intermarried Cherokee citizen; that he should be enrolled as a citizen by intermarriage of the Cherokee Nation in accordance with the provisions of section 21 of the Act of Congress approved June 28, 1898 (30 Stats., 495), and authorized this office to place said applicant's name upon the proper roll, should no further objection appear; that on December 14, 1906, the Commissioner to the Five Civilized Tribes addressed a communication to the Department

140

and recommended, before the name of Woods B. Rogers be placed upon the schedule of citizens of the Cherokee Nation and forwarded for Departmental approval, that he be summoned before it and required to establish his right to enrollment as a citizen by intermarriage of the Cherokee Nation under the decision of the Supreme Court dated November 5, 1906, in the cases of Daniel Red Bird, et al., vs. the United States, Nos. 125, 126.

THE EVIDENCE IN THIS CASE SHOWS: That the applicant herein, Woods B. Rogers, is a white man and claims his right to enrollment as a citizen of the Cherokee Nation by virtue of his marriage to Kate D. Rogers, nee Drew, who has been enrolled as a citizen of the Creek Nation, and whose name, together with that of Mary R. Rogers, a child of the said Woods B. Rogers and Kate D. Rogers, is found upon the approved partial roll of citizens by blood of the Creek Nation, opposite No. 596 and 597 respectively, in 1869, under a Cherokee tribal license issued out of the Canadian District, of the Cherokee Nation. A careful examination of Book B of the Record of Marriages and Licenses issued from the years 1869 to 1890, in the possession of this office, fails to show that any tribal license was issued for the marriage of the said applicant and the said Kate D. Rogers. It further appears from "A Record of Persons admitted to citizenship by the National Council and Supreme Court since the treaty of 1866," that the said Woods B. Rogers and the said Kate D. Rogers were not admitted to Cherokee citizenship until December 16, 1870 and that the admission of the former was conditional, in that he was "White, must marry lawfully." Said applicant did not therefore, marry in accordance with Cherokee law a recognized citizen by blood of the Cherokee Nation prior to November 1, 1875.

IT IS THEREFORE ORDERED AND ADJUDGED: That in accordance with the decision of the Supreme Court of the United States, dated November 5, 1906, in the cases of Daniel Red Bird et al., vs. the United States, Nos. 125, 126, 127, and 128, the said applicant, Woods B. Rogers, is not entitled under the provisions of section 21 of the Act of Congress approved June 28, 1898 (30 Stats., 495), to enrollment as a citizen by intermarriage of the Cherokee Nation, and his application for enrollment as such is accordingly denied.

Commissioner

Dated at Muskogee, Indian Territory

this _____

(The following is handwritten on the bottom of the page.)

There is no evidence ~~of~~ or claim that subsequent to the date of said admission the applicant was remarried to the said Kate D Rogers. Neither the names of the applicant or his wife are found upon the 1880 or 1896 rolls of the Cherokee Nation. Although duly notified to do so, the applicant has failed to offer any further evidence.

◇◇◇◇◇

COMMISSIONERS:

TAMS BIXBY,
THOMAS B. NEEDLES,
C. R. BRECKINRIDGE,
W. E. STANLEY.

ALLISON L. AYLESWORTH,
SECRETARY.

REFER IN REPLY TO THE FOLLOWING

DEPARTMENT OF THE INTERIOR, **Cherokee D-1108**
COMMISSION TO THE FIVE CIVILIZED TRIBES.

ADDRESS ONLY THE
COMMISSION TO THE FIVE CIVILIZED TRIBES.

Muskogee, Indian Territory, **February 28,** 1902.

Mr. Woods B. Rogers,
        Checotah, Indian Territory.

Sir:-

You are hereby notified that the application of **yourself**

for enrollment as ....citizen.... of the Cherokee Nation will be taken up for final consideration by the Commission to the Five Civilized Tribes, at its office in Muskogee, Indian Territory, on **the 19 day of March, 1902.**

On said date, you may, if you desire, appear before the Commission, in person or by attorney, when an opportunity will be given you to introduce any additional testimony affecting your application, **that you may deem necessary.**

You are further notified that the Representatives of the Cherokee Nation will also, at the same time, be afforded an opportunity to introduce testimony tending to disprove your right to enrollment, but said Representatives will be required to notify you of their intention to introduce such testimony before they will be permitted to do so.

Register.

                    Yours truly,

                            Commissioner in Charge.

                                    xActing Chairmanx

                    ◇◇◇◇◇

COPY   Cherokee D-1108.

Muskogee, Indian Territory, November 26, 1902.

W. W. Hastings,
        Attorney for the Cherokee Nation,
            Muskogee, Indian Territory.

Dear Sir:

There is herewith inclosed a copy of the decision of the Commission to the Five Civilized Tribes, dated November 20, 1902, granting the application of Woods B. Rogers for the enrollment of himself as a citizen by intermarriage of the Cherokee Nation.

You are advised that you will be allowed fifteen days from date hereof in which to file such protest as you desire to make against the action of the Commission in this case, a copy of which protest you will be required to serve upon the applicant. If you fail to file protest within the time allowed, this decision will be considered final.

Respectfully,

Tams Bixby
Acting Chairman.

Enc. H-186.

◇◇◇◇◇

COPY   Cherokee D 1108.

Muskogee, Indian Territory, December 13, 1902.

Woods B. Rogers,
        Checotah, Indian Territory.

Dear Sir:

There is herewith enclosed a copy of the decision of the Commission to the Five Civilized Tribes, dated November 20, 1902, granting the application for the enrollment of yourself as a citizen by intermarriage of the Cherokee Nation. There has this day been forwarded your attorney, N. A. Gibson, Muskogee, Indian Territory, a copy of the record of proceedings, together with a copy of the Commission's decision.

You are hereby advised that the Cherokee Nation protests against the action of the Commission in this case, a copy of which protest has been furnished you by the attorney for the Nation.

143

The decision, with the record of proceedings had in the case, has this day been transmitted to the Secretary of the Interior for his review and decision.

The action of the Secretary will be made known to you as soon as the Commission is informed of the same.

Respectfully,

Tams Bixby

Register.

Enclosure H. No. 185.   Acting Chairman.

◇◇◇◇◇

COPY   Cherokee D 1108.

Muskogee, Indian Territory, December 13, 1902.

N. A. Gibson,
    Attorney for Woods B. Rogers,
        Muskogee, Indian Territory.

Dear Sir:

There is herewith enclosed a copy of the record of proceedings had in the matter of the application of Woods B. Rogers for the enrollment is himself as a citizen by intermarriage of the Cherokee Nation, together with a copy of the Commission's decision, dated November 20, 1902, granting said application.

You are hereby advised that the Cherokee Nation protests against the action of the Commission in this case, a copy of which protest has been furnished the applicant by the attorney for the Nation.

The decision, with the record of proceedings had in the case, has this day been transmitted to the Secretary of the Interior for his review and decision.

The action of the Secretary will be made known to you as soon as the Commission is informed of the same.

Respectfully,

Tams Bixby

Register.   Acting Chairman.

Enclosure H. No. 186.

◇◇◇◇◇

Cherokee D 1108.

Muskogee, Indian Territory, December 13, 1902.

W. W. Hastings,
    Attorney for the Cherokee Nation,
        Muskogee, Indian Territory.

Dear Sir:

You are hereby advised that the Commission's decision, dated November 20, 1902, granting the application of Woods B. Rogers for the enrollment of himself as a citizen by intermarriage of the Cherokee Nation, a copy of which decision was furnished you on November 26, 1902, has this day been transmitted to the Secretary of the Interior for his review and decision.

The action of the Secretary will be made known to you as soon as the Commission is informed of the same.

Respectfully,

Tams Bixby

Acting Chairman.

◇◇◇◇◇

Cherokee D 1108.

COPY

Muskogee, Indian Territory, December 13, 1902.

The Honorable,
    The Secretary of the Interior.

Sir:

There is herewith transmitted the record of proceedings had in the matter of the application of Woods B. Rogers for the enrollment of himself as a citizen by intermarriage of the Cherokee Nation, including the Commission's decision, dated November 20, 1902, granting said application.

You are advised that the Cherokee Nation protests against the action of the Commission in this case, a copy of which protest is enclosed.

Respectfully,

Tams Bixby
Acting Chairman.

Through the
    Commissioner of Indian Affairs Indian Affairs.
Enclosure H. No. 187.

◇◇◇◇◇

Land.   (COPY)
                    DEPARTMENT OF THE INTERIOR
74935-1903.
                    OFFICE OF INDIAN AFFAIRS

                    WASHINGTON.   Feby. 14, 1903.

The Honorable,
        The Secretary of the Interior.

Sir

        There is transmitted herewith report from the Acting Chairman of the Commission to the Five Civilized Tribes, dated December 13, 1902, forwarding, for the Department's consideration, the record relative to the application of Woods B. Rogers, for enrollment as an intermarried citizen of the Cherokee Nation.

        November 20, 1902, the Commission held that the applicant was entitled to enrollment as an intermarried citizen of the Cherokee Nation.

        The Cherokee Nation, by its attorney, protests against the Commission's decision. The Nation's attorney invites attention to the holding of the United States Court for the Northern District of the Indian Territory in the William E. Linton case, which was appealed from the Commission's decision in 1896. The attorney does not quote from the decision, but a quotation therefrom will be found in office report of February 10, 1902, transmitting the record relative to the application of C. Howard Davis for enrollment as an intermarried citizen of the Cherokee Nation.

        The record in this case shows that the applicant applied to the Commission in 1896 for admission to citizenship in the Cherokee Nation, that his application was denied; that an appeal was taken from the Commission's decision; that the United States Court for the Northern District of the Indian Territory reversed the Commission's decision and admitted to citizenship in said Nation, as an intermarried citizen, Woods B. Rogers.

        The record also shows that the wife of the applicant, Kate D. Rogers, has elected to be enrolled as a citizen of the Creek Nation.

        From the record it appears that the applicant's wife was entitled to rights in the Cherokee and Creek Nations and that, in accordance with the provisions of the Curtis Act, she has elected to take her allotment in the Creek Nation.

        The testimony shows that the applicant and his wife were married in accordance with the laws of the Cherokee Nation in 1869.

        The Court in the Linton case held that if Pauline B. Linton elected to be enrolled as a citizen of the Cherokee Nation, her husband and minor children should also

146

be enrolled as citizens of the Nation, but that if she elected to be enrolled as a citizen of the Creek Nation, she and her children should be enrolled as citizens of the Creek Nation, and that her husband should not be enrolled as a citizen of either the Creek or Cherokee Nation.

The Court having declared that Woods B. Rogers was entitled to citizenship in the Cherokee Nation as an intermarried citizen, the office does not believe that the fact that his wife has elected to take her allotment in the Creek Nation, invalidates or in any manner whatsoever affects his rights to citizenship in the Cherokee Nation, and it therefore respectfully recommends that the Commission's decision declaring the applicant entitled to enrollment as an intermarried citizen of the Cherokee Nation be approved.

Very respectfully,

A. C. Tonner,

GAW

O

Acting Commissioner.

◇◇◇◇◇

(COPY)

D.C. 53192-1906.

Y.P.

DEPARTMENT OF THE INTERIOR

WASHINGTON.

FHE.

I.T.D. 1552-1903.

November 30, 1906.

L.R.S.

Commissioner to the Five Civilized Tribes,
    Muskogee, Indian Territory.

Sir:

December 13, 1902, the Commission to the Five Civilized Tribes transmitted the papers in the matter of the application of Woods B. Rogers for enrolment[sic] as a citizen by intermarriage of the Cherokee Nation. The case has been held awaiting the decision of the Supreme Court in the case of Daniel Red Bird, et al., vs. the United States, in which the Court rendered its decision November 5, 1906.

It is shown by the record in the Rogers case that he was admitted to citizenship in the Cherokee Nation as a citizen by intermarriage by the United State Court in the Indian Territory for the Northern District, in accordance with the provisions of the act of June 10, 1896 (29 Stat., 321). It is shown that Kate D. Rogers, the applicant's Cherokee wife, has made her election to be enroled[sic] as a citizen of the Creek Nation and to take her allotment in said nation.

The Commission to the Five Civilized Tribes, in its decision of November 20, 1902, held that inasmuch as the applicant was admitted to citizenship in the Cherokee Nation by the judgment of the United States Court, his wife's election to be enroled[sic] as a citizen of the Creek Nation is not considered to affect the applicant's rights as an intermarried Cherokee citizen, and that he should be enroled[sic] as a citizen by intermarriage of the Cherokee Nation in accordance with the provisions of section 21 of the act of June 28, 1898 (30 Stat., 495).

The Cherokee Nation by its attorney protests against the Commission's decision. The nation's attorney invites attention to the holding of the United States Court for the Northern District for the Indian Territory in the William E. Linton case. The Court in that case held that if Pauline B. Linton elected to be enroled[sic] as a citizen of the Cherokee Nation her husband and minor children should also be enroled[sic] as citizens of that nation, but that if she elected to be enroled[sic] as a citizen of the Creek Nation she and her children should be enrolled as citizens of that nation and that her husband should not be enroled[sic] as citizens[sic] of either the Creek or Cherokee Nations[sic].

The Indian Office, in letter of February 14, 1903, submitting the report of the Commission of December 13, 1902, expressed the opinion that as the Court had declared Rogers entitled to citizenship in the Cherokee Nation as an intermarried citizen, the fact that his wife had elected to take her allotment in the Creek Nation did not invalidate or in any manner affect Rogers' rights to citizenship in the Cherokee Nation, and it recommended that the decision of the Commission in favor of Rogers be affirmed.

The Court of Claims held in its decision in the case of Red Bird et al., which decision was affirmed by the Supreme Court, that such white persons residing in the Cherokee Nation as became Cherokee citizens under Cherokee laws by intermarriage with cherokees[sic] by blood prior to the first day of November, 1875, are equally interested in and have equally per capita rights with Cherokee Indians by blood in the lands constituting the public domain of the Cherokee Nation, and are entitled to be enroled[sic] for that purpose.

There is some question whether the applicant was married to his Cherokee wife in accordance with Cherokee laws; apparently he was. He states that he procured a regular license though he did not get a certificate of marriage; that he supposed that the license and certificate of marriage were destroyed. It appears that he and his wife were married in 1869, and have resided in the Indian Territory since that time. The Department considers the applicant entitled to enrolment[sic] under section 21 of the act of June 28, 1898 (30 Stat., 495), and you are authorized to place his name upon the proper roll, should no further objection appear. Advise the attorney for the Nation hereof.

A copy of the Indian Office letter is inclosed. The papers in the case have been returned to that office.

Respectfully,

(Signed Thos. Ryan,
Through the Commissioner   First Assistant Secretary.
of Indian Affairs.

1 inc. and 6 for Ind. Of.

◇◇◇◇◇

Muskogee, Indian Territory, December 14, 1906

DIRECT

The Honorable,
    The Secretary of the Interior.

Sir:

Receipt is acknowledged of Departmental letter of November 30, 1906 (I.T.D. 1552-1903), granting the application for the enrollment of Woods B. Rogers as a citizen by intermarriage of the Cherokee Nation, under Section Twenty-one of the Act of Congress approved June 28, 1898 (30 Stats., 495), and authorizing this office to place his name upon a final roll should not further objection appear.

The decision of the Commission to the Five Civilized Tribes of November 20, 1902, which the Department affirmed, granted the application for the enrollment of said Rogers, for the reason that he was admitted to citizenship in the Cherokee Nation as an intermarried citizen, by a judgment of the United States Court for the Northern District of Indian Territory, under the provisions of the Act of Congress approved June 10, 1896 (29 Stat. 321).

The applicant based his claim for admission to citizenship to the Cherokee Nation by reason of his marriage to his wife, Kate D. Rogers, who, he alleges, was a Cherokee by blood, but who, the record show, elected to be enrolled, and has received her allotment of land, as a citizen of the Creek Nation. He claims to have been married to his wife in the year 1869, but he failed to make proof to the Commission as to his compliance with Cherokee law in regard to his marriage, or that he was regularly married to her.

Under the decision of the Supreme Court of the United States of November 5, 1906, in the case of Daniel Redbird et al., versus the Cherokee Nation, the applicant is entitled to enrollment only on the condition that his wife, by reason of his marriage to whom he claims his citizenship, was a Cherokee citizen, and that he was married to her according to Cherokee law. It appears that before the applicant should be enrolled as a citizen by intermarriage of the Cherokee Nation he should be required to establish that his wife at the time of his marriage to her, was a recognized citizen of the Cherokee Nation, and that, he was married to her according to Cherokee law.

149

This office therefore respectfully recommends that before the name of Woods B. Rogers be placed upon a schedule of citizens of the Cherokee Nation and forwarded for Departmental approval, that he be summoned before it and required to establish his right to enrollment as a citizen by intermarriage of the Cherokee Nation under the decision of the Supreme Court of November 5, above referred to.

No notice of the Department's action in this case will be given the attorney for the Cherokee Nation and the applicant, until further advised by the Department.

Respectfully,

L M B   Commissioner.

◇◇◇◇◇

LAND

113106-1906
105039-1906

January 15, 1907.

The Honorable,
        The Secretary of the Interior.

Sir:

        Receipt is acknowledged of Departmental letter of December 27, 1906, enclosing a letter from the Commissioner to the Five Civilized Tribes, dated December 13, 1906, in which reference is made to Departmental letter of November 30, 1906, addressed to the Commissioner, authorizing the enrollment of Woods B. Rogers as a citizen by intermarriage of the Cherokee Nation, "should no further objection appear". The Commissioner's letter was addressed directly to the Department and was not transmitted through this Office.

        Therein he says that the applicant, Woods B. Rogers, bases his claim for admission to citizenship in the Cherokee Nation on his marriage to Kate D. Rogers, who, he alleges, was a Cherokee by blood, but who elected to be enrolled, and has received her allotment of land as a citizen of the Creek Nation. The applicant claims to have been married to his wife in the year 1869, but has failed to make proof to the Commissioner as to his compliance with the Cherokee law in regard to his marriage, or that he was legally married to her.

        Referring to the decision of the Supreme Court of the United States in the case of Daniel Red Bird, et al., vs. the United States, the Commissioner expresses the opinion that before the applicant should be enrolled as a citizen by intermarriage of the Cherokee

Nation, he should be required to establish that his wife at the time of his marriage to her was a recognized citizen of the Nation and that he was married to her according to Cherokee law, and suggests that before his name be placed on a schedule of citizens of the Nation and forwarded for Departmental approval, that the applicant be summoned before the Commissioner and required to establish his right, as above. The recommendation of this Office is requested in the matter.

It appears from the evidence in this case that Woods B. Rogers filed his application with the Commission under the Act of June 10, 1906 (29 Stat., L. 321), to be admitted to citizenship in the Cherokee Nation; that his application was denied by the Commission, and that he appealed to the United States Court for the Northern District of Indian Territory. The decision of the Commission was reversed and Woods B. Rogers was admitted as a citizen by intermarriage of the Cherokee Nation by the Court.

The wife of the applicant, Kate D. Rogers, being entitled to enrollment in both the Creek and Cherokee Nations, has selected to be enrolled as a citizen of the former.

The Office, in letter of February 14, 1903, expressed the opinion that the applicant, having been declared by the Court to be entitled to enrollment in the Cherokee Nation, as a citizen by intermarriage, his right was not affected by his wife's election to be enrolled in the Creek Nation.

This view was sustained by the Department in letter of November 30, 1906 (I.T.D. 1552-1903), in the course of which it is remarked that there is some question whether the applicant was married in accordance with Cherokee laws.

The applicant testified that he procured a regular license, although he did not get a certificate of marriage; that he supposed the license and certificate of marriage were destroyed. He and his wife were married in 1869, and have lived in the Indian Territory since that time.

In Departmental letter of December 27, 1906, (I.T.D. 25368-19060 it is said:

Presumably the United States Court which "admitted" Rogers to citizenship . . . . . in accordance with the . . . . . Act of June 10, 1896, (29 States. L., 321) considered the question whether the applicant was married in accordance with such laws.
In view of the fact that the applicant's marriage occurred in 1869, and the probabilities of the records being destroyed as he testifies, being therefore very great; that he and Kate D. Rogers have lived in the Territory as man and wife continuously since their marriage; and in view of the serious doubt as to the authority of the Commissioner to further inquire into the applicants[sic] rights which have been established by a court having jurisdiction and whose decisions are made final by the law conferring that jurisdiction, it is recommended that the applicants[sic] name be enrolled as a Cherokee intermarried citizen, in accordance with Departmental letter of November 30, 1906, above referred to.

Very respectfully,

C. F. Larrabee,

Acting Commissioner.

A. J. W.-NL

◇◇◇◇◇

J.P.
S.P.

COPY

DEPARTMENT OF THE INTERIOR,

D.C. 9329-1907.   WASHINGTON.

I.T.D. 1042-1907.

February 11, 1907.

L.N.S.

Commissioner to the Five Civilized Tribes.
    Muskogee, Indian Territory.

Sir:

Referring to your letter of December 14, 1906, relative to the application for the enrollment of Woods B. Rogers as a citizen by intermarriage in the Cherokee Nation, you are directed to enroll the applicant in accordance with decision of the Department of the Interior November 30, 1906, and the recommendation of the Indian Office of January 15, 1907, submitting your report of December 14, 1906.

A copy of Indian Office letter is enclosed.

All the papers in the matter have been sent to the Indian Office for its files.

Respectfully,

Thos. Ryan,

First Assistant Secretary.

Through the Commissioner
    of Indian Affairs.

I inc. and 8 to Ind. Of.

◇◇◇◇◇

Muskogee, Indian Territory, March 1, 1907.

SPECIAL.
Direct.

The Honorable,
The Secretary of the Interior.

Sir:

Referring to Departmental letter of February 11, 1907, (I.T.D. 1042-07), directing the enrollment of Woods B. Rogers as a citizen by intermarriage of the Cherokee Nation, There is enclosed herewith a schedule containing his name.

This schedule was not transmitted with the schedules transmitted February 28, 1907, for Departmental approval, through an inadvertence.

In the event of the approval of this schedule it is recommended that a number be placed thereon by Mr. McGarr, the employee of my office now in Washington.

Respectfully,
Tams Bixby
Commissioner.

J.O.R.
Enc. L-1.

◇◇◇◇◇◇

Cherokee D 1108   COPY

Muskogee, Indian Territory, March 14, 1907.

Woods B. Rogers,
Checotah, Indian Territory.

Dear Sir:

You are hereby advised that the decision of the Commissioner to the Five Civilized Tribes, dated December 14, 1907, granting the application for your enrollment as a citizen by intermarriage of the Cherokee Nation, was affirmed by the Secretary of the Interior, February 11, 1907.

For your information, there is enclosed herewith a copy of Departmental decision referred to.

Respectfully,

SIGNED *Tams Bixby*
Commissioner.

Enc I-64

RPI

◇◇◇◇◇◇

153

Cherokee D 1108　　　　　ʎdOϽ

Muskogee, Indian Territory, March 14, 1907.

N. A. Gibson,
　　　Attorney for Wood[sic] B. Rogers,
　　　　　Muskogee, Indian Territory.

Dear Sir:

　　　You are hereby advised that the decision of the Commissioner to the Five Civilized Tribes, dated December 14, 1907, granting the application for the enrollment of Wood[sic] Rogers, as a citizen by intermarriage of the Cherokee Nation, was affirmed by the Secretary of the Interior, February 11, 1907.

　　　For your information, there is enclosed herewith a copy of Departmental decision referred to.

　　　　　　　　　　　Respectfully,

　　　　　　　　　　　　　　SIGNED *Jams Bixby*
　　　　　　　　　　　　　　Commissioner.

Enc I-70

RPI

◇◇◇◇◇

Cherokee D 1108　　　　　COPY

Muskogee, Indian Territory, March 14, 1907.

W. W. Hastings,
　　　Attorney for the Cherokee Nation,
　　　　　Muskogee, Indian Territory.

Dear Sir:

　　　You are hereby advised that the decision of the Commissioner to the Five Civilized Tribes, dated December 14, 1907, granting the application for the enrollment of Wood B. Rogers as a citizen by intermarriage of the Cherokee Nation, was affirmed by the Secretary of the Interior, February 11, 1907.

　　　For your information, there is enclosed herewith a copy of Departmental decision referred to.

　　　　　　　　　　　Respectfully,

　　　　　　　　　　　　　　SIGNED *Jams Bixby*
　　　　　　　　　　　　　　Commissioner.

Enc I-63

RPI

◇◇◇◇◇

Department of the Interior,
Commission to the Five Civilized Tribes,
Vinita, I.T., October 2 1900.

In the matter of the application of Michael Mulcare for the enrolment[sic] of himself and children as Cherokee citizens; being sworn and examined by Commissioner Needles he testified as follows:

Q What is your name? A Michael Mulcare.
Q What is your age? A 57.
Q What is your post-office? A Vinita.
Q In what district do you live? A Delaware.
Q Are you a recognized citizen of the Cherokee Nation by blood of intermarriage?
A Intermarriage.
Q For whom do you apply for enrollment? A Four children.
Q Your wife? A No sir, she is dead.
Q Yourself and four children? A Yes sir.

Q What is the name of your wife? A I have had two wives; the mother of the four children is Tennessee.
Q She a citizen by blood? A Yes sir.
Q What was her name before you married her? A Parris.
Q Did you marry her before 1880? A No sir, since.
Q Is your name upon the roll of 1880? A Yes sir
Q Is your wife's name on the roll of 1880? A I guess it is.
Q Your last wife? A Yes sir, her name is on it, but we wasn't married then.
Q Have you been married since? A No sir.
Q Both of your wives, as I understand then, were Cherokee citizens by blood?
A They was.
Q What are the names of your children? A Minnie, she is 14 I think.
Nora, 11; Sterling P., 9; Ella, 5.
Q Are these children alive and living with you? A Yes sir.
Q How long have you lived in the Cherokee Nation? A About 30 Years.
Q What is the name of the mother of these children? A Tennessee.
Q Your last wife or first? A Last wife.
Q Got no children by your first wife? A Yes sir, but they are all grown.
1880 roll page 455 #1182 as Mike Mulcar[sic] Goingsnake District.
1880 roll page 459 #1234 as Tennie Parris Goingsnake District;
1896 roll page 581 #367 as Mike Mulcar Delaware District;
1896 roll page 507 #2169 Minnie Mulcar "
1896 roll page 507 #2170 Nora Mulcar "
1896 roll page 507 #2171 Sterling P. Mulcar "
1896 roll page 507 #2172 Ella Mulcar "

Cherokee Intermarried White 1906
Volume IX

Q   Are these children alive and living with you at this time?
A   Yes sir.
Q   Have you lived continuously in the Cherokee Nation since 1880?
A   Yes sir.
Q   Living there now?   A Yes sir
Q   Not married at the present time?   A No sir

    Com'r Needles: The name of Michael Mulcare appears upon the authenticated roll of 1880; name of his wife Tennessee appears upon the authenticated roll of 1880 as Tennie Parris, she now being deceased; his name appears upon the census roll of 1896, as well as the names of his children by his wife Tennessee, namely, Minnie, Nora, Sterling P. and Ella; they all being duly identified according to page and number of the rolls as indicated in the testimony, the sad[sic] Michael Mulcare will be duly listed for enrollment as a Cherokee citizen by intermarriage, and his children as Cherokee citizens by blood.

    M.D. Green, being first duly sworn, states that as stenographer to the Commission to the Five Civilized Tribes he correctly recorded the testimony and proceedings in this case, and the foregoing is a true and complete transcript of his stenographic notes thereof.

MD Green

Subscribed and sworn to before me this 2nd day of October 1900.

C R Breckinridge
Commissioner.

◇◇◇◇◇

Cherokee 3980.

DEPARTMENT OF THE INTERIOR,
COMMISSION TO THE FIVE CIVILIZED TRIBES.
Muskogee, I. T., October 28, 1902.

    In the matter of the application of Michal[sic] Mulcare for the enrollment of himself as a citizen by intermarriage, and for the enrollment of his four minor children, Minnie, Nora, Sterling P. and Ella Mulcare, as citizens by blood, of the Cherokee Nation.

SUPPLEMENTAL PROCEEDINGS.

MICHAL[sic] MULCARE, being sworn, testified as follows:

By the Commission,

Q What's your name?   A Michal Mulcare.
Q How old are you, Mr. Mulcare?   A Fifty-nine.
Q What is your postoffice?   A Pensecola[sic].

156

Cherokee Intermarried White 1906
Volume IX

Q Indian Territory?   A Yes, sir.

Q It was Vinita when you made your original application, was it?
A Yes, sir.

Q Are you an applicant for enrollment as an intermarried citizen of the Cherokee Nation?   A Yes, sir.

Q What's your wife's name?   A My wife's dead. Her name was Tennessee.

Q When did she die?   A Three years ago last December.

Q Three years ago?   A Yes, sir.

Q Was she a recognized citizen by blood of the Cherokee Nation?
A Yes, sir.

Q When were you married to her?   A Well, I don't believe I can tell the date.

Q Well, I don't know that I could tell you.   [sic] I guess we had been married about ten years or twelve years when she died. I don't recollect exactly.

Q Were you married to her under Cherokee license?   A No, we had been married before.

Q You were married just as one Indian married another?   A Yes, sir.

Q Had you been married before you married your wife, Tennessee?   A Yes, sir.

Q Whar[sic] was your first wife's name?   A Nancy J. Parris.

Q When were you married to your wife, Nancy J.? A I don't know whether I could tell you that ot[sic] not.

Q How long ago has it been?   A Oh, it has been over thirty years, I guess, right about thirty.

Q About thirty years ago?   A Yes, sir.

Q You're on the '80 roll with your wife, Nancy J.? A Yes, sir.

Q Now, are these two women, Nancy J. and Tennessee, the only women you have ever been married to?   A Yes, sir.

Q Did you live with your wife, Nancy J., from 1880 up until the time she died?   A Yes, sir.

Q You and Nancy J. were never separated during her lifetime?   A No, sir.

Q Then, after Nancy's death, you married your wife, Tennessee?   A Yes, sir.

Q And she was also a Cherokee?   A Yes, sir.

Q Did you and your wife, Tennessee, live together from the time of your marriage up until her death?   A Yes, sir.

Q You and she were never separated during her lifetime?   A No, sir.

Q Now, since her death, have you married again?   A No, sir.

Q Were you a widower and still a single man on the first day of September, 1902?
A Yes, sir.

Q Have you lived in the Cherokee Nation all the time since '80 up to the present time?
A Yes, sir.

Q Never lived out of the Nation since that time?   A No, sir.

Q Now, these children, Minnie, Nora, Sterling P. and Ella, are they your children by your wife, Tennessee?   A Yes, sir.

Q Are these children all living?   A Yes, sir.

Q Lived all their lives in the Cherokee Nation, have they?   A Yes, sir.

Cherokee Intermarried White 1906
Volume IX

Retta Chick, being first duly sworn, states that, as stenographer to the Commission to the Five Civilized Tribes, she recorded the testimony and proceedings in the matter of the foregoing application, and that the above is a true and complete transcript of her stenographic notes thereof.

Retta Chick

Subscribed and sworn to before me this 3rd day of December, 1902.

PG Reuter
Notary Public.

◇◇◇◇◇

DEPARTMENT OF THE INTERIOR.
COMMISSION TO THE FIVE CIVILIZED TRIBES.
AUXILIARY CHEROKEE LAND OFFICE.

Muskogee, Indian Territory, April 21, 1905.

In the matter of the application of Michal[sic] Mulcare to select allotments in the Cherokee Nation for Nora, Sterling P. and Ella Mulcare, Cherokee citizen roll No.s.[sic] 9626, 9627 & 9628, respectively, Field Card No. 3980.

Michal Mulcare, non-citizen father, being sworn, testified as follows:

Examination by the Commission:
Q   What is your name?   A Michal[sic] Mulcare.
Q   What is your post office address?   A Pensacola.
Q   What is your age?   A 62.
Q   Do you claim any rights to citizenship in the Cherokee Nation, either by blood or adoption?   A I am an adopted citizen.
Q   Is your object in appearing before the Auxiliary Cherokee Land Office of the Commission today to select allotments for you minor children?   A Yes sir.
Q   What are their names?   A Minnie, Nora, Sterling and Ella.
Q   How old is Nora?   A 16.
Q   Sterling P.?   A 13.
Q   And Ella?   A 9.
Q   Has anyone ever been appointed guardian for these children?
    A No sir.
Q   Is their mother living?   A No sir.
Q   When did she die?   A She's been dead about 6 years.
Q   What was her name?   A Tennessee Mulcare.
Q   These children make their home with you do they?   A Yes sir.

158

Q Have you been notified by the Commission to come in and file for these children?
A Yes sir.

Witness offers letter from the Commission to the Five Civilized Tribes, dated April 27[sic], 1905, in which they notify him to appear before the Cherokee Land Office and select land for his minor children, on or before April 15, 1905.

Q Is the land that you desire to have allotted to your minor children under improvement and in cultivation?   A Partly.
Q In your possession?   A Yes sir.
Q Does it lie west of the Grand and Arkansas rivers?   A Yes sir.
Q In what district?   A Delaware.
Q Has anyone ever before this time appeared at the Vinita or the Tahlequah Offices to select an allotment for them?   A Not that I know of.

WITNESS EXCUSED.

Blanch Ashton upon oath states that as stenographer to the Commission to the Five Civilized Tribes she accurately recorded the testimony in the above entitled cause and that the foregoing is a correct transcript of her notes thereof.

Blanch Ashton

Notary Public to before me this 21st day of April, 1905.

WS Haskins
Notary Public.

◇◇◇◇◇◇

F.R.   Cherokee 3980.

DEPARTMENT OF THE INTERIOR,
COMMISSIONER TO THE FIVE CIVILIZED TRIBES.
Muskogee, I. T., February 1, 1907.

In the matter of the application for the enrollment of Michal Mulcare as a citizen by intermarriage of the Cherokee Nation.
Cherokee Nation represented by H. M. Vance.

Michal Mulcare being first duly sworn by Frances R. Lane, a Notary Public for the Western District of Indian Territory, testified as follows:

By the Commissioner:
Q What is your name?   A Michal Mulcare.
Q What is your age?   A About 64
Q Your postoffice address?   A Pensacola, I. T.
Q You are a white man are you?   A Yes sir.

Q You claim right to enrollment as a citizen by intermarriage of the Cherokee nation[sic]?
A Yes sir.

Q Your claim to such right is solely by virtue of your marriage to a citizen of that nation?   A Yes sir.

Q What is the name of that citizen through whom you claim that right?   A Her name was Nancy Jane Paris[sic].

Q When were you married to Nancy Jane Paris?   A I would not be positive but it was either 1871 or 1872.

Q Where were you married?   A Going Snake District.

Q Who performed the marriage ceremony?   A I don't know whether I could tell that.

Q A judge or minister?   A No, it was not a preacher; it was either the clerk or judge.

Q Was that marriage under a license of the Cherokee nation? A Yes sir.

Q Who issued the license to you? The clerk of Going Snake District?   A Yes. I didn't go and get the license myself; the clerk or judge, whichever it was, came to my house.

Q You have no documentary evidence, papers or evidence, showing that marriage?
A No, no papers at all.

Q At the time you married Nancy Jane Paris was she a citizen by blood of the Cherokee nation?[sic] and recognized as such?   A Yes sir, she was

Q Were you ever married before you married Nancy Jane Paris?   A I never was.

Q Had she ever been married before she married you?   A Yes, she was a widow. Her first husband was Robert Paris.

Q She had been married just once before she married you?   A Yes sir.

Q Was Robert Paris living at the time she married you?   A No, he was dead.

Q Was Nancy J. Paris born in the Cherokee nation?   A Yes sir.

Q Lived there all her life until she married you?   A Yes; raised there.

Q Is she living at this time?   A No sir.

Q When did she die?   A I don't know as I can tell; been dead a number of years.

Q About how long?   A Somewhere in the neighborhood of twenty years or more.

Q Did you and Nancy Jane Mulcare live together as husband and wife and reside in the Cherokee nation until her death?   A Yes sir.

Q You never separated?   A No sir.

Q From the time of her death on until the present time have you continued to reside in the Cherokee nation?   A Yes sir.

Q Have you married since the death of Nancy Jane Mulcare? A Yes sir.

Q What is the name of your second wife?   A Tennessee Paris.

Q Was Tennessee at the time of your marriage to her a recognized citizen by blood of the Cherokee nation?   A She was.

Q Was she related to your first wife?   A She was her daughter, a step-daughter of mine.

Q Is this second wife of yours living at this time?   A No, she has been dead something like eight years.

Q Did you live in the Cherokee [sic] with her during her lifetime, that is, from the time of your marriage to her until her death?   A I did.

Q Have you married since Tennessee Paris died?   A No sir.

Q You have continued to live in the Cherokee nation?   A Yes sir.

Q Have you got any witnesses who were present at your marriage to Nancy Jane Paris?
A These two witnesses was not present but they was in the neighborhood.
Q Was there anyone present who saw you married?   A If there is anyone living I can't call it to mind.

By Mr. Vance:
Q Have you got any record at all by which you fix the date of your first marriage? Any kind of a record that helps you to remember the date of your first marriage?   A I had it put down. I[sic] was put in the bible at home, and if I am not mistaken it is put down as 1872.
Q Have you consulted it recently?   A I looked at it some two months ago.
Q Can you state positively what the record shows in the Bible?   A The Bible is an old Bible and is torn. I am pretty positive it was 1872.
Q Are you positive that is what the Bible shows?   A Yes sir,- Well, I am not really positive about it, but it is to the best of my recollection.

Q You have got the Bible at home?   A The Bible is pretty well all torn up. I had the leaves that had this record, and part of that has got destroyed, but I have got them in a trunk.
Q Have you got the leaves in the trunk that shows the date of your marriage?
A I think so.
Q Have you got any children by Nancy Jane Mulcare? A Yes sir.
Q Living at the present time?   A Yes sir.
Q What is the first one's name?   A Emet Mulcare.
Q Is he an enrolled citizen of the Cherokee Nation?   A Yes.
Q When was he born?   A He was born in the early part of 1873. Maybe the first part. I think he was born in 1873, but I don't know that I could tell positively what part of the year.

By the Commissioner:
Q Where were you born?   A I was born in Ohio.
Q When did you move to the Cherokee Nation?   A I moved to the Cherokee nation in about 1871--or I didn't move. I didn't have anything to move but myself.
Q But you came to the Cherokee nation and located there in 1871?   A I think so.
Q Then how long was it before you were married to Nancy Jane Paris?   A It was not so very long. I don't recollect the exact time; might have been six months or a year.
Q From the time of your marriage to Nancy J. Paris, did you exercise the rights of a citizen of the Cherokee nation from that time?   A Yes, I voted every election.
Q Do you remember the election you firse[sic] voted in?   A No, I don't.
Q Do you remember the name of the man you voted for the first time?   A No, I don't, but I know I voted in every election that has been held.
Q Did you ever serve on a jury?   A I don't think I was summoned on but one jury.
Q Do you remember what year that was?   A No, but it was a number of years after I was married.

Witness excused.

Cherokee Intermarried White 1906
Volume IX

     J. R. Garrett, being first duly sworn by Frances R. Lane, testified as follows:

By the Commissioner:

Q What is your name?   A J. R. Garrett.

Q Your age?   A Fifty-six.

Q Your postoffice address?   A Tahlequah, I. T.

Q Did you ever know one Michal Mulcare in the Cherokee Nation?   A Yes sir.

Q When did you first know him?   A Sometime in the spring of 1873.

Q Where was he living at that time?   A Going Snake District.

Q Were you a resident of Going Snake District too?   A Yes.

Q Was he married at that time?   A Yes, he was married when I came to the country. I came to the country in 1873, and he was married when I came.

Q What was the name of his wife?   A We always called her Nan. Nancy Paris, I suppose.

Q From the time you first knew her to the time of her death did they live together as husband and wife? A Yes sir.

Q Lived in the Cherokee nation?   A Yes sir.

Q After the death of Nancy J. Mulcare did Michal Mulcare marry again?   A Yes sir.

Q What was the name of his second wife?   A Her name was Tennessee Paris.

Q She was a step-daughter of Michal Mulcare?   A Yes sir.

Q Michal Mulcare and Tennessee Paris resided together as husband and wife and lived in the Cherokee nation up until her death?   A Yes sir.

Q Since that time Mr. Mulcare has not remarried?   A If he has married he married within the last two or three years. I have known him ever since 1873.

Q You are quite positive are you that these people were living together and regarded as husband and wife when you first got acquainted with them in 1873?   A Yes sir.

A Yes, I lived by him twenty-five years.

Witness excused.

     Frank E. Brown, being first duly sworn by Frances R. Lane, a Notary Public, testified as follows:

By the Commissioner:

Q What is your name?   A Frank E. Brown.

Q What is your age?   A Forty-eight.

Q Your postoffice address?   A Narcissa, I. T.

Q Did you ever know Michal Mulcare in the Cherokee nation[sic]

A Yes sir.

Q When did you first know him?   A Ever since I was a little boy. I couldn't tell you how long that is.

Q Was he a married man the time you first knew him?   A No

Q Did you ever know his wife, Nancy J. Paris?   A Yes, she is a half sister of mine.

Q Do you know when they were married?   A No, I can't tell you just the date.

Q Can you state about what year it was?   A I don't know that I could exactly.

Q You were not present at that marriage?   A No. She was married; I know that by what I heard over the neighborhood, but I was not there.

Q You lived in the neighborhood in which they were married? A Yes, lived about two miles away.

Q The best you can recollect you were about 14 years old at the time they were married? A Yes sir.

Q From the time you first knew of his being married they lived together from that time on as husband and wife until the death of Nancy Jane Mulcare, did they?   A Yes sir.

Q Lived in the Cherokee nation all the time did they?   A Yes sir.

Q After the death of Nancy Jane Mulcare, Michal Mulcare married his step-daughter, Tennessee Paris? A Yes sir.

Q And lived with her until her death?   A Yes sir.

Q Is it your understanding that at the time of their marriage Nancy Jane Paris was a recognized citizen by blood of the Cherokee nation?   A Yes sir.

Q Do you know the name of the oldest child of Michal Mulcare and Nancy Jane Mulcare?   A Yes, Emet.

Q Do you know how old he is now or do you remember when he was born?
A No, I don't remember just when he was born.

> The applicant, Michal Mulcare, is identified on the Cherokee authenticated tribal roll of 1880, Going Snake District opposite No. 1182, and on the Cherokee census roll of 1886, Delaware District, as Mike Mulcar[sic], page 581, No. 367.

Frances R. Lane upon oath states that as stenographer to the Commission to the Five Civilized Tribes she reported thw[sic] testimony in the above entitled cause and that the foregoing is an accurate transcript of her stenographic notes thereof.

Frances R Lane

Subscribed and sworn to before me this February 2, 1907.

Edward Merrick
Notary Public.

◇◇◇◇◇

Cherokee Intermarried White 1906
Volume IX

E.C.M.   Cherokee 3980.

DEPARTMENT OF THE INTERIOR,
COMMISSIONER TO THE FIVE CIVILIZED TRIBES,
MUSKOGEE, I. T., FEBRUARY 27, 1907.

In the matter of the application for the enrollment of MICHAEL MULCARE as a citizen by intermarriage of the Cherokee Nation.

MARGARET COSTEN ELKINS, being first duly sworn by Walter W. Chappell, Notary
    Public, testified as follows:

ON BEHALF OF THE COMMISSIONER:

Q   What is your name? A Margaret Costen Elkins.
Q   What is your age? A 45.
Q   What is your post office? A Westville.
Q   You appear here today, do you, for the purpose of giving testimony relative to the
    right of Michael Mulcare to enrollment as a citizen by intermarriage of?
    A Yes sir.
Q   Is he a white man? A He claims to be.
Q   Is his wife a Cherokee? A Yes sir.
Q   When were they married? A I cant[sic] tell you, I was small.
Q   He married your sister, did he? A Yes sir.
Q   You do not remember the date of their marriage? A Nos sir.

Q   How do you know they were married in accordance with the laws of the Cherokee
    Nation? A Simply because there were several there present, and the Clerk, and
    other people, and they came for the purpose of seeing my sister married.
Q   Who was the Clerk? A I dont[sic] remember.
Q   How do you know the Clerk came there? A Because they said he did.
Q   Then you only know it from what other people said? A Yes sir, I was only a
    small child.
Q   You didn't see the license under which they were married? A No.
Q   Then, you cannot swear, can you, that they were married under a license?
    A I didn't see the license.
Q   Do you know that they were married under a Cherokee license?
    A I never saw the license.
Q   You saw them married, did you? A Yes sir, I saw my sister and this man married.
Q   How old were you then? A 9 or 10 years old, somewhere along there.
Q   Then you dont[sic] remember much about it, do you? A I remember enough to
    know that they were married.
Q   Is your sister living? A No sir.
Q   When did she die? A I dont[sic] remember the date.
Q   About how long? A Nearly 32 or 33 years.

Q What was the name of your sister? A Nancy Jane Scott. She was a half-sister of mine, and she was a widow; her first husband was a Cherokee by blood, and his name was Parris.

Q Who is Tennie Parris? A Her daughter.

Q After the death of Nancy Jane Scott, did Michael Mulcare remarry? A Yes sir.

Q What is the name of his last wife? A Tennie Parris.

Q Then he married his daughter-in-law? A His step-daughter.

Q When did he marry her? A I cant[sic] remember dates.

Q About how long has it been since he married this last wife?
   A About 23 or 24 years.

Q She is the last wife he has married, is she? A Yes sir.

Q She is the daughter of a Cherokee by blood, is she? A Yes sir, her father and mother both were Cherokees by blood

Q Her father and mother both were Cherokees by blood? A Yes sir.

Q From the time of his first marriage has Michael Mulcare resided in the Cherokee Nation? A Yes sir.

Q He never has lived out of the Cherokee Nation? A No sir.

Q Who did you say married him to his first wife? A I dont[sic] remember.

Q But you remember it was the Clerk? A I remember there were some of the neighbors there for the wedding, and I knew that my sister married this man.

Q After their marriage did they reside together continuously as husband and wife?
   A Yes sir.

(Witness excused).

The undersigned, being first duly sworn, states that, as stenographer to the Commissioner to the Five Civilized Tribes, she correctly reported the above and foregoing testimony, and that the same is a full, true and complete transcript of her stenographic notes thereof.

Sarah Waters

Subscribed and sworn to before me this 27th day of February, 1907.

Frances R Lane
Notary Public.

◇◇◇◇◇

E C M   Cherokee 3980.

DEPARTMENT OF THE INTERIOR,
COMMISSIONER TO THE FIVE CIVILIZED TRIBES.

In the matter of the application for the enrollment of MICHAEL MULCARE as a citizen by intermarriage of the Cherokee Nation.

D E C I S I O N

THE RECORDS OF THIS OFFICE SHOW: That at Vinita, Indian Territory, October 2, 1900 application was received by the Commission to the Five Civilized Tribes for the enrollment of Michael Mulcare as a citizen by intermarriage of the Cherokee Nation. Further proceedings in the matter of said application were had at Muskogee, Indian Territory, October 28,1 902, April 21, 1905, February 1 and February 27, 1907.

THE EVIDENCE IN THIS CASE SHOWS: That the applicant herein, Michael Mulcare, a white man, was married in accordance with Cherokee law about 1872 to one Nancy J. Mulcare, formerly Parris, since deceased, who was at the time of said marriage a recognized citizen by blood of the Cherokee Nation. It is further shown that from the time of said marriage until the death of said Nancy J. Mulcare the said Michael Mulcare and Nancy J. Mulcare resided together as husband and wife and continuously lived in the Cherokee Nation. It is also shown that subsequent to the death of said Nancy J. Mulcare the said Michael Mulcare was married to one Tennessee Mulcare, nee Parris, since deceased, who was at the time of said marriage a recognized citizen by blood of the Cherokee Nation, who is identified on the Cherokee authenticated tribal roll of 1880, Going Snake District No. 1234 as "Tennie Parris", a native Cherokee marked "Dead". It is further shown that from the time of said marriage until the death of the said Tennessee Mulcare, which occurred about 1899, the said Michael Mulcare and Tennessee Mulcare resided together as husband and wife and continuously lived in the Cherokee Nation; that after the death of said Tennessee Mulcare the said Michael Mulcare remained unmarried and continuously resided in the Cherokee Nation up to and including September 1, 1902. Said applicant is identified on the Cherokee authenticated tribal roll of 1880 and the Cherokee census roll of 1896 as an intermarried citizen of the Cherokee Nation.

IT IS, THEREFORE, ORDERED AND ADJUDGED: That in accordance with the decision of the Supreme Court of the United States, dated November 5, 1906, in the cases of Daniel Red Bird, et al. vs. the United States, Nos. 125, 126, 127, and 128, the said applicant, Michael Mulcare, is entitled, under the provisions of Section Twenty-one of the Act of Congress approved June 28, 1898 (30 Stats. 495), to enrollment as a citizen by intermarriage of the Cherokee Nation, and his application for enrollment as such is accordingly granted.

Tams Bixby
Commissioner.

Dated at Muskogee, Indian Territory,
this   FEB 28 1907

◇◇◇◇◇

Cherokee 3980.

Muskogee, Indian Territory, February 28, 1907.

The Commissioner to the Five Civilized Tribes,
Muskogee, Indian Territory.

Sir:

Receipt is acknowledged of the testimony and of your decision enrolling Michal Mulcare as a citizen by intermarriage of the Cherokee Nation. Time for protesting said decision is waived, and I consent that said person may be placed upon the schedule immediately.

Respectfully,
W. W. Hastings
Attorney for Cherokee Nation.

◇◇◇◇◇

Cherokee 3980.

Muskogee, Indian Territory, February 28, 1907.

W. W. Hastings,
Attorney for the Cherokee Nation,
Muskogee, Indian Territory.

Dear Sir:

There is enclosed herewith a copy of the decision of the Commissioner to the Five Civilized Tribes, dated February 28, 1907, granting the application for the enrollment of Michal Mulcare as a citizen by intermarriage of the Cherokee Nation.

Respectfully,

Encl. E-51   Commissioner.
BLE

◇◇◇◇◇

Cherokee 3980

Muskogee, Indian Territory, February 28, 1907.

Michal Mulcare,
    Pensacola, Indian Territory.

Dear Sir:

There is enclosed herewith a copy of the decision of the Commissioner to the Five Civilized Tribes, dated February 28, 1907, granting the application for your enrollment as a citizen by intermarriage of the Cherokee Nation.

You will be advised when your name has been placed upon a schedule of citizens of the Cherokee Nation and approved by the Secretary of the Interior.

Respectfully,

Encl. E-50   Commissioner.
BLE.

◇◇◇◇◇

Cherokee
    I. W. 257

Muskogee, Indian Territory, May 1, 1907

Mike Mulcare,
    Pensacola, Indian Territory.

Dear Sir:

In reply to your letter of March 26, 1907, you are advised that your name now appears upon a roll of citizens by intermarriage of the Cherokee Nation approved by the Secretary of the Interior.

Respectfully,

LMB   Acting Commissioner

Cher IW 258

◇◇◇◇◇

(jacket missing)

Cher IW 259

<><><><><>

Department of the Interior,
Commission to the Five Civilized Tribes,
Ft. Gibson, I.T., August 25, 1900.

In the matter of the application of Rebecca Hood for the enrollment of herself as a Cherokee citizen; being sworn and examined by Commissioner Needles she testifies as follows:

Q   What is your name?   A Rebecca Hood.
Q   What is your age?   A Fifty-six.
Q   What is your post-office?   A Fawn.
Q   Are you a recognized citizen of the Cherokee Nation?   A I am an adopted citizen.
Q   What district do you live in?   A Canadian.
Q   How long have you lived in Canadian District? A About twenty-five years.
Q   About twenty-five years continuously in the Cherokee Nation?   A Yes sir.
Q   Are you married?   A No sir, my husband is dead.
Q   Do you desire to enroll any person besides yourself here?   [sic] No sir, that's all.
Q   Your father and mother living?   A No sir.
Q   They were non-citizens?   A Yes sir.
1880 roll page 25 #715 Becca Hood Canadian District.
1896 roll page 88 #129 as Lydia Hood, Canadian District.
Q   Was your name ever Lydia?   A No sir, that's my daughter's name.

Com'r Needles: The name of Rebecca Hood appears upon the authenticated roll of 1880 as Becca Hood and upon the census roll of 1896 as Lydia Hood; she being fully identified as Rebecca Hood as per page and number as indicated in the testimony, and having made satisfactory proof as to residence, she will be duly listed for enrollment by this Commission as a Cherokee citizen by intermarriage.

M.D. Green, being first duly sworn, states that as stenographer to the Commission to the Five Civilized Tribes he correctly recorded the testimony and proceedings in this case, and the foregoing is a true and correct transcript of his stenographic notes thereof.

MD Green

Subscribed and sworn to before me this 3 day of Sept 1900.

C R Breckinridge
Commissioner.

<><><><><>

CANADIAN.

CANADIAN.
Statement of Applicant Taken Under Oath.

CHEROKEE BY BLOOD AND ADOPTION.

Date...... **AUG 25 1900**............................1900.

Name ....**Fawn IT**..............
District.. Year .... Page .... No. ....
Citizen by blood .... Mother's citizenship ....
Intermarried citizen ....
Married under what law..Date of marriage ....
License₍₅₆₎... Certificate...........................
Wife's name.......... **Rebecca Hood**..............................
District................ **CANADIAN.**...................Year.... **1880**.... Page ....**25**......No. ....**715**.....
Citizen by blood........................ Mother's citizenship.............................
Intermarried citizen.. **Yes**...............
Married under what law...Date of marriage......................
License .... Certificate..........................

  Names of Children:

....Dist..............Year............Page...........No...........Age...........
....Dist..............Year............Page...........No...........Age...........
....Dist..............Year............Page...........No...........Age...........
....Dist..............Year............Page...........No...........Age...........
....Dist..............Year............Page...........No...........Age...........

  1 on 1880 roll as Becca Hood

....**#2014**......................
....
....
....

◇◇◇◇◇

Cherokee 2014.

Department of the Interior,
Commission to the Five Civilized Tribes.
Muskogee, I. T., October 17, 1902.

   In the matter of the application of Rebecca Hood for the enrollment of herself as a citizen by intermarriage of the Cherokee Nation; she being sworn and examined by the Commission, testified as follows:

Q What is your name?   A Rebecca Hood.
Q How old are you?   A Fifty-seven.
Q What is your postoffice?   A Fawn.
Q Are you a white woman?   A Yes sir.

Q Does your name appear on the roll of 1880 as an adopted white citizen?   A Yes sir.
Q What was the name of your husband at that time?   A David Hood. He has been dead sixteen years. He was living in 1880.
Q Is that the husband through whom you are claiming your citizenship? A Yes sir.
Q Did you live with David Hood from 1880 up until the time he died?   A Yes sir.
Q You were never separated from him all the time he was living and you were married to him?   A No sir.
Q Have you married since the death of David Hood?   A No sir.
Q Have you been making your home in the Cherokee Nation ever since 1880?
A Yes sir.
Q Never lived out have you?   A No sir.
Q You are still a widower[sic]?   A Yes sir.

The undersigned, being duly sworn, states that as stenographer to the Commission to the Five Civilized Tribes he correctly recorded the testimony and proceedings in this case, and the foregoing is a true and correct transcript of his stenographic notes thereof.

E.G. Rothenberger

Subscribed and sworn to before me this 17th day of November, 1902.

BC Jones
Notary Public.

◇◇◇◇◇

E.C.M.   Cherokee 2014.

DEPARTMENT OF THE INTERIOR,
COMMISSIONER TO THE FIVE CIVILIZED TRIBES.
MUSKOGEE, I. T., FEBRUARY 16, 1907.

In the matter of the application for the enrollment of REBECCA HOOD as a citizen by intermarriage of the Cherokee Nation.

REBECCA (HOOD) HILL, being first duly sworn by Walter W. Chappell,
    Notary Public, testified as follows:

ON BEHALF OF THE COMMISSIONER:

Q   What is your name?   A Rebecca.
Q   What is your age?   A 62.
Q   What is your post office address?   A Fawn.

Cherokee Intermarried White 1906
Volume IX

Q   Do you appear here today for the purpose of giving testimony relative to the right to enrollment as a citizen by intermarriage of the Cherokee Nation of Rebecca Hood?   A Yes sir.

Q   You possess no Cherokee blood?   A No sir.

Q   Then you derive whatever right you may have as a citizen of the Cherokee Nation by virtue of your marriage to a Cherokee citizen?   A Yes sir.

Q   What is the name of your husband?   A David Hood.

Q   Is he living?   A No sir.

Q   When did he die?   A He has been dead 20 years.

Q   Was he a recognized citizen by blood of the Cherokee Nation?

Q   Was he born and raised in the Cherokee Nation?   A Yes sir, in the old Nation, in Georgia or Tennessee.

Q   When did he come to this country?   A In '32 or '33; I have heard him say.

Q   He came here with the other Cherokees from the old country?   A Yes sir.

Q   When were you married to David Hood?   A In 1860.

Q   Where were you married?   A Down toward Fort Smith.

Q   Were you David Hood's first wife?   A Nos ri,[sic] his second wife.

Q   Who was his first wife?   A I dont[sic] know who she was.

Q   Was she dead at the time he married you?   A Yes sir.

Q   How long had she been dead?   A I never did hear him say how long.

Q   She was dead, though?   A Yes sir.

Q   Was David Hood your first husband?   A Yes sir.

Q   Since the death of David Hood have you remarried?   A Yes sir.

Q   Was[sic] is your second husband?   A Billy Hill.

Q   Is Billy Hill a citizen by blood of the Cherokee Nation?   A No sir

Q   Is he a white man?   A Yes sir.

Q   Not a citizen of the Cherokee Nation?   A Yes sir.

Q   When did you marry him?   A 4 weeks ago.

Q   You have never been married but twice, then?   A Nos sir, just twice.

Q   From the time of your marriage to David Hood until the present time have you continuously lived in the Cherokee Nation?   A Yes sir.

Q   Have you ever lived out of the Cherokee Nation?   A No sir.

Q   You say you have never married but twice?   A Twice.

Q   And the last time was 4 weeks ago?   A Yes sir, about that.

(Witness excused).

JEMIMA LEECH, being first duly sworn by Walter W. Chappell, Notary Public, testified as follows:

Q   What is your name?   A Jemima Leech.

Q   What is your age?   A 40.

Q   What is your post office address?   A Porum.

Q   You appear here today, do you, for the purpose of giving testimony relative to the right of Rebecca Hood to enrollment as a citizen by intermarriage of the Cherokee Nation?   A Yes sir.

Cherokee Intermarried White 1906
Volume IX

Q   Are you any relation to Rebecca Hood?   A No sir.

Q   Were you acquainted with her husband, David Hood?   A Yes sir.

Q   How long have you known Rebecca Hood and her husband, David Hood?
    A 37 years.

Q   Was David Hood at that time a recognized citizen by blood of the Cherokee Nation?
    A Yes sir.

Q   Is Rebecca Hood a white woman?   A Yes sir.

Q   At the time you first became acquainted with them were they living together as
    husband and wife?   A Yes sir.

Q   Did they continue to live together until his death?   A Yes sir.

Q   When did he die?   A I dont[sic] know

Q   Did Rebecca Hood and David Hood reside together until his death?   A Yes sir

Q   They never were separated?   A No sir.

Q   Did they hold each other out in the community as husband and wife?   A Yes sir.

Q   Were they so recognized in the community?   A Yes sir.

Q   Since the death of David Hood has Rebecca Hood remarried?   A Yes sir.

Q   How many times?   A Just once.

Q   When was that?   A About 4 weeks ago.

Q   Since you first became [sic] with the applicant, Rebecca Hood, has she continuously
    lived in the Cherokee Nation?   A Yes sir.

W. M. HUGHES, being first duly sworn by Walter W. Chappell, Notary Public, testified
    as follows:

Q   What is your name?   A W. M. Hughes.

Q   What is your age?   A 45.

Q   What is your post office address?   A Muskogee.

Q   You appear hee today, do you, for the purpose of giving testimony relative to the
    right to enrollment as a citizen by intermarriage of the Cherokee Nation of
    Rebecca Hood?   A Yes sir.

Q   Were you acquainted with her husband, David Hood?   A Yes sir.

Q   Was he a recognized citizen by blood of the Cherokee Nation?   A Yes sir.

Q   Is Rebecca Hood a white woman?   A Yes sir.

Q   How long has it been since you first became acquainted with Rebecca and David
    Hood?   A About 34 years.

Q   Were they living together as husband and wife when you first became acquainted
    with them?   A Yes sir.

Q   Did they continue to live together as husband and wife?   A Yes sir.

Q   When did he die?   A I dont[sic] know exactly.

Q   About how long ago?   A 18 or 20 years, along there.

Q   Since the death of David Hood has Rebecca Hood remarried?   A Yes sir.

Q   When did she remarry?   A Somewheres[sic] about 4 weeks ago.

Q   Is her last husband a Cherokee?   A No sir.

Q   A White[sic] man?   A Yes sir.

Q   Has Rebecca Hood continuously resided in the Cherokee Nation since you first
    became acquainted with her?   A Yes sir.

Cherokee Intermarried White 1906
Volume IX

(Witness excused).

David Hood is identified on the 1880 roll, Canadian District, Page 25, No. 714, as a native Cherokee. Rebecca Hood is identified on said roll, at No 750, as an adopted white.

The undersigned, being first duly sworn, states that, as stenographer to the Commissioner to the Five Civilized Tribes, she correctly reported the above and foregoing testimony, and that the same is a full, true and complete transcript of her stenographic notes thereof.

Sarah Waters

Subscribed and sworn to before me this 16th day of February, 1907.

Walter W. Chappell
Notary Public.

◇◇◇◇◇

E.C.M.   Cherokee 2014.

DEPARTMENT OF THE INTERIOR,

COMMISSIONER TO THE FIVE CIVILIZED TRIBES.

In the matter of the application for the enrollment of REBECCA HOOD, as a citizen by intermarriage of the Cherokee Nation.

D E C I S I O N

THE RECORDS OF THIS OFFICE SHOW: That at Fort Gibson, Indian Territory, August 25, 1900 application was received by the Commission to the Five Civilized Tribes for the enrollment of Rebecca Hood, as a citizen by intermarriage of the Cherokee Nation.   Further proceedings in the matter of said application were had at Muskogee, Indian Territory, October 17, 1902 and February 16, 1907.

THE EVIDENCE IN THIS CASE SHOWS: That the applicant herein, Rebecca Hood, a white woman married in 1860 on David Hood, since deceased, who was at the time of said marriage a recognized citizen by blood of the Cherokee Nation, who is identified on the Cherokee authenticated tribal roll of 1880, Canadian District No. 714 as a native Cherokee marked "Dead".   It is further shows[sic] that from the time of said marriage until the death of said David Hood, which occurred bout the year 1888, the said David Hood and Rebecca Hood resided together as husband and wife and continuously lived in the Cherokee Nation; that after the death of said David Hood the said Rebecca

Hood remained unmarried and continuously lived in the Cherokee Nation up to and including September 1, 1902. Said applicant is identified on the Cherokee authenticated tribal roll of 1880 and the Cherokee census roll of 1896 as an intermarried citizen of the Cherokee Nation.

IT IS, THEREFORE, ORDERED AND ADJUDGED: That in accordance with the decision of the Supreme Court of the United States, dated November 5, 1906, in the cases of Daniel Red Bird, et al. vs. the United States, Nos. 125, 126, 127, and 128, the said applicant, Rebecca Hood is entitled, under the provisions of Section Twenty-one of the Act of Congress approved June 28, 1898 (30 Stats. 495), to enrollment as a citizen by intermarriage of the Cherokee Nation, and her application for enrollment as such is accordingly granted.

Tams Bixby
Commissioner.

Dated at Muskogee, Indian Territory,
this   FEB 26 1907

◇◇◇◇◇

C.F.B.

DEPARTMENT OF THE INTERIOR,
COMMISSIONER TO THE FIVE CIVILIZED TRIBES,
CHEROKEE LAND OFFICE,
Muskogee, Indian Territory, July 8, 1907.

Cherokee I. W. 259.

- - - - -

In the matter of the application for the selection of an allotment in the Cherokee Nation for Rebecca Hill, enrolled as Rebecca Hood.

- - - - - - - - -

Wm. J. Hill, being duly sworn by S. T. Wright, Notary Public and examined by C. F. Bliss on behalf of the Commissioner, testified as follows:

Q   What is your name?
A   Wm. J. Hill.
Q   What is your age?
A   63.
Q   What is your postoffice address?
A   Fawn.
Q   Are you a citizen of the Cherokee Nation?
A   No sir

Q   What is your purpose in appearing before the Commissioner today?
A   To file on some fractions for my wife.
Q   What is your wife's name?   A Rebecca Hill.
Q   She is on the roll of citizens by intermarriage of the Cherokee Nation, is she?
A   Yes sir.
Q   What was her name before you married her?   A Rebecca Hood.
Q   When were you married?
A   Last December.
Q   Why is it that your wife does not appear in person to select her own allotment?
A   She has had a long spell of sickness and is not able.
Q   She is physically unable to attend to this matter herself, is she?
A   Yes sir.
Q   How do you represent her?
A   By power of attorney.

Wm. J. Hill present a power of attorney executed June 20, 1907, by Rebecca Hill, nee Hood, in which the said Rebecca Hill, nee Hood, constitutes and appointes[sic] the said Wm. J. Hill to act for her in the matter of completing her selection of allotment in the Cherokee Nation.

Witness excused.

- - - - -

I, May Hudson, state upon path that as stenorgapher[sic] to the Commissioner to the Five Civilized Tribes I correctly reported the testimony given above and that the foregoing is a true and complete transcript of my stenographic notes thereof.

May Hudson

Subscribed and sworn to before me
this 8th day of July, 1907.

Frances R Lane
Notary Public.

◇◇◇◇◇

REFER IN REPLY TO THE FOLLOWING:
Cherokee
20914

**DEPARTMENT OF THE INTERIOR,
COMMISSIONER TO THE FIVE CIVILIZED TRIBES.**

Muskogee, Indian Territory, February 11, 1907

SPECIAL

Rebecca Hood,
      Fawn, Indian Territory.

Dear Madam:

In connection with your application for enrollment as a citizen by intermarriage of the Cherokee Nation you are advised that before your case will be complete, it will be necessary that you appear before the Commissioner, with witnesses, to show your marriage to your Cherokee husband, by reason of which you claim the right to enrollment as a citizen by intermarriage of the Cherokee Nation, and as to his citizenship in the Cherokee Nation at the time of your marriage to him.

The Act of Congress approved April 26, 1906 provides that the Secretary of the Interior shall have no jurisdiction to approve the enrollment of any person as a citizen of the Cherokee Nation after March 4, 1907. This matter therefore demands your immediate attention.

Respectfully,

LMB   Tams Bixby   Commissioner.

◇◇◇◇◇

Cherokee
2014

Muskogee, Indian Territory, February 26, 1907.

Rebecca Hood,
         Fawn, Indian Territory.

Dear Madam:

There is enclosed herewith a copy of the decision of the Commissioner to the Five Civilized Tribes, dated February 26, 1907, granting your application for enrollment as a citizen by intermarriage of the Cherokee Nation.

You will be advised when your name has been placed upon a schedule of citizens of the Cherokee Nation and approved by the Secretary of the Interior.

Respectfully,

Encl. HJ-95.
    HJC   Commissioner.

◇◇◇◇◇

Cherokee 2014.

Muskogee, Indian Territory, February 26, 1907.

W. W. Hastings,
Attorney for the Cherokee Nation,
Muskogee, Indian Territory.

Dear Sir:

There is enclosed herewith a copy of the decision of the Commissioner to the Five Civilized Tribes, dated February 26, 1907, granting the application for the enrollment of Rebecca Hood as a citizen by intermarriage of the Cherokee Nation.

Respectfully,

Encl. HJ-96.
HJC

Commissioner.

◇◇◇◇◇

Cherokee
2014.

Muskogee, Indian Territory, February 26, 1907

The Commissioner to the Five Civilized Tribes,
Muskogee, Indian Territory.

Sir:

Receipt is acknowledged of the testimony and of your decision enrolling Rebecca Hood as a citizen by intermarriage of the Cherokee Nation. Time for protesting said decision is waived, and I consent that said person may be placed upon the schedule immediately.

Respectfully,

W. W. Hastings
Attorney for Cherokee Nation.

Cher IW 260

◇◇◇◇◇

Cherokee Intermarried White 1906
Volume IX

DEPARTMENT OF THE INTERIOR,
COMMISSION TO THE FIVE CIVILIZED TRIBES,
VINITA, I. T., SEPTEMBER 17, 1900.

In the matter of the application of Sarah B. Cheek for the enrollment of herself and children as citizens of the Cherokee Nation; said Cheek being sworn by Commissioner C. R. Breckinirdge[sic]; testified as follows:

Q   What is your full name, Madam?   A   Sarah B. Cheek.
Q   How old are you?   A   56.
Q   What is your post office?   A   Grove.
Q   In what district of you live?   A   Delaware.
Q   Who is it you want to have put on the roll?   A   Myself and two children.
Q   Do you appl7[sic] for yourself as a Cherokee by blood?   A   No, sir, white woman.
Q   When were you married?   A   --------------
Q   You have been married more than 20 years?   A   Yes, sir; married just directly after the war.
Q   Who was it you were married to?   A   Pleasant Cheek.
Q   He was a Cherokee was he?   A   Yes, sir.
Q   Dead or alive?   A   Dead.
Q   How long since he died?   A   He has been dead about 11 years.
Q   Have you ever married since his death?   A   No, sir.
Q   You are with him on the roll of 1880 are you?   A   Yes,[sic]
Q   From what district?   A   Delaware.
Q   Were you enrolled in Delaware in 1896 too?   A   Yes, sir. I have lived here every since I was 16 years old.
Q   What was your father's name?   A   Joe Blevins.
Q   Is he dead?   A   Yes, sir.
Q   How long since he died?   A   About 50 years.
Q   Your mother's given name, please?   A   Sarah.
Q   Dead or alive?   A   She is dead.
Q   How long since she died; more than 20 years?   A   Yes, sir.
Q   The names of your two children, please?   A   Lula Dora Cheek.
Q   How old is that child?   A   She is 16.
Q   The next child, please?   A   Pleasant J.
Q   How old is that child?   A   12 years old.

1880 enrollment; page 237, #547, Sarah R. Cheek, Delaware.
1896 enrollment; page 567, #102, Sarah R. Cheek, Delaware.
1896 enrollment; page 451, #632, Dora Lula Cheek, Delaware.
1896 enrollment; page 451, #633, Pleasant J. Cheek, Delware[sic].

Q   These children are both living with you now are they?   A   Yes, sir.

Com'r Breckinridge:
    The applicant applies for the enrollment of herself and two children: Her husband is dead. She is identified on the rolls of 1880 and 1896 as a Cherokee by adoption. She

has never re-married since her husband's death, and she will be listed now as a Cherokee by adoption. Her two children Lula D. and Pleasant J. Cheek, are identified with their mother on the roll of 1896. They are both living at this time, and they will be listed for enrollment now as Cherokees by blood.

---oooOOOooo---

J. O. Rosson, being first duly sworn, states that as stenographer to the Commission to the Five Civilized Tribes, he correctly recorded the testimony and proceedings in this case, and the foregoing is a true and complete transcript of his stenographic notes thereof.

JO Rosson

Subscribed and sworn to before me this 19th day of September, 1900.

TB Needles
Commissioner.

◇◇◇◇◇

Cherokee 2855.

Department of the Interior,
Commission to the Five Civilized Tribes,
Muskogee, I. T., October 6, 1902.

In the matter of the application of Sarah B. Cheek for the enrollment of herself as a citizen by intermarriage, and for the enrollment of her children, Lula D. and Pleasant J. Cheek, as citizens by blood of the Cherokee Nation.

C. F. Camp, being sworn and examined by the Commission, testified as follows:

Q   What is your name?   A C. F. Camp.
Q   What is your age?   A Fifty-three years.
Q   What is your postoffice?   A Vinita.
Q   Are you acquainted with Sarah B. Cheek who is an applicant before this Commission for enrollment as an intermarried citizen?   A Yes sir.
Q   About how old is she at this time?   A She is about sixty. I would judge 58 or 60, about 58.
Q   What is her postoffice?   A Grove.
Q   What was her husband's name?   A Pleasant B. Cheek.
Q   They were married before 1880?   A Yes sir.
Q   When did her husband die, or is he dead?   A He is dead.
Q   How long has he been dead, just about the number of years he has been dead?
A   I would judge about seven years.
Q   Did Sarah B. Cheek and her husband live together as husband and wife all the time from 1880 up until the time of his death as husband and wife?   A Yes sir.
Q   They were never separated during that time?   A No sir.

180

Q   Was Sarah B. Cheek ever married to any other man since 1880?   A No sir.
Q   Is she still a widow and single on the first day of September, 1902?
A   Yes sir.
Q   Has Sarah B. Cheek lived in the Cherokee Nation from 1880 all the time up until the present time?   A Yes sir.
Q   These two children, Lula D. and Pleasant J., are her children by her deceased husband?   A Yes sir.
Q   Have they lived in the Cherokee Nation all their lives?   A Yes sir.

The undersigned, being duly sworn, states that as stenographer to the Commission to the Five Civilized Tribes he correctly recorded the testimony and proceedings in this case, and the foregoing is a true and correct transcript of his stenographic notes thereof.

E.G. Rothenberger

Subscribed and sworn to before me this 23rd day of October, 1902.

BC Jones
Notary Public.

◇◇◇◇◇

Cher--2855

DEPARTMENT OF THE INTERIOR.
Commission to the Five Civilized Tribes,
Muskogee, I.T. October 20, 1902.

In the matter of the application of Sarah Cheek for enrollment as an intermarried citizen of the Cherokee Nation, and for the enrollment of her children Lula D., and Pleasant J. as citizens by blood of the Cherokee nation[sic].

Sarah B. Cheek, called as a witness, being duly sworn by the Commission, testified as follows:

Q   What is your name?   A Sarah B. Cheek.
Q   How old are you?   A 56 years.
Q   What is your postoffice address?   A Grove, I.T.
Q   Are you a white woman?   A Yes sir.
Q   Is your name on the roll of 1880 as an intermarried white citizen?   A Yes sir.
Q   What is your husband's name?   A Pleasant Cheek.
Q   He is dead?   A Yes sir.
Q   Was Pleasant Cheek your husband in 1880?   A Yes sir.
Q   He is the husband through whom you are claiming citizenship?   A Yes.
Q   When did he die?   A Twelve years ago.

Cherokee Intermarried White 1906
Volume IX

Q   Did you live with your husband in the Cherokee nation from 1880 up to the time he died?   A Yes sir.

Q   You were never separated, were you?   A No sir.

Q   Have you married since your husband's death?   A No sir.

Q   Have you been residing in the Cherokee nation from 1880 up to this time?
A   Yes sir.

Q   You never lived anywhere else?   A No sir.

Q   How many children have you?   A Five living.

Q   How many under age?   A Two.

Q   The two children under age are living at your home with you, are they?
A   Yes sir.

-------------0----------

Frances R. Lane upon oath states that as stenographer to the Commission to the Five Civilized Tribes she correctly recorded the testimony taken in this case and that the foregoing is a full, true and correct transcript of her stenographic notes thereof.

Frances R Lane

Subscribed and sworn to before me this October 25th, 1902.

BC Jones
Notary Public.

◇◇◇◇◇

(The Affidavit below was originally handwritten on the microfilm and is typed as given.)

Grove I.T.
Jan 26 - 07.

This is to certify that Mrs. Sarah B. Cheek is in very poor health. She is at present confined to her room all the time. I have been her family Physician for three years am a regular practicing Physician for 5 years.

Respt
C.F. Walker M.D.

The within affidavit subscribed and sworn to this 26th day of January A.D. 1907

T S Remsen Notary Public
My comp expires May 2nd 1908

◇◇◇◇◇

Cherokee Intermarried White 1906
Volume IX

(The Affidavit below was originally handwritten on the microfilm and is typed as given.)

2nd Recording District
Indian Territory

Grove January 26th 1907

Personally appeared before me a Notary Public in and for said Dist and Territy. Stephen D Brown to me well known and entitled to credit who after being duly sworn declares as follows: I am 66 years of age. My Post office and residence is Grove Ind Ter have been acquainted with Sarah B. Cheek, wife of Pleasant Cheek for the past 36 years. And know that she lived with him until he died And was always recognized as his lawful wife. And Pleasant Cheek was a recognized Cherokee Citizen by blood. And said Sarah B. Cheek has not remarried since his death. They were living together as man and wife in 1870. And lived together as such until his death which was about 1890.

Stephen D Brown

The within affidavit subscribed and sworn to this 26th day of January A.D. 1907

T S Remsen
Notary Public
My Comp expires May 2d 1908

◇◇◇◇◇

(The Affidavit below was originally handwritten on the microfilm and is typed as given.)

2nd Recording District
Indian Territory

Grove January 26th 1907

Personally appeared before me a Notary Public in and for said District and Territory George M Ward. Age 64 years. Whose post office and residence is Grove Ind. Tery. to me well known and entitled to credit who after being duly sworn declares as follows: Have been personally acquainted with Sarah B. Cheek wife of Pleasant Cheek for the past 35 years. And know that she lived with him until he died which was about 1890. She is still living and has not remarried since his death. They were living together as man and wife in 1870. And ever since. And raised a family of children who have been recognized as Cherokee citizens.

George M. Ward

183

The within affidavit subscribed and sworn to this 26th day of January AD 1907

T S Remsen
Notary Public
My comp expires May 2d 1908

◇◇◇◇◇

(The Affidavit below was originally handwritten on the microfilm and is typed as given.)

2nd Recording District
Indian Territory

Grove Feby 5th 1907

Personally appeared before me a Notary Public in and for said District and Territory Sarah B. Cheek age 64 years; whose Post office and residence is Grove, Ind Terry to me well known and entitled to credit. Who after being duly sworn declares as follows: I am an invalid and have been for the past year. I am hardly able to get from one room to another in my house. Am not able to go anywhere. I therefore respectfully ask the Commission to the 5 Civilized Tribes to send a person to my home at Grove to take my deposition as to my right of enrollment as a citizen of the Cherokee Nation as per decision of the Supreme Court and Court of Claims "Cherokee Nation vs Intermarried Whites"

<table>
<tr><td>Witness to mark</td><td>her</td></tr>
<tr><td>William F. Sager</td><td>Sarah B x Chick</td></tr>
<tr><td>Jay Cheek</td><td>mark</td></tr>
</table>

The within affidavit Subscribed
and sworn to this 5th day of
February AD 1907
T S Remsen
Notary Public
My Comp expires May 2d 1908

◇◇◇◇◇

Cherokee 2855.

DEPARTMENT OF THE INTERIOR.

COMMISSIONER TO THE FIVE CIVILIZED TRIBES.

In the matter of the application for the enrollment of Sarah B. Cheek as a citizen by intermarriage of the Cherokee Nation.

Sarah B. Cheek being first duly sworn by Frances R. Lane, a Notary Public, testifies as follows:

By the Commissioner:

Q   What is your name?   A Sarah B. Cheek.
Q   What is your age?   A I am going on 64--will be 64 years in March.
Q   What is your Post Office?   A Grove, Post Office.
Q   Mrs. Cheek you appear here today for the purpose of giving testimony relative to your right to enrollment as a citizen by intermarriage of the Cherokee Nation?
A   Yes sir.
Q   What is the name of your husband through whom you claim the right to enrollment?
A   Pleasant Cheek.
Q   Is Pleasant Cheek living now?   A No sir, if he was alive I wouldn't be here now.
Q   When did he die?   A He has been dead going on about 18 or 19 years.
Q   Was he a citizen by blood of the Cherokee Nation?   A Yes, yes, he was a citizen by blood.
Q   When were you and Pleasant Cheek married?   A We was married -- I've got our marriage certificate right here, I sent it here. We was married just after the war about one year after peace was made. Its[sic] been a long time, I don't know exactly.
Q   Was Pleasant Cheek your first husband?   A No sir, my first husband got killed in the war.
Q   What was the name of your first husband?   A Ward.
Q   Was he dead when you married your last husband?   A Yes, he was killed in the war and the wolves--the wolves et[sic] him up. He had been dead three or four years.
Q   You have only been married twice? A Yes sir, that is all.
Q   Had Pleasant Cheek ever been married before you married him? A No sir.
Q   Then you were his first wife and he was your second husband? A Yes sir.
Q   From the time of your marriage until the death of Pleasant Cheek did you live together as husband and wife in the Cherokee Nation? A Yes sir.
Q   Since the death of your husband you have continuously resided in the Cherokee Nation?   A Yes sir. Never knowed[sic] anything else, lived here ever since I was going on 16.
Q   You have not remarried since the death of your husband?   A No sir.

Witness Excused.

Cherokee Intermarried White 1906
Volume IX

W. F. Slater being duly sworn by Frances R. Lane, a Notary Public, testifies as follows:

By the Commissioner.

Q   What is your name?   A W. F. Slater.

Q   How old are you?   A Will be 55 next birthday.

Q   What is your Post Office address?   A Grove, I.T.

Q   Mr. Slater, you appear here today for the purpose of giving testimony relative to the right of Sarah B. Cheek to enrollment as a citizen by intermarriage of the Cherokee Nation? A Yes sir.

Q   How long have you known the applicant?   A 25 years, or right close to it.

Q   Were you acquainted with her husband, Pleasant Cheek?   A Oh yes.

Q   How long had you been acquainted with him?   A I have been acquainted with him before he died three or four years before I knowed[sic] her. He had a mill and I got lumber there all the time.

Q   Were you acquainted with him prior to November 1, 1875?   A Yes, I must have been.

Q   You don't know positively how long you have been acquainted with him?

A   I have been living in this territory thirty years and he was one of the first men I got acquainted with.

Q   Was he married at that time?   A Oh yes, I married their daughter.

Q   Since the death of Pleasant Cheek has the applicant Sarah B. Cheek remarried?

A   Oh no, no.

Witness Excused.

I, Cora E. Glendenning, a stenographer to the Commissioner to the Five Civilized Tribes on oath state that I reported the foregoing proceedings had in the above entitled cause, and that the foregoing is a true and correct transcript of my stenographic notes therein.

Cora E Glendenning

Subscribed and sworn to before me this 13th day of February 1907.

Walter W. Chappell
Notary Public.

◇◇◇◇◇

ECM   Cherokee 2855.

DEPARTMENT OF THE INTERIOR,

COMMISSIONER TO THE FIVE CIVILIZED TRIBES.

In the matter of the application for the enrollment of Sarah B. Cheek as a citizen by intermarriage of the Cherokee Nation.

D E C I S I O N

THE RECORDS OF THIS OFFICE SHOW: That at Vinita, Indian Territory, September 17, 1900, application was received by the Commission to the Five Civilized Tribes for the enrollment of Sarah B. Cheek as a citizen by intermarriage of the Cherokee Nation. Further proceedings in the matter of said application were had at Muskogee, Indian Territory, October 6, 1901, October 20, 1902, and February 13, 1907.

THE EVIDENCE IN THIS CASE SHOWS: That the applicant herein, Sarah B. Cheek, a white woman, married prior to November 1, 1875, one Pleasant Cheek, since deceased, who was at the time of said marriage, a recognized citizen by blood of the Cherokee Nation, who is identified on the Cherokee Authenticated Tribal Roll of 1880, Delaware District, No. 546, is a native Cherokee marked "dead"; it appearing from the 1880 Roll that they had at that time three children, aged respectively, seven, five, and one, and it is further shown that from the time of said marriage until the death of said Pleasant Cheek, which was about the year 1890. Said Pleasant Cheek and Sarah N[sic]. Cheek resided, together as husband and wife and continuously lived in the Cherokee Nation, and that after the death of said Pleasant Cheek, the said Sarah B. Cheek remained unmarried and continuously remained in the Cherokee Nation up to and including September 1, 1902.   Said applicant is idnetified[sic] on the Cherokee Authenticated Tribal Roll of 1880 and the Cherokee Census Roll of 1896, as an intermarried citizen of the Cherokee Nation.

IT IS, THEREFORE, ORDERED AND ADJUDGED: That in accordance with the decision of the Supreme Court of the United States, dated November 5, 1906, in the cases of Daniel Red Bird, et al., vs. the United States, Nos. 125, 126, 127, and 128, the said applicant, Sarah B. Cheek, is entitled, under the provisions of Section Twenty-one of the Act of Congress approved June 28, 1898 (30 Stats. 495), to enrollment as a citizen by intermarriage of the Cherokee Nation, and her application for enrollment as such is accordingly granted.

Tams Bixby

Commissioner.

Dated at Muskogee, Indian Territory,
this   FEB 26 1907

◇◇◇◇◇

State of Missouri |
| I certify that I have on this 29th day of Nov. 1866
County of McDonald |
solemnized the rites of matrimony between Pleasant Cheek and Sarah Ward both of the county and state aforesaid.

(Signed) D. C. Hopkins, J. P.

State of Missouri |
|SS
County of McDonald | I S. G. Sutter Clerk of the Circuit Court and exofficio[sic]
Recorder do hereby certify the above is a true, full and correct copy as the same appears of Record in my office in Marriage Record "A" page 9.

In testimony whereof I have hereunto set my hand and official seal of office in Pineville Mo. this the 2nd day of August a. D. 1897.

(Signed) S. G. Sutter
Circuit Clerk and Exofficio
Recorder.

On Back:

Marriage Certificate

of

Sarah B. Cheak[sic].

---ooOoo---

DEPARTMENT OF THE INTERIOR,
COMMISSIONER TO THE FIVE CIVILIZED TRIBES.

Muskogee, Oklahoma, March 30, 1908.

I, the undersigned, a stenographer to the Commissioner to the Five Civilized Tribes, do hereby certify that the above and foregoing is a true and correct copy of the original offered in evidence in the matter of application for the enrollment of Sarah B. Cheek as a citizen by intermarriage of the Cherokee Nation.

Louise Smith

◇◇◇◇◇

(Copy of original document from case.)

◇◇◇◇◇

DEPARTMENT OF THE INTERIOR,
COMMISSIONER TO THE FIVE CIVILIZED TRIBES.

Muskogee, Indian Territory, February 2, 1907

Sarah B. Cheek,
Grove, Indian Territory.

Dear Madam:

There has been this day sent you the following telegram:

"Appear before Commissioner immediately and testify in your Cherokee intermarried case."

The Act of Congress approved April 26, 1906 provides that the Secretary of the Interior shall have no jurisdiction to approve the enrollment of any person as a citizen of the Cherokee Nation after March 4, 1907. This matter therefore demands your immediate attention.

Respectfully,

L M B   Tams Bixby   Commissioner

◇◇◇◇◇

189

Cherokee
2855

Muskogee, Indian Territory, February 26, 1907.

Sarah B. Cheek,
Grove, Indian Territory.

Dear Madam:

There is enclosed herewith a copy of the decision of the Commissioner to the Five Civilized Tribes, dated February 26, 1907, granting your application for enrollment as a citizen by intermarriage of the Cherokee Nation.

You will be advised when your name has been placed upon a schedule of citizens of the Cherokee Nation and approved by the Secretary of the Interior.

Respectfully,

Encl. HJ-93.
HJC

Commissioner.

◇◇◇◇◇

Cherokee
2855.

Muskogee, Indian Territory, February 26, 1907.

W. W. Hastings,
Attorney for the Cherokee Nation,
Muskogee, Indian Territory.

Dear Sir:

There is enclosed herewith a copy of the decision of the Commissioner to the Five Civilized Tribes, dated February 26, 1907, granting the application for the enrollment of Sarah B. Cheek as a citizen by intermarriage of the Cherokee Nation.

Respectfully,

Encl. HJ-94.
HJC

Commissioner.

◇◇◇◇◇

Cherokee
2855

Muskogee, Indian Territory, February 26, 1907.

The Commissioner to the Five Civilized Tribes,
Muskogee, Indian Territory.

Sir:

Receipt is hereby acknowledged of the testimony and of your decision enrolling Sarah B. Cheek as a citizen by intermarriage of the Cherokee Nation. Time for protesting said decision is waived, and I consent that said person may be placed upon the schedule immediately.

Respectfully,

W. W. Hastings

Attorney for Cherokee Nation.

◇◇◇◇◇

Cherokee I.W. 260
9606-1908.

Muskogee, Oklahoma, March 31, 1908.

Mrs. Sarah B. Cheek,
Grove, Oklahoma.

Madam:

As requested in your letter of March 25, 1908, there is enclosed marriage certificate of yourself and Pleasant Cheek which was filed in the matter of your application for enrollment as such is accordingly granted. a citizen by intermarriage of the Cherokee Nation. Copies of the same have been retained in the files of this office.

Respectfully,

LS   Acting Commissioner.
Incl. S-20

◇◇◇◇◇

(Copy of original document from case.)

Cher IW 261

◇◇◇◇◇

ECM

DEPARTMENT OF THE INTERIOR,

COMMISSIONER TO THE FIVE CIVILIZED TRIBES.

In the matter of the application for the enrollment of

LEWIS MOORE

As a citizen by intermarriage of the Cherokee Nation.

CHEROKEE NO, 3297.

◇◇◇◇◇

DEPARTMENT OF THE INTERIOR.

COMMISSION TO THE FIVE CIVILIZED TRIBES.

Vinita, I.T. September 22, 1900.

IN THE MATTER OF THE APPLICATION OF BETTIE MOORE FOR THE ENROLLMENT OF HERSELF, HER HUSBAND AND CHILDREN AS CHEROKEE CITIZENS.

The said Bettie Moore, being called, sworn and examined by the Commissioner, Hon. T. B. Needles, testified as follows:

Q What is your name?   A Bettie Moore.
Q How old are you?   A I am forty-five years old.
Q What is your post office address?   A Afton.
Q What district do you live in?   A Delaware.
Q Are you a recognized citizen of the Cherokee Nation? A Yes, sir.
Q By blood?   A Yes, sir.
Q For whom do you apply for enrollment?   A My husband, myself and family.
Q Is your husband here?   A No, sir; he is not here; he is at home.
Q He is taking care of the children while you are here, is he? A Yes, sir. Oh, he was busy and he couldn't come.
Q What was your father's name?   A Goodwin
Q What is his first name?   A John.
Q Is he living?   A No, sir.
Q What was your mother's name?   A Katie.
Q Is she living?   A No, sir.
Q What is the name of your husband?   A Lewis Moore.
Q Is he a citizen by blood?   A No, sir; he is a white man.
Q When were you married to him?   A In 1855, I believe.
Q Have you a certificate of marriage?   A No, sir; preacher Thompson has the marriage certificate, and of course henever[sic] did, send it back to us, and the offices got burned up at Tahlequah, and the certificate got burned up there. Mr. McGhee was a clerk then.
Q Is the preacher living?   A Yes, sir.
Q Are you on the 1880 roll?   A Yes, sir; I am on every roll, and my husband is too.
Q How old is your husband?   A Why, he is forty-six, somewhere along there. He is pretty near a year older than I am.
Q You don't mean to say you were married in 1855?   A No, I expect,--I don't remember what year it was.
Q How long ago was it?   A Well, it has been about twenty-five years, I expect.
Q Then you were married in 1875?   A Yes, sir; I guess it is about 1875, or '74. I expect about seventy-four.
Q Now, what are the names of your children under twenty-one years of age?

A   Why, Sammie Moore.

Q   How old is he?   A Eighteen. She is a girl.

Q   Now, the next one, Mrs. Moore. A She is a girl, Jimmie.

Q   How old is Jimmie?   A She is seventeen.

Q   What is the name of the next one?   A Josie.

Q   How old is Josie?   A She is about fifteen, I guess.

Q   What is the name of the next one?   A Johnie.

Q   How old is Johnie now?   A He is thirteen.

Q   What is the name of the next one?   A Mary Moore.

Q   How old is Mary?   A She is about 11.

Q   What is the name of the next one?   A The next one is Lewis Moore, Jr.

Q   How old is he?   A Nine.

Q   What is the name of the next one?   A Fred.

Q   How old is he?   A Seven.

Q   What is the name of the next one?   A Stein. He is named after a Cherokee.

Q   How old is he?   A He is about four years old.

Q   What is the name of the next one?   A That is all.

Q   That is eight? A Yes, sir.

Q   Are these children all alive and living with you at home? A Yes, sir.

Q   Lewis, is at home at work, isn't he?   A Yes, sir; he is putting up hay.

Q   He ought to be with a family the size of this. A He went up and tried to get in two days, but he was so busy he could not stay.

1880 Roll, page 291, No. 1839, Bettie Moore, Delaware District.
1880 Roll, page 291, No. 1838, Lewis Moore, Delaware District.
1880 Roll, page 506, No. 2131, Bettie Moore, Delaware District.
1880 Roll, page 506, No. 2133, Sammie Moore, Delaware District.
1880 Roll, page 506, No. 2134, Jimmie Moore, Delaware District.
1880 Roll, page 506, No. 2135, Josie Moore, Delaware District.
1880 Roll, page 506, No. 2136, Johnie Moore, Delaware District.
1880 Roll, page 506, No. 2137, Mary Moore, Delaware District.
1880 Roll, page 506, No. 2138, Lewis Moore, Delaware District.
1880 Roll, page 506, No. 2139, Fred Moore, Delaware District.

Q   Have you always lived in the Cherokee Nation?   A Yes, sir.

Q   And your husband since you married him?   A Yes, sir.

Q   Are these children all alive and living with you?   A Yes, sir.

Q   Were you and your husband living together four years ago? A Yes, sir.

Q   You have always lived together?   A Yes, sir.

THE COMMISSIONER: The name of Bettie Moore appears upon the authenticated roll of 1880, and the name of her husband, Lewis Moore also appears upon the authenticated roll of 1880. The name of Lewis Moore does not appear upon the census roll of 1896, but the name of his wife appears upon the census roll of 1896 as well as the names of his children, Sammie, Jimmie, Josie, Johnie, Mary, Lewis, Jr., and Fred; consequently the said Bettie Moore and her said children as enumerated in the testimony will be duly listed for enrollment by this Commission as Cherokee citizens by blood, and the said Lewis Moore as a Cherokee citizen by intermarriage. The applicant's child Stein, whose name does not appear upon the census roll of 1896, will also be duly listed for enrollment by this Commission as a Cherokee citizen by blood, upon the filing of satisfactory proof of birth.

-----0-----

The undersigned, being sworn, stated that as stenographer to the Commission to the Five Civilized Tribes he correctly recorded the testimony and other proceedings in this application for enrollment, and that the foregoing is a correct and complete transcript of his stenographic notes thereof.

Wm S. Meeshean

Subscribed and sworn to before me this 4th day of October A. D. 1900.

C R Breckinridge
Commissioner.

◇◇◇◇◇

R.

DEPARTMENT OF THE INTERIOR.
Commission to the Five Civilized Tribes.
Muskogee, Indian Territory, October 1st, 1902.

In the matter of the application of Lewis Moore for the enrollment of himself as a citizen by intermarriage of the Cherokee Nation and for the enrollment of his wife, Bettie Moore, and his children, Sammie Thomas and Jimmie, Josie, Johnie, Mary, Lewis Jr., Fred and Stein S. Moore, as citizens by blood of the Cherokee Nation.

Supplemental to #3297.

Appearances:
Benjamin C. England for Applicant.
J. C. Starr for Cherokee Nation.

BENJAMIN C. ENGLAND, being duly sworn, testified as follows:
Examination by the Commission.
Q.   Give him your name and age and post office?   A.   Benjamin C. England, Afton, 54.

Q.   Are you acquainted with Lewis Moore, whose post office is Afton, I. T., and who is an applicant before this Commission for enrollment as an intermarried citizen of the Cherokee Nation?   A. Yes, sir.

Q.   Are you acquainted with his wife, Bettie?   A Yes, sir.

Q.   Is she a citizen by blood of the Cherokee Nation?   A. By blood; yes, sir.

Q.   How long have you known Lewis Moore?   A. I have known Lewis Moore at least 20 years.

Q.   Did you know him before his marriage to his wife Bettie?   A. Yes, sir.

Q.   Do you know whether he was married prior to his marriage to her?
A.   No, sir; he never was married before.

Q.   Was she ever married prior to her marriage to him?   A. No, sir.

Q.   How long have they been married?   A. Oh, 20 years. They have got children married off.

Q.   Have Lewis Moore and his wife Bettie lived together continuously as husband and wife from the time of their marriage up to the present time?   A. Yes, sir.

Q.   Were they living together on the first of September, 1902?   A. Yes, sir.

Q.   Where has Lewis Moore lived for the last 20 years?   A.   In the Cherokee Nation; Delaware district.

Q.   He never has lived outside the Cherokee Nation for the last 20 years?   A. No, sir.

Q.   His wife has lived with him in the Cherokee Nation for the last 20 years?
A.   Yes, sir.

Q.   Are you acquainted with Lewis Moore and Bettie Moore's daughter, Sammie?
A.   Yes, sir.

Q.   Do you know whether or not she has married since the original application was made for her enrollment?   A. Yes, sir; I believe she was. Yes, I am satisfied she was.

Q.   You know she was married?   A. Yes, I am satisfied they were married. I didn't see them married. I was there afterwards.

Q.   You didn't see them married but you were present the night they were married and present at the entertainment?   A. Yes, sir.

Q.   Her name is now Thomas?   A. Yes, sir.

Q.   Do you know her husband's name?   A. No, I don't believe I can call it at present.

Jesse O. Carr, being first duly sworn, states that as stenographer to the Commission to the Five Civilized Tribes he reported the above entitled case and that the foregoing is a true and complete transcript of his stenographic notes thereof.

Jesse O. Carr

Subscribed and sworn to before me this 24th day of October, 1902.

BC Jones
Notary Public.

◇◇◇◇◇

Cherokee Intermarried White 1906
Volume IX

C. F. B.   Cherokee 3297.

DEPARTMENT OF THE INTERIOR,
COMMISSION TO THE FIVE CIVILIZED TRIBES.
Muskogee, Indian Territory, January 7, 1907.

In the Matter of the Application for the Enrollment of Lewis Moore as a citizen by intermarriage of the Cherokee Nation.

APPEARANCES:

Applicant appears in person.

Cherokee Nation represented by W. W. Hastings, Attorney.

Lewis Moore being first duly sworn by John E. Tidwell, Notary Public, testified as follows:

ON BEHALF OF COMMISSIONER.

Q What is your name?   A Lewis Moore.
Q What is your age?   A 53 the 7th of February.
Q What is your post office address?
A Afton.
Q Are you an applicant for enrollment as a citizen by intermarmiage[sic] of the Cherokee Nation?
A Yes sir.
Q You have no Cherokee blood?
A No sir.
Q Your only claim to the right to enrollment as a citizen of the Cherokee Nation is by virtue of your marriage to a citizen by blood of the Nation?
A Yes sir.
Q What is the name of the citizen through whom you claim that right?
A Bettie Goodwin.
Q Was she a recognized citizen of the Cherokee Nation at the time you married her?
A Yes sir.
Q Where did you marry her?
A Hickory Grove School House.
Q In the Cherokee Nation?
A Yes sir.
Q In what year?
A '71.
Q Did you marry her in accordance with the law of the Cherokee Nation?
A Yes sir; I got my license from Mr. McGee.
Q In what district was the license issued?
A Delaware.

197

Cherokee Intermarried White 1906
Volume IX

Q You say your wife is living at this time?
A Yes sir.
Q Since your marriage to her, have you and she continuously lived together as husband and wife?
A Yes sir.
Q And have lived all these years in the Cherokee Nation?
A Yes sir.
Q There has never been any separation of any king?
A No sir.
Q Was she your first wife?
A Yes sir.
Q Are you her first husband?
A Yes sir.

The apllicant[sic], Lewis Moore, is identified on the Cherokee Authenticated Tribal Roll of 1880, Delaware District, No. 1838. His wife, Bettie Moore, is identified on said roll at No. 1837 and her name is also included in the approved partial roll of citizens by blood of the Cherokee Nation opposite No. 8120.

Q You have no documentary evidence to show your marriage to your wife, have you?
A No sir; not here with me.
Q Who issued you marriage license?
A Jeff McGee.

Thomas J. McGee being first duly sworn by John E. Tidwell, Notary Public, testified as follows:

ON BEHALF OF COMMISSIONER.

Q State your name, age and post office address.
A Thomas J. McGee; Afton, Indian Territory.
Q You desire to give testimony relative to the right to enrollment of Lewis Moore as a citizen by intermarriage of the Cherokee Nation?
A Yes sir.
Q How long have you known Lewis Moore?
A I guess about 35 years.
Q He is not a Cherokee by blood?
A No sir.
Q His only claim to the right to enrollment is by virtue of his marriage to a citizen by blood?
A Yes sir.
Q What is the name of his citizen wife?
A Bettie Moore.
Q Did you know her before they were married?
A Yes sir.

Q   Qhat[sic] was her maiden name?
A   Bettie Goodwin.
Q   Was she a citizen of the Cherokee Nation at the time he married her?
A   Yes sir; so recognized.
Q   Living in the Cherokee Nation, were they?
A   Yes sir.
Q   Do you know of your own personal knowledge that Lewis Moore was married to his wife, Bettie Goodwin, in accordance with the laws of the Cherokee Nation?
A   I have no reason to doubt it. The records will show.
Q   Do you know in what district they were living at the time they were married?
A   Delaware District.
Q   Did you see them married?
A   No sir; I did not.
Q   Do you know about what year they were married?
A   Well, not just exactly. The records ought to show just what year they were married.
Q   Did you issue this license to them?
A   It occurs to me that I did. The records ought to show if I did.
Q   Do you know of your own personal knowledge that since about the year 1869 or 1870, these parties have continuously lived together as husband and wife?
A   Yes sir; they have been together as far back as I recollect; are living together yet.
Q   And since you became acquainted with Lewis Moore, has he been recognized as a citizen by intermarriage of the Cherokee Nation?
A   Yes sir; he has been a voter there in our district.

Q   He has enjoyed all the rights and privileges as a citizen of the Cherokee Nation by intermarriage?
A   Yes sir.

ON BEHALF OF CHEROKEE NATION.

Q   You don't remember specifically whether you issued the license or not?
A   I stated a while ago that the records would show.

The undersigned being first duly sworn states that as stenographer to the Commission to the Five Civilized Tribes, she correctly recorded the testimony taken in this case and that the foregoing is a full, true and correct transcript of her stenographic notes thereof.

Myrtle Hill

Subscribed and sworn to before me this the 8th day of January, 1907.

John E. Tidwell
Notary Public.

◇◇◇◇◇

E.C.M.   Cherokee 3297.

DEPARTMENT OF THE INTERIOR,
COMMISSIONER TO THE FIVE CIVILIZED TRIBES.
MUSKOGEE, I. T., FEBRUARY 21, 1907.

In the matter of the application for the enrollment of LEWIS MOORE as a citizen by intermarriage of the Cherokee Nation.

CHEROKEE NATION represented by W. W. HASTINGS, ATTORNEY.

LOUISA J. TROTT, being first duly sworn by Walter W. Chappell, Notary Public, testified as follows:

ON BEHALF OF THE COMMISSIONER:

Q   What is your name?   A Louisa J. Trott.
Q   What is your age?   A 56.
Q   What is your post office address?   A Vinita.
Q   Do you appear here today for the purpose of giving testimony relative to the right of Lewis Moore to enrollment as a citizen by intermarriage of the Cherokee Nation? A Yes sir.
Q   How long have you been acquainted with the applicant, Lewis Moore? A All his life.
Q   Are you any relation to Lewis Moore?   A He is my brother.
Q   He is a white man, is he?   A Yes sir.
Q   Through whom does he claim the right to enrollment?
      A His wife, Elizabeth Goodwin.
Q   The same as the one listed here as Bettie?   A Yes sir.
Q   Is she a Cherokee?   A Yes sir, a half-breed.
Q   When were Lewis Moore and his wife, Bettie Moore, married?
      A I dont[sic] know the day of the month, but it was in July, 1874.
Q   Were you present at the marriage?   A No sir.
Q   Was he married under a license issued by the authorities of the Cherokee Nation? A Yes sir.
Q   Did you see the license?   A No sir.
Q   But you know that he was married under a license?   A Yes sir.
Q   Are both Lewis Moore and his wife living?   A Yes sir.
Q   Since their marriage have they continuously resided together as husband and wife, and remained residents of the Cherokee Nation?
      A Yes sir.
Q   In what District were they married?   A Delaware, I think.
Q   Did he secure the license in Delaware District?   A Yes sir, and the Clerk's name was McGhee.

BY MR. HASTINGS:

Q   How do you know that they were married under a license?
    A   Well, I know as far as anybody can without seeing it.
Q   Upon what do you base your judgment?   A   Well, I know that the[sic] would not
    be living any other way, and he has always voted at all the elections and
    everything like that, and has been recognized as a citizen.
Q   It is for these reasons that you draw the conclusion that he was married under a
    Cherokee license?   A   Yes sir.
Q   You didn't actually see the license?   A   No sir, I think Preacher Joe Thompson
    who married them lived at Tahlequah, but I think he is now at the Orphan
    Asylum.

JOHN H. MILLER, being first duly sworn by Walter W. Chappell, Notary Public,
    testified as follows:

Q   What is your name?   A   John M. Miller.
Q   What is your age?   A   64.
Q   What is your post office address?   A   Needmore.
Q   Do you appear here today for the purpose of giving testimony relative to the right of
    Lewis Moore to enrollment as a citizen by intermarriage of the Cherokee Nation?
    A   Yes sir.
Q   How long have you been acquainted with Lewis Moore?   A   Ever since 1872.
Q   Is he a white man?   A   Yes sir.
Q   Through whom does he claim the right to enrollment?   A   His wife.
Q   Is she a Cherokee?   A   Yes sir.
Q   When were they married?   A   In 1873 or 1874.
Q   Were you present at their marriage?   A   Yes sir.
Q   Was he married under a license?   A   Not that I know of.
Q   You didn't see the license?   A   I didn't see the license.

Q   Who married them?   A   Joe Thompson.
Q   Since their marriage have they continuously resided together as husband and wife,
    and remained residents or the Cherokee Nation?
    A   Yes sir.

(Witness excused).

LEWIS MOORE, being first duly sworn by Walter W. Chappell, Notary Public, testified
    as follows:

Q   What is your name?   A   Lewis Moore.
Q   What is your age?   A   53.
Q   What is your post office address?   A   Afton.
Q   You are the applicant in this case, are you?   A   Yes sir.
Q   Do you care to make any statement relative to your case?

A I have forgot the date, but I got the license from Jeff McGhee; he knows me, and he says I am right.

BY MR. HASTINGS:

Q What is the correct date of your marriage?   A Well, the way I get it is by the childrens'[sic] ages. We was married in July, 1874, and the oldest child was born the 17th of the next July comin'[sic], and he died in November; Billie was born February 7, 1877, and he was 30 years old last February.

(Witness excused).

The undersigned, upon oath, states that, as stenographer to the Commissioner to the Five Civilized Tribes, she correctly reported the above and foregoing testimony, and that the same is a full, true and complete transcript of her stenographic notes thereof.

Sarah Waters

Subscribed and sworn to before me this 23d day of February, 1907.

Frances R Lane
Notary Public.

◇◇◇◇◇◇

(The Affidavit below was originally handwritten on the microfilm and is typed as given.)

In the matter of the application of Louis Moore for citizenship by intermarriage, of the Cherokee Nation.

Northern District ⎤
Indian Territory ⎦

Personally appeared before me, AW Harlan who after being duly sworn states: That he was present and saw Louis Moore and Bettie Moore married in the Hickory Grove school house in the then Delaware District, Cherokee Nation, Indian Territory. That this was before the year 1875 about 1871. That he has lived in the Hickory Grove school house neighbourhood[sic] since 1869 and is of the age of sixty years, and has no interest in the applicants[sic] claim.

A W Harlan

Subscribed and sworn to before me this the 23 day of January 1907

C G James

My Commission expires Sept. 7th, 1908.   *Notary Public.*

◇◇◇◇◇◇

Cherokee Intermarried White 1906
Volume IX

(The Affidavit below was originally handwritten on the microfilm and is typed as given.)

In the matter of the application of Louis Moore for citizenship by intermarriage, of the Cherokee Nation.

Northern District ⎫
Indian Territory ⎭

Personally appeared before me Alexander Copeland who after being duly sworn states:

That he was present and saw Louis Moore and Bettie Moore married in the Hickory Grove school house in the then Delaware District, Cherokee Nation, Indian Territory. That this was before 1875 and was about 1871. That he was unable to give more definate[sic] dates. That he is of the age of Sixty-seven years and has resided and gone to said Hickory Grove school house since 1869 or 1870. That he has no interest in the applicant's claim.

	his
Witnesses	Alexander x Copeland
Edward Barnett	mark
William T Kelly	

Subscribed and sworn to before me this the 23 day of January 1907.

C G James

My Commission expires Sept. 7th, 1908.　　　　*Notary Public.*

◇◇◇◇◇

E C M　　　　　　　　　　　　　　　　　　　　　　　Cherokee 3297.

DEPARTMENT OF THE INTERIOR,

COMMISSIONER TO THE FIVE CIVILIZED TRIBES.

In the matter of the application for the enrollment of LEWIS MOORE as a citizen by intermarriage of the Cherokee Nation.

D E C I S I O N

THE RECORDS OF THIS OFFICE SHOW: That at Vinita, Indian Territory, September 22, 1900 application was received by the Commission to the Five Civilized Tribes for the enrollment of Lewis Moore as a citizen by intermarriage of the Cherokee Nation. Further proceedings in the matter of said application were had at Muskogee, Indian Territory, October 1, 1902 and January 7, 1907 and February 21, 1907.

THE EVIDENCE IN THIS CASE SHOWS: That the applicant herein, Lewis Moore, a white man, was married in accordance with Cherokee law in the year 1871 to his wife Bettie Moore, nee Goodwin, who was at the time of said marriage a recognized citizen by blood of the Cherokee Nation, who is identified on the Cherokee authenticated

203

tribal roll of 1880, Delaware District No. 1839, as a native Cherokee by blood of the Cherokee Nation opposite No. 8120. It is further shown that from the time of said marriage the said Lewis Moore and Bettie Moore resided together as husband and wife and continuously lived in the Cherokee Nation up to and including September 1, 1902. Said applicant is identified on the Cherokee authenticated tribal [sic] of 1880 and the Cherokee census roll of 1896 as an intermarried citizen of the Cherokee Nation.

IT IS, THEREFORE, ORDERED AND ADJUDGED: That in accordance with the decision of the Supreme Court of the United States, dated November 5, 1906, in the cases of Daniel Red Bird et al. vs. the United States, Nos. 125, 126, 127, and 128, the said applicant, Lewis Moore is entitled, under the provisions of Section Twenty-one of the Act of Congress approved June 28, 1898 (30 Stats. 495), to enrollment as a citizen by intermarriage of the Cherokee Nation, and his application for enrollment as such is accordingly granted.

Tams Bixby

Commissioner.

Dated at Muskogee, Indian Territory,
this   FEB 26 1907

◇◇◇◇◇

THE WESTERN UNION TELEGRAPH COMPANY.
INCORPORATED
23,000 OFFICES IN AMERICA.   CABLE SERVICE TO ALL THE WORLD.
ROBERT C. CLOWRY, President and General Manager.

Form No. 260.

Receiver's No.	Time Filed	Check

SEND the following message subject to the terms on back hereof, which are hereby agreed to.   Muskogee, I.T. February 19, 1907.

ECM   Cherokee 3297

Lewis Moore,

Afton, Indian Territory.

Affidavits insufficient. Present witnesses immediately.

Bixby

O.E.G.R. PAID.   Commissioner.

☞ READ THE NOTICE AND AGREEMENT ON BACK. ☜

(Copy of original document from case.)

◇◇◇◇◇

Cherokee Intermarried White 1906
Volume IX

Cherokee
   3297

Muskogee, Indian Territory, February 19, 1907.

Lewis Moore,
   Afton, Indian Territory.

Dear Sir:

There has been sent you this day the following telegram:

"Affidavit insufficient. Present witnesses immediately."

The Act of Congress approved April 26, 1906, provides that the Secretary of the Interior shall have no jurisdiction to approve the enrollment of any person as a citizen of the Cherokee Nation after March 4, 1907.

This matter therefore demands your immediate attention.

Respectfully,

MTM   Commissioner.

◇◇◇◇◇

Form No. 260.
THE WESTERN UNION TELEGRAPH COMPANY.
INCORPORATED
23,000 OFFICES IN AMERICA.   CABLE SERVICE TO ALL THE WORLD.
ROBERT C. CLOWRY, President and General Manager.

Receiver's No.	Time Filed	Check

SEND the following message subject to the terms on back hereof, which are hereby agreed to.   Muskogee, I.T. February 19, 1907.

E.C.M.   Cherokee 3297

   Lewis Moore

      Afton, Indian Territory.

         Affidavit not sufficient, Present evidence at once.

                        Bixby

O.B.G.R. PAID.   Commissioner.

☞ READ THE NOTICE AND AGREEMENT ON BACK. ☜

(Copy of original document from case.)

◇◇◇◇◇

Cherokee
3297

Muskogee, Indian Territory, February 19, 1907.

Lewis Moore,
Afton, Indian Territory.

Dear Sir:

There has been sent you this day the following telegram:

"Affidavit not sufficient. Present evidence at once."

The Act of Congress approved April 26, 1906, provides that the Secretary of the Interior shall have no jurisdiction to approve the enrollment of any person as a citizen of the Cherokee Nation after March 4, 1907.

This matter therefore demands your immediate attention.

Respectfully,

MTM   Commissioner.

◇◇◇◇◇

Cherokee
3297

Muskogee, Indian Territory, February 26, 1907.

W. W. Hastings,
Attorney for the Cherokee Nation,
Muskogee, Indian Territory.

Dear Sir:

There is enclosed herewith a copy of the decision of the Commissioner to the Five Civilized Tribes, dated February 26, 1907, granting the application for the enrollment of Lewis Moore as a citizen by intermarriage of the Cherokee Nation.

Respectfully,

Enc I-1   Commissioner.

RPI

◇◇◇◇◇

Cherokee Intermarried White 1906
Volume IX

Cherokee
3297

Muskogee, Indian Territory, February 26, 1907.

Lewis Moore,
Afton, Indian Territory.

Dear Sir:

There is enclosed herewith a copy of the decision of the Commissioner to the Five Civilized Tribes, dated February 26, 1907, granting the application for your enrollment as a citizen by intermarriage of the Cherokee Nation.

You will be advised when your name has been placed upon a schedule of citizens of the Cherokee Nation and approved by the Secretary of the Interior.

Respectfully,

I-2

Commissioner.

RPI

◇◇◇◇◇

Cherokee 3297

Muskogee, Indian Territory, February 26, 1907.

The Commissioner to the Five Civilized Tribes,
Muskogee, Indian Territory.

Sir:

Receipt is acknowledged of the testimony and of your decision enrolling Lewis Moore as a citizen by intermarriage of the Cherokee Nation. Time for protesting said decision is waived and I consent that said person may be placed upon the schedule immediately.

Respectfully,
W. W. Hastings
Attorney for the Cherokee Nation.

Cher IW 262

◇◇◇◇◇

Cherokee Intermarried White 1906
Volume IX

Department of the Interior,
Commission to the Five Civilized Tribes,
Vinita, I.T., September 25, 1900.

In the matter of the application of Robert D. Knight for the enrollment of himself, wife and three children as Cherokee citizens; being sworn and examined by Commissioner Breckinridge he testified as follows:

Q   What is your name?   A Robert D. Knight.
Q   How old are you?   A 53 years old.
Q   What is your post-office?   A Vinita.
Q   What district do you live in?   A Delaware District.
Q   Who is it you want to have put on the roll?   A Myself, wife and three children.
Q   Are you a Cherokee by blood?   A Yes sir.
Q   What proportion of Cherokee blood do you claim?   A About 1/8
Q   Is your wife Cherokee?   A No sir.
Q   White woman?   A Yes sir.
Q   How long have you lived in the Cherokee Nation?   A 53 years.
Q   What district are you from in 1880?   A Delaware.
Q   In 1896 what district?   A Delaware.
Q   Give me your wife's name?   A Martha Louisa.
Q   How old is she?   A 44.
Q   When did you marry her?   A 1875.
Q   What was her maiden name?   A Martha Louisa West
Q   She living with you at this time?   A Yes sir.
Q   Has lived with you ever since you were married?   A Yes sir.
Q   Give me the names of your children?   A Robert Franklin, 19 years old; Grover Cleveland, 16; William Dew, 8.
Q   All living now are they?   A Yes sir.
1880 roll page 276 #1451 Robert D. Knight, Delaware Dist, native
1880 roll page 276 #1452 Martha L. Knight, Delaware, adopted white
1880 roll page 276 #1454 Robert F. Knight, Delaware District;
1896 roll page 490 #1701 Robert Dew Knight, Delaware
1896 roll page 579 #298 Martha L. Knight   "
1896 roll page 490 #1703 Robert Frank Knight   "
1896 roll page 490 #1704 Grover Cleaveland Knight   "
1896 roll page 490 #1705 William Dew Knight   "

Com'r Breckinridge: The applicant applies for the enrollment of himself, wife and three children. He is identified on the rolls of 1880 and 1896 as a native Cherokee; he has lived in the Cherokee Nation all his life and he will be listed now for enrollment as a Cherokee by blood.

His wife is identified with him on the rolls of 1880 and 1896; she has lived with him ever since their marriage in 1875, and she will be listed now for enrollment as a Cherokee by adoption; His oldest child, Robert F. Knight, is identified on the rolls of 1880 and 1896 with his parents; he will be listed now for enrollment as a Cherokee by blood; The two younger children, Grover C. and William Dew are identified with their parents on the roll of 1896; they are living at this time and they will be listed now for enrollment as Cherokees by blood.

M. D. GREEN, being first duly sworn, states that as stenographer to the Commission to the Five Civilized Tribes he correctly recorded the testimony and proceedings in this case and the foregoing is a true and correct transcript of his stenographic notes thereof.

MD Green

Subscribed and sworn to before me this 26 day of Sept 1900.

C R Breckinridge
Commissioner.

◇◇◇◇◇

Cherokee 3502.

Department of the Interior,
Commission to the Five Civilized Tribes,
Muskogee, I. T., October 3, 1902.

In the matter of the application of Robert D. Knight for the enrollment of himself and children, Robert F., Grover C., and William D. Knight, as citizens by blood, and for the enrollment of his wife, Martha L., as a citizen by intermarriage of the Cherokee Nation.

Preston S. Davis, being sworn and examined by the Commission, testified as follows:
Q What is your name?   A Preston S. Davis, 32 years old, postoffice Vinita.
Q Are you acquainted with Robert D. Knight who is an applicant before this Commission for enrollment as a citizen by blood of the Cherokee Nation?   A I am.
Q Are you acquainted with his wife, Martha L., who is an applicant as an intermarried citizen?   A Yes sir.
Q How long have you known his wife, Martha L.? A I have known Mr. Knight and his wife since 1883.
Q Were they married when you first knew them?   A Yes sir, I think they were.
Q Have they lived together as husband and wife all the time since 1883 up until the present time?   A Yes sir, ever since I have known them.
Q Have they ever been separated at all during that time?   A No sir.
Q Living together as husband and wife on the first day of September, 1902?   A They were and are now.
Q Has Robert D. Knight and Martha L., his wife, lived in the Cherokee Nation from the time you knew them up until the present time?   A Yes sir.

209

Q Their children, Robert F., Grover C. and William D., lived all their lives in the Cherokee Nation? A Yes sir.
Q Are all three of these children living at the present time? A Yes sir.

The undersigned, being duly sworn, states that as stenographer to the Commission to the Five Civilized Tribes he correctly recorded the testimony and proceedings in this case, and the foregoing is a true and correct transcript of his stenographic notes thereof.

E.G. Rothenberger

Subscribed and sworn to before me this 21st day of October, 1902.

BC Jones
Notary Public.

◇◇◇◇◇

Cher # 3502

Department of the Interior,
Commission to the Five Civilized Tribes,
Muskogee, I. T., October 13, 1902.

In the matter of the application of ROBERT D. KNIGHT, for the enrollment of himself, and his children, ROBERT F., GROVER C. AND WILLIAM D. KNIGHT, as citizens by blood, and his wife, MARTHA L. KNIGHT, as a citizen by intermarriage, of the Cherokee Nation.

MARTHA L. KNIGHT, called as a witness, being duly sworn and examined by the Commission, testified as follows:

Q What is your name ? A Martha L. Knight.
Q What is your age ? A Forty seven.
Q What is your post office address ? A Vinita.
Q Are you the same Martha L. Knight for whom application was made to the Commission for enrollment as an intermarried citizen of the Cherokee Nation in 1900 ?
A Yes sir.
Q What is the name of your husband ? A Robert D. Knight.
Q When were you married ? A In 1875.
Q Were you ever married before you married Mr. Knight ? A No sir.
Q Was he ever married before he married you ? A No sir.
Q Have you and he lived together continuously since 1880 as husband and wife up to the present time ? A Yes sir.
Q Were you living together as husband and wife on the first day of September, 1902 ?
A Yes sir.

Q   Never been separated ?   A No sir.

Q   Have you and he lived together in the Cherokee Nation since 1880 ?   A Yes sir.

Q   Are these children, Robert F., Grover C. and William D., your children by your husband Robert Knight ?   A Yes sir.

Q   Are they living with you in the Cherokee Nation ?   A Yes sir.

Q   Have they lived in the Cherokee Nation all their lives ?   A Yes sir.

E. C. Bagwell, on oath states that, as stenographer to the Commissioner to the Five Civilized Tribes, he correctly recorded the testimony and proceedings had in the above entitled cause, and that the foregoing is an accurate transcript of his stenographic notes thereof.

E.C. Bagwell

Subscribed and sworn to before me this October 21, 1902.

BC Jones
Notary Public.

◇◇◇◇◇

E.C.M.   Cherokee 3502.

DEPARTMENT OF THE INTERIOR
COMMISSIONER TO THE FIVE CIVILIZED TRIBES.
MUSKOGEE, I. T., FEBRUARY 18, 1907.

In the matter of the application for the enrollment of MARTHA L. KNIGHT as a citizen by intermarriage of the Cherokee Nation.

MARTHA L. KNIGHT, being first duly sworn by Walter W. Chappell, Notary Public, testified as follows:

ON BEHALF OF THE COMMISSIONER:

Q   What is your name?   A Martha Louisa Knight.

Q   What is your age?   A 51.

Q   What is your post office address?   A Needmore, I.T.

Q   Do you appear here today for the purpose of giving testimony relative to your right to enrollment as a citizen by intermarriage of the Cherokee Nation?   A Yes sir.

Q   You have no Cherokee blood?   A No sir.

Q   Then you derive whatever right you may have to enrollment as a citizen of the Cherokee Nation by virtue of your marriage to a citizen by blood of the Cherokee Nation?   A Yes sir.

Q   What is the name of your Cherokee husband?   A Robert D. Knight.

Q   When were you married to Robert D. Knight?   A April 1, 1875.

Q   Was Mr. Knight, at the time of your marriage to him, a recognized citizen by blood of the Cherokee Nation?   A Yes sir.

Cherokee Intermarried White 1906
Volume IX

Q Born and raised in the Cherokee Nation?   A Born and raised on Grand River.
Q Was he ever married before he married you?   A No sir.
Q Were you ever married before you married him?   A No sir.
Q Then he is your first husband, and you are his first wife?   A Yes.
Q Since the date of your marriage, have you and Robert D. Knight continuously
    resided together as husband and wife, and remained residents of the Cherokee
    Nation?   A Yes sir.
Q You have never been separated?   A No sir.
Q Have you any children, Mrs Knight?   A Yes sir, four.
Q What is the name of the eldest child?   A Herman Knight.
Q How old is Herman?   A 29.

BY MR. VANCE:

Q How long subsequent to your marriage was Herman born?   A 2 years.
Q Have you any marriage certificate?   A No sir.
Q Who married you?   A Jim Ketcham.
Q Is he living?   A No sir.
Q Is any one living who witnessed your marriage?   A No sir.
Q Did your husband secure a license?   A There were no licenses in those days.
Q There is no one living who was present at your marriage?   A No sir
Q Your son Herman is 29 years old?   A Last September.
Q And he was born two years subsequent to your marriage?   A Yes sir.
Q Have you any record of the date of your marriage?   A No sir.
Q Then you just give the date from your own independent knowledge?
    A Yes sir.
Q Are you enrolled upon the Cherokee authenticated tribal roll of 1880?
    A I guess I was; I dont[sic] remember.
Q You do not remember when you were enrolled?   A I was enrolled soon after I was
    married; I dont[sic] remember just when the census takers came around, but in
    May or June, I think.
Q How long had you know your husband prior to your marriage to him?
    A About a year.
Q What you say as to his not having been married before he married you is just your
    understanding from what he told you?   A Yes, and from everybody else,
    because he has live right there always.

ROBERT D. KNIGHT, being first duly sworn by Walter W. Chappell, Notary Public,
    testified as follows:

ON BEHALF OF THE COMMISSIONER:

Q What is your name?   A Robert D. Knight.
Q What is your age?   A 61.
Q What is your post office address?   A Needmore.

Cherokee Intermarried White 1906
Volume IX

Q   Do you appear here today for the purpose of giving testimony relative to the right of
    Martha L. Knight to enrollment as a citizen by intermarriage of the Cherokee
    Nation?   A Yes sir.
Q   What relation are you to the applicant?   A Husband.
Q   When were you married to her?   A April 1, 1875.
Q   Are you a citizen by blood of the Cherokee Nation?   A Yes sir.
Q   Born and raised in the Cherokee Nation?   A Yes sir.
Q   Were you ever married prior to your marriage to Martha L. Knight?
    A No sir.
Q   Since your marriage have you and your wife continuously resided together as
    husband and wife, and lived in the Cherokee Nation?
    A Yes sir.
Q   You have never been out of the Cherokee Nation to live?   A No sir.
Q   What is the name of you eldest child?   A Herman.
Q   When was he born?   A In '77.
Q   Do you remember the month?   A No sir, but it was late in the summer, or early in
    the fall.
Q   Are you identified on the 1880 roll?   A I expect so.
Q   What is your occupation?   A Well, I am a carpenter.
Q   Have you ever had any other occupation?   A I dont[sic] know; some people call
    me an architect; I never claimed to be, but I do that kind of work.

BY MR. VANCE:

Q   Can you give the exact date of the birth of Herman?   A No sir.
Q   Is your next oldest child named Robert F. Knight?   A Yes sir.
Q   Can you give the date of his birth?   A I think it was February 25.
Q   Mrs. Knight, do you know Herman's birthday?   A September 19.
Q   Mrs. Knight, do you know Robert F.'s birthday?   A February 25.

ON BEHALF OF THE COMMISSIONER:

The applicant, Martha L. Knight, is identified on the Cherokee authenticated
tribal roll of 1880, Delaware District, Page 276, at No. 1452, as an adopted white. Her
husband, Robert D. Knight, is identified on said roll, at No. 1451, as a native Cherokee.
Two children are identified on said roll,- Herman Knight, age two years, at No. 1453, and
Robert F. Knight, age two months, at No. 1454.

Q   Mr. Knight, were you ever a harness and saddlemaker?   A I work at everything,
    nearly; I believe I did have a little harness shop for about two months once.
Q   When was that?   A I can't tell you what year; way back yonder, maybe somewhere
    along in '76 or '77.
Q   Do you think it would be impossible for you to produce witnesses who have
    knowledge of your marriage prior to November 1, 1875?
    A Yes sir, I could probably get 50, as many as you wish.

Q Mrs. Knight, what is the difference in the ages of your children, Herman and Robert F.? A Herman was born in September, 1877, and Frank was born on February 25, 1880.

(Witnesses excused).

The undersigned, being first duly sworn, states that, as stenographer to the Commissioner to the Five Civilized Tribes, she correctly reported the above and foregoing testimony, and that the same is a full, true and complete transcript of her stenographic notes thereof.

Sarah Waters

Subscribed and sworn to before me this 18th day of February, 1907.

Frances R Lane
Notary Public.

◇◇◇◇◇

E.C.M.   Cherokee 3502.

DEPARTMENT OF THE INTERIOR,
COMMISSIONER TO THE FIVE CIVILIZED TRIBES.
MUSKOGEE, I.T., FEBRUARY 21, 1907.

SUPPLEMENTAL PROCEEDINGS in the matter of the application for the enrollment of MARTHA L. KNIGHT as a citizen by intermarriage of the Cherokee Nation.

CHEROKEE NATION represented by W. W. HASTINGS, Attorney.

LOUISA J. TROTT, being first duly sworn by Walter W. Chappell, Notary Public, testified as follows:

ON BEHALF OF THE COMMISSIONER:

Q What is your name?   A Louisa J. Trott.
Q What is your age?   A 56.
Q What is your post office address?   A Vinita.
Q Do you appear here today for the purpose of testifying relative to the right of Martha L. Knight to enrollment as a citizen by intermarriage of the Cherokee Nation? A Yes sir.
Q How long have you been acquainted with the applicant in this case?
   A Ever since they were married, and a little while before.

Q   Is she a white woman?   A Yes sir.

Q   Are you acquainted with her husband, Robert D. Knight?   A Yes sir.

Q   Is he a Cherokee?   A Yes sir.

Q   Mrs. Trott, I want you to tell me when they were married?   A They were married in April, 1875.

Q   How do you fix the date of that marriage?   A I only fix it by the childrens'[sic] birth.

Q   When was the first child born?   A In the winter or early fall; it must have been in the same fall.

Q   When was the next child born?   A September, 1877.

Q   You can fix that date positively?   A Yes sir.

Q   Then you are willing to swear that the second child born of that marriage was born in September, 1877?   A Yes sir.

Q   And that they were married in April, or in the early spring, but you think it was April, of 1875?   A Yes sir.

(Witness excused).

The undersigned, upon oath, states that, as stenographer to the Commissioner to the Five Civilized Tribes, she correctly reported the above and foregoing testimony, and that the same is a full, true and complete transcript of her stenographic notes thereof.

Sarah Waters

Subscribed and sworn to before me this 23d day of February, 1907.

Frances R Lane
Notary Public.

◇◇◇◇◇

E C M   Cherokee 3502.

DEPARTMENT OF THE INTERIOR,
COMMISSIONER TO THE FIVE CIVILIZED TRIBES.

In the matter of the application for the enrollment of MARTHA L. KNIGHT as a citizen by intermarriage of the Cherokee Nation.

D E C I S I O N

THE RECORDS OF THIS OFFICE SHOW: That at Vinita, Indian Territory, September 25, 1900 application was received by the Commission to the Five Civilized Tribes for the enrollment of Martha L. Knight as a citizen by intermarriage of the

Cherokee Nation. Further proceedings in the matter of said application were had at Muskogee, Indian Territory, October 3 and October 13, 1902 and February 18, 1907 and February 21, 1907.

THE EVIDENCE IN THIS CASE SHOWS: That the applicant herein, Martha L. Knight, a white woman, was married April 1, 1875 to one Robert D. Knight, who was at the time of said marriage a recognized citizen by blood of the Cherokee Nation, who is identified on the Cherokee authenticated tribal roll of 1880, Delaware District No. 1451 as a native Cherokee, and whose name is included on the approved partial roll of citizens by blood of the Cherokee Nation opposite No. 8519. It is further shown that from the time of said marriage the said Robert D. Knight and Martha L. Knight resided together as husband and wife and continuously lived in the Cherokee Nation up to and including September 1, 1902. Said applicant is identified on the Cherokee authenticated tribal roll of 1880 and the Cherokee census roll of 1896 as an intermarried citizen of the Cherokee Nation.

IT IS, THEREFORE, ORDERED AND ADJUDGED: That in accordance with the decision of the Supreme Court of the United States, dated November 5, 1906, in the cases of Daniel Red Bird, et al. vs. the United States, Nos. 125, 126, 127, and 128, the said applicant, Martha L. Knight, is entitled, under the provisions of Section Twenty-one of the Act of Congress approved June 28, 1898 (30 Stats. 495), to enrollment as a citizen by intermarriage of the Cherokee Nation, and her application for enrollment as such is accordingly granted.

Tams Bixby

Commissioner.

Dated at Muskogee, Indian Territory,
this   FEB 26 1907

◇◇◇◇◇

(Copy of original document from case.)

◇◇◇◇◇

(The letter below typed as given.)

REFER IN REPLY TO THE FOLLOWING:

Cherokee 3502

DEPARTMENT OF THE INTERIOR,
COMMISSIONER TO THE FIVE CIVILIZED TRIBES.

ECM   Muskogee, Indian Territory, February 21, 1907.

SPECIAL

    Martha L. Knight,
        Needmore, Indian Territory.
    Dear Madam:-

        The Commission sent you this day a telegram as follows:

        "Appear immediately with witnesses to prove
date of your marriage."

Cherokee Intermarried White 1906
Volume IX

The act of Congress approved April 26, 1906, provides that the Secretary of the Interior shall have no jurisdiction to approve the enrollment of any person as a citizen of the Cherokee Nation after March 4, 1907.

This matter, therefore, dem   Commissioner.

◇◇◇◇◇

Cherokee 3502

Muskogee, Indian Territory, February 26, 1907.

Martha L. Knight,
    Vinita, Indian Territory.

Dear Madam:

There is enclosed herewith a copy of the decision of the Commissioner to the Five Civilized Tribes, dated February 26, 1907, granting the application for your enrollment as a citizen by intermarriage of the Cherokee Nation.

You will be advised when your name has been placed upon a schedule of citizens of the Cherokee Nation and approved by the Secretary of the Interior.

Respectfully,

Encl. H-110   Commissioner
   JMH

◇◇◇◇◇

Cherokee 3502

Muskogee, Indian Territory, February 26, 1907.

The Commissioner to the Five Civilized Tribes,
    Muskogee, Indian Territory.

Sir:

Receipt is acknowledged of the testimony and of your decision enrolling Martha L. Knight as a citizen by intermarriage of the Cherokee Nation. Time for protesting said decision is waived, and I consent that said person may be placed upon the schedule immediately.

Respectfully,

W. W. Hastings
Attorney for Cherokee Nation.

◇◇◇◇◇

Cherokee
3502

Muskogee, Indian Territory, February 26, 1907.

W. W. Hastings,
Attorney for the Cherokee Nation,
Muskogee, Indian Territory.

Dear Sir:

There is enclosed herewith a copy of the decision of the Commissioner to the Five Civilized Tribes, dated February 26, 1907, granting the application for the enrollment of Martha L. Knight as a citizen by intermarriage of the Cherokee Nation.

Respectfully,

Encl. H-111   Commissioner.
JMH

Cher IW 263

◇◇◇◇◇

DEPARTMENT OF THE INTERIOR,
COMMISSION TO THE FIVE CIVILIZED TRIBES,
VINITA, I.T., OCTOBER 3d, 1900.

In the matter of the application of John Johnson Caldwell for the enrollment of himself and four children as citizens of the Cherokee Nation; said Cladwell[sic] being sworn by Commissioner C. R. Breckinridge, testified as follows:

Q Give me your name, please?   A John Johnson Caldwell
Q How old are you?   A I am about 51.
Q What is your post office?   A Vinita.
Q In what district do you live?   A Delaware.
Q Who is it you want to have put on the roll?   A Myself and four children.
Q Are you Cherokee by blood?   A No, sir, white man.
Q Have you your marriage certificate and license?   A I have part of it.
Q When were you married?   A About 1874 or 1875.
Q To whom were you married?   A Martha J. Foster, that is my first marriage, I have been married twice.
Q How long did you live with your wife Martha J?   A She died about two years after I was married.

Q When did you marry again?   A I guess it was about '79.
Q To whom?   A Callie M. Thompson.
Q Are you still living with yer[sic]?   A No, sir, she is dead.
Q When did she die?   A She died about 1895.
Q Is she Cherokee?   A Yes, sir, Cherokee by blood.
Q Did you live with her from the time you married her until she died?   A Yes, sir.
Q And all the time in the Cherokee Nation?   A Yes, sir.
Q Give me the names of your children?   A Oldest on is John L.
A How old is that child?   A 17.
Q The next child?   A Mariah F.
Q How old is she?   A 13.
Q The next child?   A Benjamin Morris.
Q How old is he?   A 11.
Q The next child?   A Joella May.
Q How old is that child?   A She is nine.
Q All alive now[sic] A Yes, sir.

1880 enrollment; page 239, #609, John J. Caldwell, Delaware.
1880 enrollment; page 239, #610, Callie M. Cladwell[sic], Delaware.
1896 enrollment; page 567, #109, John J. Cladwell, Delaware.
1896 enrollment; page 448, #541, John Lynch   "   "
1896 enrollment; page 448, #542, Mariah Francis   "

1896 enrollment; page 448, #543, Benjamin Morris,   "
1896 enrollment; page 448, #544, Joella May,   "

Q You never re-married since your wife died?   A No, sir.

Com'r Breckinridge:--The applicant applies for the enrollment of himself and four children: He is identified with his Cherokee wife on the roll of 1880. She has been dead some five years, and he has not re-married since her death. He salso[sic] identified on the roll of 1896, and he will be listee[sic] now for enrollment as a Cherokee by adoption. His four children enumerated in the testimony are all minors and are identified on the roll of 1896. They are alive at this time and will be listed for enrollment as Cherokees by blood.

---oooOOOooo---

J.O. Rosson, being first duly sworn, states that as stenographer to the Commission to the Five Civilized Tribes, he correctly recorded the testimony and proceedings in this case, and that the foregoing is a true and complete transcript of his stenographic notes thereof.

JO Rosson

Subscribed and sworn to before me this 8th day of October, 1900.

C R Breckinridge
Commissioner.

Cherokee Intermarried White 1906
Volume IX

◇◇◇◇◇

Cher
Supp'l to # 4101

Department of the Interior,
Commission to the Five Civilized Tribes,
Muskogee, I. T., October 16, 1902.

In the matter of the application of JOHN J. CALDWELL, for the enrollment of himself as a citizen by intermarriage, and his children, JOHN L., MARIAH F., BENJAMIN M., and JOELLA M. CALDWELL, as citizens by blood, of the Cherokee Nation.

JOHN J. CALDWELL, being duly sworn and examined by the Commission, testified as follows:

Q   What is your name ?   A   John J. Caldwell.
Q   How old are you ?   A   Fifty three years old.
Q   What is your post office address ?   A   Vinita.
Q   Are you a white man ?   A   Yes sir.
Q   Is your name on the 1880 roll as an adopted white citizen ?   A   Yes sir.
Q   What was your wife's name in 1880 ?   A   Callie N. Thompson.
Q   Is she the wife through whom you claim your citizenship ?
A   Well, I was married before that to a Cherokee woman.
Q   Then you claim you citizenship through your first wife ?
A   They were both Cherokees.
Q   You married the first one under a Cherokee marriage license ?
A   Yes sir.
Q   When did your first wife die ?   A   A year after we were married; we were married in 1874 or 5.
Q   Then she died about 1876 ?   A   Yes sir.
Q   Then you married Callie N ?   A   In 1878 I think it was.
Q   How long did you live with Callie ?   A   Until she died, in 1893
Q   You haven't married since, have you ?   A   No sir.
Q   Have you been living and making your home in the Cherokee Nation since 1880 ?
A   Yes sir, been there since --
Q   How many children have you ?   A   Five.
Q   How many are living at home ?   A   They are all at home part of the time, the oldest boy is away from home a good deal of the time with his uncle, right close.
Q   John L., is that the oldest child ?   A   Yes sir.
Q   The next one is Mariah ?   A   They call her Fannie.
Q   Benjamin M., is next ?   A   Yes sir.
Q   And Joella ?   A   Yes sir. And Lula.
Q   She is the youngest ?   A   Yes sir. She is not at home, Mrs. Webb at Adair has her. They enrolled her I guess.

Q These four children have lived in the Cherokee Nation all their lives ? A Yes sir.

Examined by J. C. Starr:

Q Did you live with you second wife until she died ?
A Yes sir.

E. C. Bagwell, on oath states that, as stenographer to the Commission to the Five Civilized Tribes, he correctly recorded the testimony and proceedings had in the above entitled cause, and that the foregoing is an accurate transcript of his stenographic notes thereof.

E.C. Bagwell

Subscribed and sworn to before me this November 20, 1902.

BC Jones
Notary Public.

◇◇◇◇◇

C. F. B.   Cherokee 4101.

DEPARTMENT OF THE INTERIOR,
COMMISSION TO THE FIVE CIVILIZED TRIBES.
Muskogee, Indian Territory, January 7, 1907.

In the Matter of the Application for the Enrollment of John J. Caldwell as a citizen by intermarriage of the Cherokee Nation.

Applicant appears in person.

APPEARANCES:

Cherokee Nation represented by H. M. Vance, in behalf of W. W. Hastings, Attorney.

John J. Caldwell being first duly sworn by John E. Tidwell, Notary Public, testified as follows:

ON BEHALF OF COMMISSIONER.

Q What is your name?   A   John J. Caldwell.
Q What is your age?   A   56.
Q What is your post office address?
A Vinita, Indian Territory.

Q   Are you an applicant for enrollment as a citizen by intermarriage of the Cherokee Nation?

A   Yes sir.

Q   You have no Cherokee blood?

A   No sir.

Q   Your only claim to the right to enrollment as a citizen of the Cherokee Nation is by virtue of your marriage to a citizen by blood of the Nation?

A   Yes sir.

Q   What is the name of the citizen through whom you claim that right?

A   Martha J. Foster.

Q   When did you marry her?

A   In December, '74.

Q   Is she living at this time?

A   No sir.

Q   Was she a recognized citizen of the Cherokee Nation at the time you married her?

A   Yes sir; always was.

Q   Living in the Cherokee country?

A   Yes sir.

Q   When did she die?

A   October, 1875.

Q   From the time of your marriage to her, did you and she continuously live together as husband and wife?

A   Yes sir.

Q   Was Martha J. Fozter[sic] your first wife?

A   Yes sir.

Q   Were you her first husband?

A   Yes sir.

Q   Have you married since her death?

A   Yes sir.

Q   What is the name of your second wife?

A   Callie N. Thompson.

Q   Was she a citizen by blood of the Cherokee Nation.

A   Yes sir.

Q   What is the name of her father?

A   Joe L. Thompson.

Q   What is her mother's name?

A   Francis D. Thompson.

Q   Is she living at this time?

A   No sir.

Q   When did she die?

A   In '94.

Q   Did you and she live together as husband and wife from the time of your marriage until the time of her death?

A   Yes sir.

Q   Have you married since the death of your second wife?

A   No sir.

Q   Has your residence been continuous in the Cherokee Nation since your marriage to your first wife?

A   Yes sir.

Q   Did you marry your first wife in accordance with the law of the Cherokee Nation?

A   Yes sir.

Q   Did you secure a license?

A   Yes sir.

Q   In what district was that license issued?

A   Delaware District.

Q   Have you a copy of the license?

A   Yes sir; a part of one. It has been badly damaged.

Q   Who married you?

A   The first time, Parson J. F. Thompson, I believe, of Tahlequah. He lived at Locust Grove at the time he married us.

Q   In what district was your license issued?

A   Delaware.

Q   In 1874?

A   Yes sir.

The applicant presents parts of original marriage license and certificate showing that on the 23rd of December, 1874, license was issued by J. E. Harlin, Clerk Delaware District, Cherokee Nation, authorizing the marriage of John J Caldwell, a citizen of the United States and Miss Marther[sic] J. Foster, a citizen of the Cherokee Nation.

Q   Is your deceased wife, Martha J. Caldwell, identical with the person mentioned in this marriage license as Marther J. Foster?

A   Yes sir.

Q   They are one and the same person, are they?

A   Yes sir.

Q   Who married you?

A   Joe F. Thompson.

Q   Did he put his certificate on the back of this license?

A   Yes sir.

Q   But the part that is torn off from this instrument is the part that contains his certificate?

A   No sir; that was written here with red ink and has faded out. At the time I was enrolled here with the Dawes Commission, you could see a good many of the letters.

The applicant, John J. Caldwell is identified on the Cherokee Authenticated Tribal Roll of 1880, Delaware District, No. 609. Applicant states that he drew what they called "bread money" in 1875.

The undersigned being first duly sworn states that as stenographer to the Commission to the Five Civilized Tribes, she correctly recorded the testimony taken in this case and that the foregoing is a full, true and correct transcript of her stenographic notes thereof.

Myrtle Hill

Subscribed and sworn to before me this the 8th day of January, 1907.

John E. Tidwell
Notary Public.

◇◇◇◇◇

C. F. B.   Cherokee 4101.

DEPARTMENT OF THE INTERIOR,
COMMISSIONER TO THE FIVE CIVILIZED TRIBES.
Muskogee, Indian Territory, February 6, 1907.

In the matter of the application for the enrollment of John J. Caldwell as a citizen by intermarriage of the Cherokee Nation.

SUPPLEMENTAL.

Cherokee Nation represented by W. W. Hastings.

Samuel C. Foster being first duly sworn by Mrs. Lyman K. Lane, Notary Public, testified as follows:

ON BEHALF OF COMMISSIONER.

Q   What is your name?   A   Samuel C. Foster.
Q   What is your age?   A   48 past.
Q   What is your post office address?
A   Claremore.
Q   Are you a citizen by blood of the Cherokee Nation?
A   Yes sir.
Q   Are you acquainted with one John J. Caldwell?
A   Yes sir.
Q   Is he a married man?   A   No sir; not now.
Q   He has been married?   A   Yes sir.
Q   What was his wife's name?
A   His first wife's name was Martha Foster.
Q   Did you know him prior to his marriage to Martha Foster?
A   Yes sir; I had known him about a year.

225

Cherokee Intermarried White 1906
Volume IX

Q   Martha Foster is not living at this time?
A   No sir
Q   Was she a Cherokee by blood?   A   Yes sir.
Q   Do you remember when John J. Caldwell married Martha Foster?
A   Well, it was about '74; just a day or two days after Christmas.
Q   It was in the year 1874 was it?
A   Yes sir.
Q   She was a recognized citizen by blood of the Cherokee Nation at the time he married
    her?   A   Yes sir.
Q   They were married in the Cherokee Nation, were they?
A   Yes sir; on Grand River, at old man Red Bird Sixkiller's house.
Q   Were you present at the marriage ceremony?
A   Yes sir.

Q   Did John J. Caldwell secure a license before his marriage?
A   Well, I can't say as to that.
Q   You can't testify as to whether or not he secured a license?
A   No; I didn't see the license.
Q   By whom was he married?   A   By Joe Thompson.
Q   Was he a Judge or minister of the Gospel?
A   He was a Minister of the Gospel, I think.
Q   Do you know of your own personal knowledge, that since that time John J. Caldwell
    has been recognized as a citizen by intermarriage of the Cherokee Nation?
A   Yes; she only lived about a year after he married her and he married again; he
    married a Thompson,- another Joe Thompson's daughter.
Q   But since his marriage to her, has he been recognized as a citizen by intermarriage of
    the Cherokee Nation?
A   Yes sir.
Q   Exercised all the rights and enjoyed all the privileges of that class of citizens?
A   Yes sir.
Q   Do you know of his voting at the elections?
A   No, I never was at the elections; I live in Cooweescoowee District and they live in
    Delaware.
Q   He lived with his first wife until her death, did he?
A   Yes sir.
Q   Then who did he marry?   A   This Thompson girl.
Q   Was she a citizen by blood of the Cherokee Nation?
A   I think she was.
Q   Of Cherokee blood, was she?   A   Yes sir.
Q   Is she living?   A   No sir; she's dead.
Q   Did they live together as man and wife until her death?
A   I think so.
Q   Since her death, has he re-married?
A   No, I think not.

BY MR. HASTINGS:

Q Was his first wife related to you?

A She was a half sister to my father.

Q No, Mr. Foster, is there anything particular that you fix the date of this marriage with reference to the year or has your attention just been recently called to it by Mr. Caldwell?

A No, it hasn't; I was in Going Snake until the fall of '73, we moved up in Cooweescoowee District; I was just a boy and we lived up there that fall and in the spring of '74, I went to Jim Foster's and lived there, and that fall then, I went to Grand River to visit my aunt; I had been there before along in the summer and then that fall I went over there again along about Christmas time and I was there when they got married.

Q Were you there the next year, in '75, visiting your aunt, or in '76?

A Well, I was backward and forward all the time while they lived.

Q You visited them every year from that time on, didn't you?

A No, they moved away from there and I never seen her any more.

Q Your aunt?

A Yes sir; to Delaware District.

Q How long did they live over there where you talked about visiting them?

A They didn't live there long; they went back up in Delaware District.

Q About what year did they leave that locality?

A About '74 or '75; along about the first of '75.

Q Are you positive about that?

A Well, I can't say as to be real positive about it; that's the best of my knowledge.

Q Is there any memoranda or anything that you have in your possession that fixes this date as being near Christmas of '74?

A No, I didn't keep any memoranda of it.

Q What was Mr. Caldwell's wife's first name?

A Martha.

Q Do you know whether her name was Callie M?

A No, that was his second wife.

Q When did he marry his second wife?

A I don't know but her name was Callie Thompson. I knew her before he married her.

ON BEHALF OF COMMISSIONER.

Q Are you positive as to the date of the marriage of John J. Caldwell to his first wife?

A Well, that's to the best of my knowledge.

Q To the best of your knowledge, it was a day or two after Christmas in 1874?

A Yes sir.

Q Is there any way by which you fix that date,- any circumstance that happened in your life that would make you remember the year?

A No, except I hadn't been in this country very long and we came in the fall of '73 and in the spring of '74, I went on the river and in the fall I went to my aunt's.

Q   Then it was the next fall after you came here that this marriage occurred?
A   Yes sir; that's all I know.

Sarah Mayfield being first duly sworn by Mrs. Lyman K. Lane, Notary Public, testified as follows:

ON BEHALF OF COMMISSIONER:

Q   What is your name?   A   Sarah Mayfield.
Q   What is your age?   A   70 years old.
Q   What is your post office address?
A   Oolagah.
Q   Are you a citizen by blood of the Cherokee Nation?
A   Yes sir.
Q   Do you know a person in the Cherokee Nation by the name of John J. Caldwell?
A   Yes sir.
Q   How long have you known him?
A   I guess over 20 years.
Q   Did you know him before he was married?
A   No, I didn't; but just shortly after he was married.
Q   Were you acquainted with his first wife?
A   O[sic] yes; she was my neice[sic].
Q   She was a Cherokee by blood?   A   Yes sir.
Q   And she was residing in the Cherokee country at the time of her marriage to John J. Caldwell?
A   Yes sir.
Q   She was a recognized citizen of the Cherokee Nation at that time?
A   Yes sir.
Q   Were you present at the marriage?
A   No sir; I just heard they was married; her mother told me.
Q   You can't state positively then that he secured a marriage license and married his first wife in accordance with the law of the Cherokee Nation?
A   No sir, I can't; but I heard they did.
Q   It is your understanding and you believe that he did secure a license?
A   Yes sir.
Q   Did he live with his first wife until her death?
A   Yes sir.
Q   When did she die?   A   I can't tell.
Q   Were you acquainted with his second wife?
A   Yes sir; I knew her too.
Q   She was a Cherokee by blood?   A   Yes sir.
Q   Is she living?   A   No sir; she's dead.
Q   Did he live with his second wife continuously until her death?
A   Yes sir; they had one child.

Q   Has he to your knowledge ever been married to anyone other than these two women you have mentioned?

A   No sir.

Q   To you own personal knowledge, has his residence been continuously in the Cherokee Nation since his marriage to his first wife?

A   Yes sir; so far as I know.

BY MR. HASTINGS.

Q   How long did he live with his first wife?

A   I forget just how long; I can't tell you just exactly.

Q   What is your best recollection?

A   About two years I reckon.

Q   Did you know when she died?

A   No, not when she died I didn't, but I heard it just after she died.

Q   You don't know what year you heard she died in?

A   No sir, I don't.

Q   Do you know where she died?

A   Yes sir; on Grand River, at her mother's.

Q   How far did you live from them at that time?

A   I lived way up at what they called Big Cabin and they lived on Grand River; about 30 miles I guess.

Q   Were you living that far away when they were said to have been married?

A   Yes sir; I was living up there when I heard they were married.

Q   You are not testifying as to the date of the marriage,- only that you heard they were married?

A   Yes sir; and I saw them shortly after they were married.

Q   Have you any recollection of that date of your own personal knowledge?

A   Well, I can't tell you just the real truth about it.

ON BEHALF OF COMMISSIONER.

Q   Did John J. Caldwell have any children by his first wife?

A   Yes sir; one,- a little boy.

Q   How long did it live?

A   I think it lived about,- nearly a year as well as I can recollect. I know Mrs. Collier taken care of it.

Q   The child died?   A   Yes sir.

Q   Before or after its mother died?

A   After its mother died.

BY MR. HASTINGS.

Q   Is your name John J. Caldwell?   A   Yes sir.

Cherokee Intermarried White 1906
Volume IX

Q   Were you ever married previous to your marriage to this woman through whom you claim citizenship, whom you claim you married in '74?

A   No sir.

Q   That was your first marriage? A Yes sir.

Q   Have you ever been married but the two times,- to the Foster woman first and the Thompson woman the second time?

A   No sir.

Q   Your first wife was a Miss Forter[sic]? Had she been married when she married you? A No sir.

Q   You had no children by your first wife?

A   Yes sir; one boy.

Q   Is he living? A No sir.

Q   How long did he live?

A   Just a little over a year; a year and a month I think.

Q   How long did you live with your first wife?

A   Just a little over a year.

Q   Did you first wife die about the birth of this child?

A   Yes sir.

Q   When did she die?

A   She died in '75; I can't tell you the date; I can't remember dates unless I set them down.

Q   Then you don't know independently, the time you were married?

A   Yes sir; I set it down. I got the license the 23rd day of December, '74.

Q   You have today left with the Commissioner, the original license through which you claim?

A   Yes sir.

Q   Now, I want to call your attention in this regard to the original license which you present here, and I desire to call your particular attention to the fact that an examination of this license shows that it was first dated as having been issued by J. E. Harlin, Clerk Delaware District, on the 23rd day of December, 1875, and by an examination it can clearly be seen by the naked eye that a 4 is written over the 5. Had your attention ever been invited to that?

A   No sir; it can't be that way sir I don't think, because I know it was before the bread money payment in '75. We were enrolled in the Delaware District and drew money in '75.

Q   Have you any explanation about what seems to be clear, namely, that this license was first dated '75 and was changed to '74?

A   No sir; that was not the case I reckon.

Q   You didn't know anything about it?

A   No sir.

Q   Since your attention has been called to it and you have examined it, you see what I have stated to be what the license shows is correct, don't you?

A   That's a four but whether there is a 5 under there or not I don't know anything about it. I got the license in '74.

Q   You don't know the date though of the death of your wife?

A   I have it down.

Q   I am asking you if you know it. You don't know the date of the birth of this child?

A   In October, '75; and he died, I think it was sometime in November, '76; its[sic] on the tomb stone in the grave yard at Vinita.

Q   Was your first wife buried at Vinita?

A   No sir; she was buried on Grand River.

Q   Near what place?

A   Close to Red Bird Sixkiller's in Saline District; she was at her mother's when she died.

Q   Do Henry Ross' folks live there?

A   I don't know; I haven't been there for several years.

Q   And your child in[sic] buried in the Vinita grave yard?

A   Yes sir.

The undersigned being first duly sworn states that as stenographer to the Commission to the Five Civilized Tribes, she recorded the testimony taken in this case and that the foregoing is a true and correct transcript of her stenographic notes thereof.

Myrtle Hill

Subscribed and sworn to before me this the 11th day of February, 1907.

J L Gary
Notary Public.

◇◇◇◇◇

(The Marriage License and Certificate below is transcribed by this author immediately following the copies of the said documents.)

(Copies of original document from case.)

The Rites of *(illegible)* according to the *(illegible)* and *(illegible)* usually of server and performed in such cases. Between John J Caldwell a citizen *(paper torn)* States and Miss Martha J Foster a *(paper torn)* the Cherokee Nation.

Said John *(paper torn)* having fully conformed to the act *(paper torn)* and act passed by the National *(paper torn)* Regulate Entermarriages of Ci *(paper torn)*

Given from under my
hand in office this the
23 day of Dec 1874
J.E. Harlin Clerk
   Del Dist

of March 1895 In conformity with the act entitled an act regulating entermarriages

In Testimony whereof I
have hereunto set my hand
and the Seal of Del Dist
on the 27 Day March AD 1895
J E Harlen Clerk
   Del Dist
    C N

◇◇◇◇◇

E.C.M.   Cherokee 4101.

DEPARTMENT OF THE INTERIOR,
COMMISSIONER TO THE FIVE CIVILIZED TRIBES.

In the matter of the application for the enrollment of John J. Caldwell as a citizen by intermarriage of the Cherokee Nation.

D E C I S I O N .

THE RECORDS OF THIS OFFICE SHOW: That at Vinita, Indian Territory, October 3, 1900, application was received by the Commission to the Five Civilized Tribes for the enrollment of John J. Caldwell as a citizen by intermarriage of the Cherokee Nation. Further proceedings in the matter of said application were had at Muskogee, Indian Territory, October 16, 1902, and January 7, and February 6, 1907.

THE EVIDENCE IN THIS CASE SHOWS: That the applicant herein, John J. Caldwell, a white man, was married in accordance with the Cherokee law in December, 1874, to his wife, Martha J. Caldwell (nee Foster), since deceased, who was at the time of said marriage, a recognized citizen by blood of the Cherokee Nation. It appears that the original license issued in this case was, at some time, changed as to the date of its issuance, but from the Recorder's certificate on the back showing it to have been recorded in March, 1875, it is conclusive that said license was issued prior to that date. It is further shown that from the time of said marriage until the death of said Martha J. Caldwell, which occurred in October, 1875, the said John J. Caldwell and Martha J. Caldwell resided together as husband and wife, and continuously lived in the Cherokee Nation. It is also shown that about 1879, said John J. Caldwell was married to one Callie M. Caldwell (nee Thompson), since deceased, who was at the time of said marriage a recognized citizen by blood of the Cherokee Nation, who is identified on the Cherokee authenticated tribal roll of 1880, Delaware District, No. 610, as a native Cherokee marked "Dead". It is further shown that from the time of said marriage until the death of said Callie M. Caldwell, which occurred about 1894, the said John J. Caldwell and Callie M. Caldwell resided together as husband and wife and continuously lived in the Cherokee Nation. That since the death of Callie M. Caldwell, said John J Caldwell has not re-married, and has continuously lived in the Cherokee Nation up to and including September 1, 1902. The said applicant is identified on the Cherokee authenticated tribal roll of 1880, and on the Cherokee census roll of 1896, as an intermarried citizen of the Cherokee Nation.

IT IS, THEREFORE, ORDERED AND ADJUDGED: That in accordance with the decision of the Supreme Court of the United States, dated November 5, 1906, in the cases of Daniel Red Bird, et al., vs. the United States, Nos. 125, 126, 127, and 128, the said applicant, John J. Caldwell, is entitled, under the provisions of Section 21 of the Act of Congress approved June 28, 1898 (30 Stats. 495), to enrollment as a citizen by intermarriage of the Cherokee Nation, and his application for enrollment as such is accordingly granted.

Tams Bixby

Commissioner.

Dated at Muskogee, Indian Territory,
this   FEB 26 1907

◇◇◇◇◇

Cherokee 4101

Muskogee, Indian Territory, January 24, 1907.

John J. Caldwell,
    Vinita, Indian Territory.

Dear Sir:

    In connection with your application for enrollment as a citizen by intermarriage of the Cherokee Nation, you are advised that it will be necessary for you to furnish this office with the original marriage license and certificate or a certified copy of same, showing your marriage to Martha J. Foster.

    If you are unable to obtain said marriage license and certificate, the testimony of two witnesses who have actual personal knowledge of your marriage to said Martha J. Foster, will be necessary to establish your marriage.

    This matter should receive your immediate attention.

Respectfully,

Commissioner.

MMP

◇◇◇◇◇

Form No. 260.

THE WESTERN UNION TELEGRAPH COMPANY.
INCORPORATED
23,000 OFFICES IN AMERICA.   CABLE SERVICE TO ALL THE WORLD.
ROBERT C. CLOWRY, President and General Manager.

Receiver's No.	Time Filed		Check

SEND the following message subject to the terms on back hereof, which are hereby agreed to.

Muskogee, I.T. Feb. 1, 1907.

John J. Caldwell,

Vinita, I.T.

Your are directed to forward to the Commissioner immediately, original or certified copy of marriage license and certificate, or with witnesses to establish your marriage to Martha Foster.

BIXBY

O T O K Paid.   Commissioner.

☞ READ THE NOTICE AND AGREEMENT ON BACK. ☜

(Copies of original documents from case.)

Form No. 168.

THE WESTERN UNION TELEGRAPH COMPANY.
INCORPORATED
23,000 OFFICES IN AMERICA.   CABLE SERVICE TO ALL THE WORLD.

This Company TRANSMITS and DELIVERS messages only on conditions limiting its liability, which have been assented to by the sender of the following message. Errors can be guarded against only by repeating a message back to the sending station for comparison, and the Company will not hold itself liable for errors or delays in transmission or delivery of Unrepeated Messages, beyond the amount of tolls paid thereon, nor in any case where the claim is not presented in writing within sixty days after the message is filed with the Company for transmission.
This is an UNREPEATED MESSAGE, and is delivered by request of the sender, under the conditions named above.
ROBERT C. CLOWRY, President and General Manager.

RECEIVED at

12 KB GH C 25 Paid Govt.

Muskogee,I.T.Feb 2'0.

John   J.Calldwell,

Vinita,I.T.

Forward immediately original or certified copy of marriage license and certificate or appear with witnesses to establish your marriage.

BIxby,Commissioner..... 25&P

Cherokee 4101

COPY

Muskogee, Indian Territory, February 26, 1907.

W. W. Hastings,
　　　Attorney for the Cherokee Nation,
　　　　　Muskogee, Indian Territory.

Dear Sir:

　　　There is enclosed herewith a copy of the decision of the Commissioner to the Five Civilized Tribes, dated February 26, 1907, granting the application for the enrollment of John J. Caldwell as a citizen by intermarriage of the Cherokee Nation.

Respectfully,

SIGNED *Tams Bixby*

Enc I-39
　　　　　　　　　　　　Commissioner.

RPI

◇◇◇◇◇

Cherokee 4101

Muskogee, Indian Territory, February 26, 1907.

The Commissioner to the Five Civilized Tribes,
　　　Muskogee, Indian Territory.

Sir:

　　　Receipt is acknowledged of the testimony and of your decision enrolling John J. Caldwell as a citizen by intermarriage of the Cherokee Nation. Time for protesting said decision is waived and I consent that said person may be placed upon the schedule immediately.

Respectfully,
W. W. Hastings
Attorney for the Cherokee Nation.

◇◇◇◇◇

Cherokee 4101

Muskogee, Indian Territory, February 26, 1907.

John J. Caldwell,
Vinita, Indian Territory.

Dear Sir:

There is enclosed herewith a copy of the decision of the Commissioner to the Five Civilized Tribes, dated February 26, 1907, granting the application for your enrollment as a citizen by intermarriage of the Cherokee Nation.

You will be advised when your name has been placed upon a schedule of citizens of the Cherokee Nation and approved by the Secretary of the Interior.

Respectfully,

SIGNED *Jams Bixby*

Enc I-40

Commissioner.

RPI

Cher IW 264

◇◇◇◇◇

R.

Department of the Interior,
Commission to the Five Civilized Tribes,
Chelsea, I.T., November 19, 1900.

In the matter of the application of James Goddard for the enrollment of himself and child as Cherokees by blood and his wife as a Cherokee by intermarriage; he appearing before the Commission, and being sworn and examined, testified as follows:

Q What is your name? A James Goddard.
Q How old are you? A I am 65.
Q What is your post office address? A Kinnison[sic].
Q Are you a Cherokee by blood? A Yes, sir.
Q For whom do you make application, for yourself? A For myself and my wife and one baby.
Q What degree of Cherokee blood do you claim? A About 1/16 part.
Q How long have you lived in the Cherokee Nation? A Raised right here.

Q Live here continuously?   A   All but about five years, when I left Tennessee; I was born in Tennessee.
Q When was that?   A   When I was quite a small boy.
Q Doe your name appear upon the roll of 1880?   A   Yes, sir.
Q What district were you living in at that time?   A   Delaware.
Q What was the name of your father?   A   Ira Goddard.
Q Was he a Cherokee?   A   No, sir, my mother was a Cherokee.
Q What is the name of your mother?   A   Elizabeth Blair.
Q Was she a Cherokee?   A   Yes, sir.
Q Your parents are both dead, are they?   A   Yes, sir.
Q What is the name of your wife?   A   Phoebe.
Q Is she living?   A   Yes, sir.
Q How old is she?   A   She is 54.
Q When were you married to her?   A   In 1870.
Q Is she a Cherokee or a white woman?   A   White woman.
Q Does her name appear with your name on the 1880 roll?   A   Yes, sir.
Q Have you lived with her continuously since your marriage?   A Yes, sir.
Q Were you ever married before?   A   No, sir, except before the war.
Q Was that first wife dead before you married this wife?   A   Yes, sir.
Q Was she ever married before?   A   No, sir.
Q What is the name of your child?   A   James William, 17 years old.
Q This child alive and living with you at the present time?   A   Yes, sir.
Q You are the father of the child?   A   Yes, sir.
Q And Phoebe Goddard is the mother?   A   Yes, sir.
(James Goddard on 1880 roll, page 261, No. 1120, Delaware district; on 1896 roll, page 473, No. 1320, James Goddard, Delaware district. Phoebe Goddard on 1880 roll, page 261, No. 1121, Phebe Goddard, Delaware district, adopted white; on 1896 roll, page 573, No. 204, Phoeba Goddard, Delaware district. James W. Goddard on 1896 roll, page 473, No. 1234, James William Goddard, Delaware district.)

The applicant applies for the enrollment of himself and one child as citizens by blood and his wife as a citizen by intermarriage. He is identified upon the authenticated roll of 1880 and the census roll of 1896 as a naïve Cherokee, he has lived almost all his life in the Cherokee Nation, and he will be listed for enrollment by this Commission as a Cherokee citizen by blood. His child, James W., is identified upon the census roll of 1896 as a native Cherokee, and the residence of this child has been established to the satisfaction of the Commission, and it will be listed for enrollment with its father as a citizen by blood. His wife, Phoebe, is identified upon the authenticated roll of 1880 as an adopted white, and upon the census roll of 1896 as an adopted white. She and her husband have lived continuously together since their marriage, and she will be listed for enrollment as a citizen by intermarriage of the Cherokee Nation.

--------0--------

Bruce C. Jones, being duly sworn, says that as stenographer to the Commission to the Five Civilized Tribes he correctly recorded the proceedings and testimony in the above case, and the foregoing is a true and complete transcript of his stenographic notes thereof.

Bruce C Jones

Sworn to and subscribed before me this the 20th of November, 1900.

C R Breckinridge
Commissioner.

◇◇◇◇◇

Cherokee 5579.

Department of the Interior,
Commission to the Five Civilized Tribes,
Muskogee, I. T., October 16, 1902.

In the matter of the application of James Goddard for the enrollment of himself and child, James W. Goddard, as citizens by blood, and for the enrollment of his wife, Phoebe Goddard, as a citizen by intermarriage of the Cherokee Nation; said Phoebe Goddard being sworn and examined by the Commission, testified as follows:

Q What is your name? A Phoebe Goddard.
Q How old are you? A Fifty-six.
Q What is your postoffice? A Catale.
Q Are you a white woman? A Yes sir.
Q Does you name appear on the roll of 1880 as an adopted white citizen? A Yes sir.
Q What is your husband's name? A James Goddard.
Q Was he your husband in 1880? A Yes sir.
Q Is he the husband through whom you are claiming your citizenship? A Yes sir.
Q Have you and your husband, James, been living together ever since 1880?
A Yes sir.
Q You have separated? A Yes sir, we are separated now.
Q When were you separated from your husband? A Just about eight years.
Q What was the cause of this separation? A Non-support.
Q He didn't support you? A Yes sir, he didn't.
Q Did you live with him from 1880 up until about eight years ago? A Yes sir.
Q What was your husband's business, his occupation? A We lived on a farm.
Q In what way did he fail to provide for you? A He didn't provide anything scarcely.
Q Clothing? A No sir, no clothing.
Q Nor enough to eat? A I had some means before I married him; he didn't help me.
Q What were his habits, did he drink any? A Yes sir.
Q Did he stay away from home much? A Yes sir, a good deal.
Q Did you leave him or he leave you? A He left me; the place belonged to me and he left me.
Q He went away and left you didn't he? A Yes sir.
Q Did you give him any cause to leave you? A No any -- we just didn't agree.

239

Cherokee Intermarried White 1906
Volume IX

Q On account of the fact he didn't support you?   A   Yes sir, that is the trouble.
Q You were quite willing to let him go?   A   I would rather for him to have stayed, but he wouldn't support the family.
Q He has never lived with you since that first separation?   A   No sir.
Q He hasn't contributed to your support at all?   A   Nothing at all.
Q Did either of you ever bring any suit for divorce?   A No sir.
Q You haven't married gain since he left you?   A   No sir.
Q Have you been living in the Cherokee Nation ever since 1880?   A   Yes sir.
Q How many children have you by your husband, James?   A   Three.
Q How many are living at home with you?   A   Two living at home.
Q What are their names?   A   Henry M.
Q How old is Henry M.? A   I believe he is twenty-six.
Q He enrolled himself?   A Yes sir.
Q The other one James W.? A Yes sir.
Q He is living at home?   A   Yes sir.
Q He has lived in the Cherokee Nation all his life?   A Yes sir.
J.C. Starr: How many times have you been married?   A Only one time.
Q Where did you and your husband live at the time this separation took place?
A On Grand River, Delaware District, Cherokee Nation.
Q What was your postoffice at that time?   A   Fairland.
Q How far did you live from Fairland?   A   Seven or eight miles.
Q In which direction?   A   Southeast I guess; down the river.
Q Who owned the place that you lived on at that time?   A   I did.
Q How long had you owned it?   A   I don't believe I could tell you.
Q Did you own that place before you were married to Mr. Goddard?   A   No sir, after that.
Q How did you come to by this place?   A I bought this place.
Q You bought it and paid for it of your own means?   A   I did, yes sir.
Q How long did you and Mr. Goddard live on that place?   A   I don't really know; we lived just about two and a half miles from that place and sold it and moved down on the other place and lived there fifteen or sixteen years some where in the neighborhood of that; I don't know exactly.
Q Where did Mr. Goddard go when this separation took place?   A   He went to Kinnison[sic].
Q Did you have any trouble before that?   A   Disagreement, yes sir.
Q What was the cause of that?   A   Just the same cause.
Q Just because he wouldn't provide for you?   A   Yes sir, because he didn't provide for me.
Q Who were living neighbors at that time of the separation?   A   Ab. Harlin.
Q Who else lived here by you?   A   Henry Keefer.
Q Did you go and try to get Mr. Goddard to come back and live with you? A No sir.
Q Didn't make any effort?   A No sir.
Q Didn't care if he come back?   A   No.
Q You didn't go out to Centralia to get him to come back?   A   No sir.
Q Quite willing for him to go?   A   Yes sir, quite willing under those circumstances if he wanted to go.

Cherokee Intermarried White 1906
Volume IX

The undersigned, being duly sworn, states that as stenographer to the Commission to the Five Civilized Tribes he correctly recorded the testimony and proceedings in this case, and the foregoing is a true and correct transcript of his stenographic notes thereof.

E.G. Rothenberger

Subscribed and sworn to before me this 13th day of November, 1902.

BC Jones
Notary Public.

◇◇◇◇◇

Cherokee No. 5579.

DEPARTMENT OF THE INTERIOR,
COMMISSIONER TO THE FIVE CIVILIZED TRIBES.

Muskogee, Indian Territory, January 4, 1906.

In the matter of the application for the enrollment of Phoebe Goddard, as a citizen by intermarriage of the Cherokee Nation.

Phoebe Goddard, being first duly sworn by Charles E. Webster, Notary Public, testified as follows:

BY THE COMMISSIONER:

Q   State your name, age and postoffice address?   A   Phoebe Goddard; 50; Catalee, Indian Territory.
Q   You claim to be a citizen by intermarriage of the Cherokee Nation do you?
A   Yes, sir.
Q   Through whom do you claim that right?   A   My husband, James Goddard.
Q   Is he living at the present time?   A   Yes, sir.
Q   What is his citizenship?   A   Cherokee.
Q   By blood?   A   By blood.
Q   When were you married to Mr. Goddard?   A   June 15, 1871.
Q   Cherokee Nation?   A   Yes, sir.
Q   Who married you?   A   Preacher Adams. I have forgotten his given name.
Q   Did this man Adams furnish you with a certificate of marriage?   A   He did not.

241

Cherokee Intermarried White 1906
Volume IX

Q   Do you know whether or not he issued ne?   A   No, sir, I don't.

Q   If one was issued in which district would it be recorded?

A   It would be recorded in Delaware District, I suppose.

Q   Had either you or your husband been married prior to 1871?

A   My husband had.

Q   Was his wife dead when you and he were married?   A   No, sir.

Q   Had they separated?   A   Yes, sir.

Q   How long prior to your marriage?   A   I don't know - about a year. Perhaps a little more.

Q   Was your husband and his wife divorced?   A   I don't know whether they were or not; I guess they was for she married.

Q   Did she marry prior to your marriage to Mr. Goddard?

A   No, sir, I think we married first.   We was married in June and her the following fall as well as I remember.

Q   What was the citizenship of Mr. Goddard's first wife?

A   She was a white woman.

Q   Is his first wife living at the present time?   A   No, sir, she is dead.

Q   When did she die?   A   I think it is between 15 and 20 years ago.

Q   Have you and your husband lived together continuously ever since your marriage in 1871?   A   We have been parted about 10 or 12 years.

Q   Hs either one of you secured a divorce?   A   No, sir.

Q   Have you married since your separation?   A   No, sir.

Q   Has he?   A   No, sir.

Q   At the time of your marriage to Mr. Goddard he was a citizen of the Cherokee Nation, was he?   A   Yes, sir.

Q   Was he a native born citizen or did he emigrate to this country from the east?

A   He was three years old when he come with the emigrants; that is the way I understand it.

Q   Your husband has made application for enrollment has he?   A   Yes, sir, he is enrolled.

The records of this office show that James Goddard, husband of the applicant is included in an approved partial roll of Cherokee by blood opposite No. 13393.

The applicant, Phoebe Goddard, is identified on the authenticated Cherokee Tribal Roll of 1880, and Cherokee census roll of 1896, Delaware District, opposite numbers 1121 and 204, respectively, as an intermarried white.

Q   Is ~~her~~ your husband present today?   A   No, sir, he isn't; he isn't able to come he is sick.

Q   Where does he live at the present time?   A   His postoffice is Catalee; he lives about 2 1/2 miles or three from where I live.

Q   Do you know when your husband married his first wife?   A   No, sir, I don't know.

Q   Do you know where they were married?   A   No, sir, but I think they was married in Missouri, I think in Jasper County, Missouri.

Q   At the time of his first marriage your husband was a Cherokee citizen was he?
A   Yes, sir.
Q   Have you lived in the Cherokee Nation continuously since your marriage to Mr. Goddard in 1871?   A   Yes, sir.
Q   What was your maiden name, Mrs. Goddard?   A   Wright.

The marriage records for Delaware District furnished this office by the Cherokee Nation fails to show that a certificate of the marriage ceremony alleged to have been performed between the applicant and her husband, James Goddard, is filed for record therein.

Q   Have you any witnesses that can testify as to your marriage to Mr. Goddard?
A   There was two the last time I knew they were living, but I don't know where they are.
Q   Is your husband confined to his room?   A   No, sir, he wasn't.
Q   Do you know if you can get him to appear here as a witness in your behalf?
A   Yes, sir, he will come if it is absolutely necessary.

Q   Do you think you could secure any witnesses to your marriage to Mr. Goddard in 1871?   A   Not more than one; there is one woman.
Q   Where is this witness living that you think you can produce the last time you heard of her?   A   I heard that she was living here in Muskogee, but I don't know whether it is so or not. I heard it last summer.
Q   What is her name?   A   Her name is Wasson.

WITNESS EXCUSED.

Katherine Wasson, being first duly sworn, by W. W. Chappell, testified as follows:

BY THE COMMISSIONER:

Q   What is your name, age and postoffice?   A   Katherine Wasson; 51; Muskogee.
Q   Are you acquainted with the applicant in this case, Phoebe Goddard?   A   Yes sir.
Q   How long have you know her?   A   Ever since she was married; she was married at my house.
Q   When was she married?   A   In 1871.
Q   Where did you say she was married?   A   Married up on Neosho River at my home in the territory.
Q   Cherokee Nation?   A   Yes, sir.
Q   Which district?   A   Delaware.
Q   Whom did she marry?   A   James Goddard.
Q   Was he a citizen of the Cherokee Nation a[sic] that time?   A   Yes, sir.
Q   Do you know whether or not the applicant or her husband, James Goddard, has been married prior to that time?   A   He had.
Q   Was his first wife living when he married the applicant?   A   Yes, sir.

Q   Do you know whether or not he had secured a divorce from his first wife when he married the applicant?   A   I don't know about that, but they hd[sic] separated and she got married again. About the time that I first knew anything about them she was married; she had married another man and went to the states. I wasn't very well acquainted with her, but I had seen her.

Q   Do you know where James Goddard and his first wife were married?

A   No, sir, I don't, must have ben[sic] in the states.

Q   Do you knw[sic] when they were married?   A   No, sir

Q   Have you known the applicant ever since her marriage to James Goddard?

A   Yes, sir, I have known her or known of her; I haven't been right where she lived.

Q   Has she lived in the Cherokee Nation continuously since then?   A   Yes, sir.

Q   How do you identify the date of her marriage to Mr. Goddard?

Q[sic]   They were married at our house.

Q   You say that was in the year 1871?   A   Yes, sir.

Q   What causes you to remember that particular year?   A   Well, because we hadn't been married very long ourselves, Mr. Goddard and I. We was living down on the river then, my son was just a baby.

Q   You were married at that time yourself were you?   A   Yes, sir.

Q   And your husband's name was Goddard?   A   Larkin Goddard.

Q   Was Larkin Goddard related to James Goddard?   A   Brother.

Q   When were you and Larkin Goddard married?   A   Married in 1869. In the winter of '69.

Q   Is the son that you refer to as being a baby in 1871 living now?   A   Yes, sir.

Q   Has he been enrolled?   A   Yes, sir.

Q   What is his name?   A   W. P. Goddard.

Q   How old was he when the applicant Phoebe Goddard married James Goddard?

A   I don't know; he was born in '70, and she was married in '71 in June I think; he was born in November, '70.

Q   Mrs. Goddard and her husband are not living together at the present time are they?

A   I don't think they are. I haven't heard much of them since Mr. Wasson and I were married; I understood that they are separated.

Q   You don't know of your own knowledge that they are separate; just what you have heard?   A   Just what I have heard.

Q   Do you know whether the applicant has married since she separated from her first husband?   A   I don't know anything about it if she has; I don't think she has, I never heard of it.

Q   You are a citizen by blood of the Cherokee Nation are you?

A   Yes, sir.

WITNESS EXCUSED.

F. Elma Lane, upon oath, states that she reported the proceedings in the above entitled and numbered cause, and that the foregoing is a true and correct transcript of her stenographic notes therein.

F Elma Lane

Subscribed and sworn to before me this 6th day of January, 1907.

Chas E Webster
Notary Public.

◇◇◇◇◇

C. F. B.   Cherokee 5579.

DEPARTMENT OF THE INTERIOR,
COMMISSIONER TO THE FIVE CIVILIZED TRIBES.
Muskogee, Indian Territory, February 11, 1907.

In the matter of the application for the enrollment of Phoebe Goddard as a citizen by intermarriage of the Cherokee Nation.

SUPPLEMENTAL.

Applicant appears in person.

APPEARANCES:

Cherokee Nation represented by
W. W. Hastings, Attorney.

James Goddard being first duly sworn by J. L. Garey[sic], Notary Public, testified as follows:

ON BEHALF OF COMMISSIONER.

Q   What is your name?   A   James Goddard.
Q   What is your age?   A   71; soon be 72; 14th day
                                              of this month.
Q   What is your post office address?   A   Cattale.
Q   You are a citizen by blood of the Cherokee Nation, are you?
A   Yes sir; I am.
Q   Have you always lived in the Cherokee Nation?
A   Never lived any other place; on every roll that was made since '35.
Q   You have lived continuously in the Cherokee Nation since your birth?
A   Yes sir.
Q   How many times have you been married:
A   Well, supposed to be married twice, but the first proved to be a fraud. I was married in '61 at the beginning of the war.
Q   What was the name of your first wife?
A   Elizabeth Nichols.
Q   Was she a Cherokee by blood?
A   No sir; she was a white woman.
Q   When did you marry her?   A   '61.

Q   You married her just before the war, then?
A   Just at the commencment[sic] of the war.
Q   Did you and she live together until her death?
A   No sir.
Q   How long did you live together?
A   Well, we didn't live together more than about five years.

Q   What became of her at the end of the five years?
A   Why, after the war was over, she married another man.
Q   She married another man, then, did she, directly after the war?
A   Yes sir.
Q   Did she leave you?   A   Yes sir.
Q   What was the cause of her leaving you?
A   Nothing in the world that I could find out only she found out, -- we was not lawfully married she said, and she wouldn't live with me, and I couldn't get her to marry me again.
Q   Then you and she were never married?
A   No; there was a man pretended to marry us, and she went to see the man and found out we wasn't married.
Q   Then you claim to have gone through a marriage ceremony?
A   Yes.
Q   But you claim that the man who married you to your first wife had no authority to perform a marriage ceremony?
A   That's the way she told me herself.
Q   At the time of her leaving you, you claim that she refused to re-marry you in accordance with the law?
A   Yes sir.
Q   Did you own a home when she left you?
A   Yes sir.
Q   You were living in your own house, were you?
A   Yes sir.
Q   Did she leave your house?   A   Yes sir.
Q   And you, after she left you, continued to live in the same house, did you?
A   I stayed there for two years after and she never came back; she married.
Q   Did she ever secure a divorce?
A   No, it was hard to get them days.
Q   Did you attempt to get a divorce from her?
A   No; after she was married, I just thought I would marry too.
Q   She married, did she, before you married your second wife?
A   Yes sir.
Q   What is the name of your second wife?
A   Phoebe Wright.
Q   Wright was her maiden name?   A   Yes sir.
Q   Was she ever married before she married you?
A   No sir.

Q When did you marry her?
A In '70 or '71 I guess; I can't hardly remember.
Q You say you married you second wife in '70 or '71?
A Yes sir.
Q Since your marriage to her, have you and she continuously lived together as husband and wife?
A We haven't exactly lived together all the time; we are not living together now.

Q How long did you and she after your marriage, continuously live together as husband and wife?
A 10 or 15 years; I guess 20 years.
Q Where are you living now or with whom are you living?
A With my renter.
Q How long have you been living with him, apart from your wife?
A I have been living with him now right at a year.
Q Where did you live prior to that time?
A With my brother part of the time.
Q With whom have you lived since you and your wife have been living apart?
A Just with my brother and my renter.
Q What is the cause of your living at one place and your wife living at another?
A We somehow didn't agree altogether; she said that I didn't exactly provide well enough, I guess; something that way.
Q Did you own a home when she left you?
A Yes sir; owned a home and I left the place; she didn't leave me.
Q You left her?   A   Yes sir.
Q And she continued to live in the home in which you and she had lived as husband and wife?
A Yes sir.

BY MR. HASTINGS.

Q Is the only reason of your separation because of difference of temper?
A No, it wasn't temper.
Q How long have you been living apart from your wife, Phoebe Goddard?
A About 11 years as well as I remember.
Q Have you been living apart continuously for 11 years, all the time?
A Yes sir.
Q Did you ever separate before that?   A   No sir.
Q Did you live together up until about 11 years ago?
A Yes sir.
Q What was the immediate cause of your separation; did you disagree because your wife complained that you didn't provide well enough for her?
A Yes.
Q Is that the only reason?
A That's the only reason I know anything about,- with me.
Q Did you have a falling out at the time?

A   Yes sir; we had a few words and she said she wasn't going to live with me and I left.

Q   Did you and she have any children?

A   Yes sir; We've got three.

Q   Who kept the children?

A   She took them and kept them there on the place?

Q   And they have always lived there?

A   Yes sir, right with her.

Q   She has never re-married?   A   No sir.

Q   Is what you stated here the sole and only reason of this separation?

A   That's the only thing we ever had any trouble about; that I didn't provide.

Q   This man that married you to your first wife, did he claim to be a preacher?

A   Why, he claimed to be a preacher but then she found out afterwards that he wasn't.

Q   Did you know the man?

A   No, I didn't know the man.

Q   Where were you married to your first wife?

A   In the edge of Missouri; Newton County.

Q   How far did you live from him at the time you married you first wife?

A   5 or 6 miles.

Q   You had known him before?

A   I had seen him a few times.

Q   Well, he was a recognized minister?   A   No sir.

Q   Didn't you know it at that time?

A   No, I didn't know it then; I was sent to him by some of the neighbors.

Q   Well, didn't you hear at the time, that he had been in the habit of preaching around there?

A   If he had been preaching, I never heard it.

Q   Well, how come you to go to him if you didn't hear he was a preacher?

A   I was sent to him by some of my neighbors.

Q   How long did you and she live together,- 5 or 6 years?

A   Yes, we lived together during the war. When the war was over she left me.

Q   You and she recognized that a marriage for that length of time, didn't you?

A   Well, you see, I was a soldier and I wasn't at home all the time.

Q   How long did you remain there in that community, immediately after you married and before you went to the war?

A   About 6 months.

Q   How far from where this preacher lived?

A   He left there,-- left that country.

Q   And where did he go to?

A   Over about Springfield, Missouri,-- the last I heard of him.

Q   How long did he live there after you were married, before leaving?

A   Two or three months.

Q   During that two or three months, he was recognized as a preacher wasn't he?

A   Not that I heard of.

Q   You didn't take any steps immediately after you were married to be re-married nor to separate, did you?

A   No, not until after the war was over; we couldn't in that country.

Cherokee Intermarried White 1906
Volume IX

Q   Were you living over in Missouri at the time or in the Cherokee Nation?
A   On the neutral land
Q   Where were you living when you married this present applicant, Phoebe Gardner?
A   On Grand River in the Cherokee Nation.
Q   When did you come to the Cherokee Nation after the war?
A   I came right back; I was one of the first ones back here.
Q   You were always recognized as a citizen here?
A   Yes sir.
Q   You didn't take any allotment on the neutral land?
A   No sir.
Q   When you and your preset wife here, the applicant, first separated, how far did you go from there?
A   I went about 25 miles to my brother's and stayed there.
Q   Did you get a license over in Missouri to marry your first wife?
A   No sir; it wasn't required at that time.

ON BEHALF OF COMMISSIONER.

Q   You say that after you and your present wife separated, she remained at your old home and the children remained with her?
A   Yes sir.
Q   Have you visited them frequently since then?
A   Sometimes --- well, I didn't for about 5 years and then I would go there I guess once every two or three months.

(Witness Excused)

Phoebe Goddard being first duly sworn by J. L. Garey, Notary Public, testified as follows:

BY MR. HASTINGS.

Q	Your name is Phoebe Goddard?	A	Yes sir.
Q	You are the applicant in this case?	A	Yes sir.
Q	Where if[sic] your post office?	A	Cattalee.
Q	How old are you?	A	60.

Q   You claim the right to enrollment through your marriage to Mr. James Goddard, who just left the stand?
A   Yes sir.
Q   Were you ever married before you married him in '71?
A   No sir.
Q   Where were you living at the time of your marriage?
A   My home was in Cherokee County, Kansas; I had come down here on a visit.
Q   About how long did you and he live together as husband and wife?
A   It must have been 30 years.

Q   He says until about 11 years ago; is that right?
A   It has been longer than that.
Q   About how long ago was it?
A   It was after the strip payment; I don't know whether it was a year after the strip payment or not.
Q   Did you and he have some children?
A   Yes, we have three.
Q   With whom did the children remain?
A   They remained with me.
Q   Boys or girls?
A   Two boys and a girl.
Q   They continuously lived with you, did they?
A   Yes sir.
Q   Are they grown?   A   Yes sir.
Q   All of them?
A   Yes sir; my youngest one is 23.
Q   Now, Mrs. Goddard, what was the cause of this separation?
A   Well, I don't like to tell.
Q   Was that the cause of the separation,- the statement he made?
A   Yes, partly; he didn't provide; we had trouble over that and when he used whiskey too much.
Q   The reason then was that he dissipated and he didn't provide?
A   Yes sir.
Q   I suppose dissipation was the main cause of the trouble?
A   Yes; of course we got mad and had words and he was drinking---
Q   You have never married since?   A   No sir.
Q   That was your only marriage?   A   Yes sir.
Q   You have continued to remain on the place since he left?
A   No, I don't live there now; we sold out.
Q   Did you remain for a while at the same place?
A   7 or 8 years I think.
Q   You had heard of his previous marriage, had you?
A   Yes sir.
Q   He is reputed to have been married to some woman before the war?
A   Yes sir.
Q   What do you know about that?
A   I know very little about it; only just hearsay.
Q   Did you know of him living with this woman personally, yourself?
A   No sir.
Q   Did you know when you married him that he had lived with this woman?
A   She said so.
Q   What representations did she make?
A   She said she was never married; she said she was fixing to get married; I think that was in '70 I saw her.

Q   Did she say she had ever gone through any form of any marriage ceremony or that she had not?

A   She didn't say; she just said she had never been married. At that time I hadn't even seen him and she was fixing to get married at that time, she said.

Q   She was fixing to marry someone else?   A   Yes sir.

Q   Is this woman with whom your husband first lived dead?

A   Yes sir; she's dead.

Q   You heard him give some testimony about the man who should have married him; do you know whether that man lives up there in the community or not?

A   I never did know him but I don't think he does.

Q   Would it be impossible for you to get any additional witnesses with reference to the fraudulency of this first marriage of your husband?

A   No, I don't know of anything at all at the present time.

Q   Did this woman with whom your husband first lived, marry again?

A   Yes sir.

Q   And where did she marry?

A   Well, I can't tell you for certain but I understand she married in Kansas.

Q   Did she ever afterwards live in the community where she lived with your husband?

A   No sir; they went to Colorado; she died in Colorado.

Q   And she ran off with another man and left the country?

A   That is the information I have. I think she moved to Texas first and then from there to Colorado and she died in Colorado.

Q   But you claim to have understood from her before you married your husband, that she had investigated and found that she and your husband had never been lawfully married previous to that time.

A   That's what she said and that's what others said.

Q   Did you talk to others in the community about it?

A   Yes.

Q   Did they claim that this man who attempted to perform the marriage ceremony was not an ordained minister of the gospel?

A   Some said that they was married by a man that was not ordained and others said they never was married at all; that's all I can tell you; she just said that she was not married and that she had a lawful right to marry whenever she wanted to.

Q   Has the legality of your marriage to James Goddard ever been questioned up to this time?

A   No, not that I know of.

Q   Never been troubled about it in any way?

A   No, nothing that I ever knew anything about at all.

ON BEHALF OF COMMISSIONER.

Q   You were under the impression, were you Mrs. Goddard, when you married James Goddard, from what you had heard concerning his former marriage, that you had lawful right to marry him?

A   Yes sir; I married him in good faith.

Q   And the legality of your marriage to him never has been questioned?
A   No, not that I ever heard of.

The undersigned being first duly sworn states that as stenographer to the Commission to the Five Civilized Tribes, she recorded the testimony taken in this case and that the foregoing is a true and correct transcript of her stenographic notes thereof.

Myrtle Hill

Subscribed and sworn to before me this the 13th day of February, 1907.

Walter W. Chappell
Notary Public.

◇◇◇◇◇

E C M   Cherokee 5579.

DEPARTMENT OF THE INTERIOR,
COMMISSIONER TO THE FIVE CIVILIZED TRIBES.

In the matter of the application for the enrollment of PHOEBE GODDARD as a citizen by intermarriage of the Cherokee Nation.

D E C I S I O N

THE RECORDS OF THIS OFFICE SHOW: That at Chelsea, Indian Territory, November 19, 1900 application was received by the Commission to the Five Civilized Tribes for the enrollment of Phoebe Goddard as a citizen by intermarriage of the Cherokee Nation.   Further proceedings in the matter of said application were had at Muskogee, Indian Territory, October 16, 1902, January 4, 1907 and February 11, 1907.

THE EVIDENCE IN THIS CASE SHOWS: That the applicant herein, Phoebe Goddard, a white woman, married June 15, 1871 on James Goddard, who was at the time of said marriage a recognized citizen by blood of the Cherokee Nation, who is identified on the Cherokee authenticated tribal roll of 1880, Delaware District No. 1120 as a native Cherokee, and whose name is included on the approved partial roll of citizens by blood of the Cherokee Nation opposite No. 13393.   It is further shown that about 1892 the said Phoebe Goddard and James Goddard were separated, the cause of said separation being "failure to support" and abandonment by the said James Goddard of his wife, the said Phoebe Goddard.   It is also shown that the said James Goddard had contracted a reputed marriage to another woman prior to his marriage to the said Phoebe Goddard; that said marriage was not contracted in accordance with law, the ceremony not having been performed by a duly authorized minister; that no presumption of a common law marriage can be asserted as against his subsequent formal marriage to the said Phoebe Goddard. Said applicant is identified on the Cherokee authenticated tribal roll of 1880 and the Cherokee census roll of 1896 as an intermarried citizen of the Cherokee Nation.

IT IS, THEREFORE, ORDERED AND ADJUDGED: That in accordance with the decision of the Supreme Court of the United States, dated November 5, 1906, in the cases of Daniel Red Bird, et al. vs. the United States, Nos. 125, 126, 127, and 128, the said applicant, Phoebe Goddard is entitled, under the provisions of Section Twenty-one of the Act of Congress approved June 28, 1898 (30 Stats. 495), to enrollment as a citizen by intermarriage of the Cherokee Nation, provisions of Section Twenty-one of the Act of Congress approved June 28, 1898 (30 Stats., 495), to enrollment as a citizen by intermarriage of the Cherokee Nation and her application for enrollment as such is accordingly granted.

Tams Bixby
Commissioner.

Dated at Muskogee, Indian Territory,
this   FEB 26 1907

◇◇◇◇◇

THE WESTERN UNION TELEGRAPH COMPANY.

INCORPORATED

23,000 OFFICES IN AMERICA.   CABLE SERVICE TO ALL THE WORLD.

This Company TRANSMITS and DELIVERS messages only on conditions limiting its liability, which have been assented to by the sender of the following message. Errors can be guarded against only by repeating a message back to the sending station for comparison, and the Company will not hold itself liable for errors or delays in transmission or delivery of Unrepeated Messages, beyond the amount of tolls paid thereon, nor in any case where the claim is not presented in writing within sixty days after the message is filed with the Company for transmission.

This is an UNREPEATED MESSAGE, and is delivered by request of the sender, under the conditions named above.

ROBERT C. CLOWRY, President and General Manager.

RECEIVED 436 PM.   Sg Jn   Js Ck 25 paid Govertment.

Mail from Chelsea,
Muskogee, I.T. 2nd.

James Goddart,

Catale I.T.

Forward immeaditely original or certified copy of your Divorce from

first wife or appear with witnesses to give testimonia...

Bixby Commissioner?////

(Copy of original document from case.)

◇◇◇◇◇

Cherokee
5579

Muskogee, Indian Territory, February 26, 1907.

W. W. Hastings,
     Attorney for the Cherokee Nation,
          Muskogee, Indian Territory.

Dear Sir:

      There is enclosed herewith a copy of the decision of the Commissioner to the Five Civilized Tribes, dated February 26, 1907, granting the application for the enrollment of Phoebe Goddard as a citizen by intermarriage of the Cherokee Nation.

Respectfully,

Enc I-9   Commissioner.

RPI

◇◇◇◇◇

Cherokee 5579

Muskogee, Indian Territory, February 26, 1907.

The Commissioner to the Five Civilized Tribes,
     Muskogee, Indian Territory.

Sir:

      Receipt is acknowledged of the testimony and of your decision enrolling Phoebe Goddard as a citizen by intermarriage of the Cherokee Nation. Time for protesting said decision is waived and I consent that said person may be placed upon the schedule immediately.

Respectfully,
                W. W. Hastings
                Attorney for the Cherokee Nation.

◇◇◇◇◇

Cherokee
5579

Muskogee, Indian Territory, February 26, 1907.

Phoebe Goddard,
      Catale, Indian Territory.

Dear Madam:

      There is enclosed herewith a copy of the decision of the Commissioner to the Five Civilized Tribes, dated February 26, 1907, granting the application for your enrollment as a citizen by intermarriage of the Cherokee Nation.

      You will be advised when your name has been placed upon a schedule of citizens of the Cherokee Nation and approved by the Secretary of the Interior.

Respectfully,

Enc I-10
Commissioner.
RPI

Cher IW 265

◇◇◇◇◇

DEPARTMENT OF THE INTERIOR,
COMMISSION TO THE FIVE CIVILIZED TRIBES,
TAHLEQUAH, I.T., NOVEMBER 28th, 1900.

      In the matter of the application of Robert F. Wyly for the enrollment of himself, wife and child as citizens of the Cherokee Nation; said Wyly being sworn and examined by Commissioner Needles, testified as follows:

Q What is your name? A Robert F. Wyly.
Q What is your age, Mr. Wyly? A 73 years old.
Q What is your post office address? A Tahlequah.
Q In what district do you live? A Tahlquah[sic].
Q Are you a recognized citizen of the Cherokee Nation? A Yes, sir.
Q By blood? A No, sir.
Q By intermarriage? A Yes, sir.
Q Who do you want to enroll? A I want to enroll myself and wife and child,
Q What is your wife's name? A Mary Jane.
Q What is her age? A 60 years old.
Q Is she a citizen by blood? A Yes, sir.

255

Cherokee Intermarried White 1906
Volume IX

Q What is the name of your child? A Zoe August.
Q How old is she? A 21 years old.
Q Is she single and unmarried? A Yes, sir.

> 1880 Roll; page 342, #3041, R. F. Wiley, Delaware.
> 1880 Roll; page 342, #3042, Mary J. Wiley, Delaware.
> 1880 Roll; page 342, #3049, Zoe Wiley, Delaware.
> 1896 Roll; page 1291, #280, Robert F. Wyly, Tahlequah.
> 1896 Roll; page 1264, #3601, Mary J. Wyly, Tahlequah.
> 1896 Roll; page 1264, #3602, Zoe A. Wyly, Tahlequah.

Q You have been living with your wife continuously, Mr. Wyly once you married her?
A Yes, sir, some 40 odd years ago.
Q Zoe is making her home with you? A Yes, sir.

Com'r Needles:--The name of Robert F. Wyly appears upon the authenticated roll of 1880 and the census roll of 1896 as an intermarried white. He being duly identified, he will be duly listed for enrollment as a Cherokee citizen by intermarriage. His wife, Mary J., appears upon the authenticated roll of 1880 and the census roll of 1896 as a Cherokee citizen by blood. The name of their child, Zoe A., appears upon the authenticated roll of 1880 and the census roll of 1896 as Zoe A. Wyly. They being duly identified and having made satisfactory proof as to residence, said Mary J. and Zoe A. Wyly will be duly listed for enrollment as Cherokee citizens by blood.

---oooOOOooo---

J. O. Rosson, being first duly sworn, states that as stenographer to the Commission to the Five Civilized Tribes, he correctly recorded the testimony and proceedings in this case, and the foregoing is a true and complete transcript of his stenographic notes thereof.

J O Rosson

Subscribed and sworn to before me this 28th day of November, 1900.

T B Needles
Commissioner.

R.
Cher. 5788.

Department of the Interior.
Commission to the Five Civilized Tribes.
Tahlequah, I. T., September 29,1 902.

SUPPLEMENTAL TESTIMONY AND PROCEEDINGS in the matter of the application for the enrollment of ROBERT F. WYLY as a citizen by intermarriage of the Cherokee Nation.

ROBERT F. WYLY, being first duly sworn, and being examined, testified as follows:

BY COMMISSION: What is your name?   A   Robert F. Wyly.
Q How old are you?   A   Seventy-five.
Q What is your post office address?   A   Tahlequah, I. T.
Q Are you a white man?   A   Yes sir.
Q   Have you heretofore made application for your own enrollment as a citizen by intermarriage of the Cherokee Nation?   A   Yes sir.
Q What is the name of your wife?   A   Mary J. Wyly.
Q Is she living?   A   No sir.
Q You have just executed an affidavit as to her death on the 4th day of June, 1902?
A   Yes sir.
Q She was a Cherokee by blood?   A   Yes sir.
Q Did you live with her continuously until the date of her death?   A   Yes sir.
Q Have you married since she died?   A   No sir.
Q Have you resided in the Cherokee Nation continuously since you made application for enrollment?   A   Yes sir.

> This testimony will be filed with and made a part of the record in the matter of the application for the enrollment of Robert F. Wyly as a citizen by intermarriage of the Cherokee Nation, Cherokee straight card field No. 5788.

Wm. Hutchinson, being first duly sworn, states that as stenographer to the Commission to the Five Civilized Tribes he correctly recorded the testimony and proceedings in this case, and that the foregoing is a true and complete transcript of the stenographic notes thereof.

Wm Hutchinson

Subscribed and sworn to before me this 29th day of September, 1902.

John O Rosson
Notary Public.

Cherokee Intermarried White 1906
Volume IX

◇◇◇◇◇

Cherokee 5788.

Department of the Interior,
Commission to the Five Civilized Tribes,
Tahlequah, I. T, May 6, 1903.

In the matter of the application of Robert F. Wyly for the enrollment of himself as a citizen by intermarriage, and for the enrollment of his wife, Mary J. Wyly, and his child, Zoe A., and his grandchild, Mildred W. Watts, as citizens by blood of the Cherokee Nation.

Robert F. Wyly, being duly sworn, and examined by the Commission, testified as follows:

Q   State your full name?   A   Robert F. Wyly.
Q   How old are you?   A   I am seventy-five years old.
Q   What is your postoffice?   A   Tahlequah.
Q   You are a white man?   A   Yes sir.
Q   And a citizen by marriage of the Cherokee Nation?   A   Yes sir.
Q   How long have you lived in the Cherokee Nation?   A   I came to this country forty-six years ago this next fall.
Q   Have you lived in the Cherokee Nation continuously since then?
A   Except in the time of the war I was out.
Q   Since '80, the past twenty-three years?   A   Yes sir.
Q   You have always been here continuously?   A   Yes sir, since the spring of '68.
Q   Your wife, Mary J., was a Cherokee by blood?   A   Yes sir.
Q   She is the wife through whom you claim?   A   Yes, I had two Cherokee wives, but she is the last one.
Q   She is dead is she?   A   Yes sir.
Q   When did she die?   A   The fourth of June next will be a year.
Q   You have a daughter named Zoe A. Wyly?   A   Yes.
Q   She is married now?   A   Yes.
Q   Her name is Zoe A. Watts?   A   Yes.
Q   Is he a citizen of the Cherokee Nation?   A   By marriage only.
Q   By marriage with her?   A   Yes.
Q   When were they married?   A   I am not certain, but I think it will be three years this next fall.
Q   Was he ever married before?   A   No sir.
Q   He is not claiming any right through that marriage, is he?   A   No sir.
Q   How many children has he?   A   He as one.
Q   Mildred?   A   Yes.
Q   That child is living?   A   It was the last I knew of, a few days ago it was.
Q   Your daughter and husband have been living in the Cherokee Nation since their marriage?   A   Yes sir; they first lived at Muldrow and then at Sallisaw.

258

Q   Your daughter has lived with you all her life until she was married?   A   Yes sir, born and raised right here, not here in town but in Delaware District, and raised principally here.

The undersigned, being duly sworn, states that as stenographer to the Commission to the Five Civilized Tribes he correctly recorded the testimony and proceedings in this case, and the foregoing is a true and correct transcript of his stenographic notes thereof.

E.G. Rothenberger

Subscribed and sworn to before me this 12th day of May, 1903.

Samuel Foreman
Notary Public.

◇◇◇◇◇

C. F. B.   Cherokee 5788.

DEPARTMENT OF THE INTERIOR,
COMMISSION TO THE FIVE CIVILIZED TRIBES.
Muskogee, Indian Territory, January 10, 1907.

In the matter of the application for the enrollment of Robert F. Wyly, as a citizen by intermarriage of the Cherokee Nation.

Cherokee Nation represented by W. W. Hastings.

L. B. Bell being first duly sworn by B. P. Rasmus, Notary Public, testified as follows:

Q   What is your name?   A   L. B. Bell.
Q   What is your age?   A   Will soon be 69 years old.
Q   What is your post office address?
A   Vinita, Indian Territory.
Q   You desire to make a statement in the matter of the application for the enrollment of Robert F. Wyly as a citizen by intermarriage of the Cherokee Nation?
A   Yes sir. I knew this Robert F Wyly, now dead, as far back as 1858. I think he came there in '57. In 1858, in Delaware District, Cherokee Nation, he married my step sister, Mary Buffington. That was along about February of that year. Well, they were married in the Cherokee Nation at our house , regularly, and they lived together from that on until the time Mary died. He lived in this country continuously except a visit he made in Georgia after he married. He went back to Texas to settle some matters of his father's estate; otherwise, he has been in this country. We were out during the war but we never county that.

259

Q   During all that time after his marriage, he considered the Cherokee Nation his home whether he was in the Cherokee Nation or absent from it?

A   I presume so; he didn't have one anywhere else.

Q   Do you know that he and his wife were married in accordance with the laws of the Cherokee Nation?

A   I can't swear to that but that is what I have always understood.

Q   You witnessed the ceremony?   A   Yes sir.

Q   In what year did that marriage occur?

A   I think it was in February, 1858.

Q   In what district were they married?

A   Delaware District.

Q   Was either party ever married prior to that marriage?

A   Yes, he was married prior to that and his other wife was a Cherokee.

Q   She was dead?

A   Yes, had been dead several years.

ON BEHALF OF CHEROKEE NATION.

Q   It was your understanding that he was married then in accordance with the Cherokee law?

A   Yes; it seems to me that I was busy getting his license but I can't recollect.

Q   Since the war and up to the time of his death, was he continuously recognized as a citizen here?

A   Yes; he came here and lived continuously except when his father died, he went back down to Texas and settled up that estate; but his farm and everything he had was here.

Q   What offices did he hold here in the Cherokee Nation?

A   He was Judge of Delaware District.

Q   About how long?   A   Two terms

Q   He was attorney general for the Cherokee Nation?

A   Yes sir.

Q   Superintendent of the Cherokee Female Seminary for a while?

A   One or two years, I think.

Q   You know that he voted since September 1, 1902?

A   Yes sir.

The undersigned being first duly sworn states that as stenographer to the Commission to the Five Civilized Tribes. she recorded the testimony taken in this case and that the foregoing is a full, true and correct transcript of her stenographic notes thereof.

Myrtle Hill

Subscribed and sworn to before me this the 16th day of January, 1907.

B.P. Rasmus
Notary Public.

◇◇◇◇◇◇

F.R.   Cherokee 5788.

DEPARTMENT OF THE INTERIOR,
COMMISSIONER TO THE FIVE CIVILIZED TRIBES.
Muskogee, I. T. January 24, 1907.

In the matter of the application for the enrollment of Robert F. Wylie as a citizen by intermarriage of the Cherokee Nation.

W. W. Hastings, being first duly sworn by Frances R. Lane, a Notary Public for the Western District of Indian Territory, testified as follows:

By the Commissioner:
Q You desire to testify relative to the right to enrollment of Robert F. Wylie as a citizen by intermarriage of the Cherokee Nation?   A   Yes, I have been asked to give some testimony. My name is W. W. Hastings: age Forty, postoffice address, Tahlaquah[sic], I.T.
Q Please state what you know with reference to this case?
A When I can first remember, say when I was 6, 7 or 8 years old, I knew the applicant, Robert F. Wylie, and I knew his wife, Mary Wylie, who were living within about a mile of my parents in Delaware District, Cherokee Nation. His wife, Mary Wylie was a recognized citizen by blood of the Cherokee Nation, and Robert F. Wylie was living with her as her husband, and I know they were at that time, and ever after until his death, he was recognized as a citizen by intermarriage of the Cherokee Nation. He was District Judge in Delaware District, according to my recollection some eight years; he was also a candidate for the Senate in Delaware District; he was afterwards attorney general of the Cherokee nation, and was also steward in charge of the Female Seminary some four years, and represented the Cherokee Nation before what is known as the Adair Commission for some 3 or 4 years I think, beginning in 1887. I am not positive as to the date of his death, but it was November, in my judgment, in 1903. Anyhow, I know it was subsequent to September, 1902. He lived with his wife until her death some two years before his death.

Frances R. Lane, upon oath states that as stenographer to the Commission to the Five Civilized Tribes she reported the testimony in the above entitled cause and that the foregoing is an accurate transcript of her stenographic notes thereof.

Frances R Lane

Cherokee Intermarried White 1906
Volume IX

Subscribed and sworn to before me this January 24, 1907.

Edward Merrick
Notary Public.

◇◇◇◇◇

C.F.B.   Cherokee 5788.

DEPARTMENT OF THE INTERIOR,
COMMISSIONER TO THE FIVE CIVILIZED TRIBES.
Muskogee, I. T., February 23, 1907.

In the matter of the application for the enrollment of Robert F. Wyly as a citizen by intermariage[sic] of the Cherokee Nation.

Cherokee Nation represented by H. M. Vance.

J. F. Thompson being first duly sworn by Walter W. Chappell, testified as follows:

By the Commissioner:
Q What is your name?   A   J. F. Thompson.
Q Your age?   A   I am in my sixty-sixth year.
Q Your postoffice address?   A   Tahlequah, I. T.
Q Are you acquainted with one Robert F. Wyly, who is the husband of Mary J. Wyly?
A Yes sir.
Q How long have you known these people?   A   Known Mary J. Wyly, she was a first cousin of mine; knew hr[sic] since childhood; raised together; knew Robert F. Wyly since 1858.
Q Are they both living at this time?   A   No, both dead.
Q When did Robert F. Wyly die?   A   He died I think in 1905, the fall.
Q He was living September 1, 1902?   A   Yes sir.
Q Do you know whether Robert F. Wyly and Mary J. Wyly were married?   A   Yes sir.
Q When were they married?   A   In February, 1858.

Q Mary J. Wyly was a recognized citizen by blood of the Cherokee Nation at the time of that marriage?   A   Yes sir.
Q And living in the Cheroke[sic] country, was she?   A   Yes sir.
Q Do you know who married them?   A   Yes, Rev. E. J. Mack, I think was the name, a Bavarian missionary.
Q Were you present at the marriage ceremony?   A   Yes sir.
Q Do you know anything about Robert F. Wyly securing a marriage license? Do you know whether he did secure one?   A   I only know from the record the man made. His daughter came to this country after sometime since the civil[sic] war[sic] and he would have her re-married according to the Cherokee law, and then he held office for a number of years and was District Judge in Delaware District, which he could not have done

262

unless he had been married according to the law. But I could not swear that he had a license. I believe he had because he was such a stickler for--

Q You have every reason to believe that he did comply with the law of the Cherokee nation[sic]?   A Yes sir.

Q Did they live together continuously as husband and wife from the time of their marriage until the death of the said Mary J. Wyly?   A Yes sir.

Q And continuously lived in the Cherokee nation did they?   A Not continuously; they left there during the civil war and went to Texas, and moved back in 1867 or 8, and lived there until his death.

Q Any absence that they may have had from the Cherokee Nation was merely temporary?   A No, there was no forfeiture of citizenship.

Q You say that Robert F. Wyly held office?   A Yes sir.

Q Please make a statement of all the different positions he held as near as you can remember?   A The three different offices I recall now was District Judge of Delaware District; and he was afterwards attorney general for the Cherokee Nation or District attorney for the Cherokee nation[sic]. Then he was special delegate to Washington in 1894. He was also attorney for the commissions on citizenship. These are the four that I remember

Q You never heard this man's right as a citizen by intermarriage of the Cherokee Nation questioned in any way?   A No sir.

Frances R. Lane upon oath states that as stenographer to the Commission to the Five Civilized Tribes she reported the testimony in the above entitled cause and that the foregoing is an accurate transcript of her shorthand notes thereof.

Frances R Lane

Subscribed and sworn to before me this February 23, 1907.

Walter W. Chappell
Notary Public.

◇◇◇◇◇

Cherokee Intermarried White 1906
Volume IX

E C M   Cherokee 5788.

DEPARTMENT OF THE INTERIOR,
COMMISSIONER TO THE FIVE CIVILIZED TRIBES.

In the matter of the application for the enrollment of ROBERT F. WYLY as a citizen by intermarriage of the Cherokee Nation.

D E C I S I O N

THE RECORDS OF THIS OFFICE SHOW: That at Tahlequah, Indian Territory, November 28, 1900 application was received by the Commission to the Five Civilized Tribes for the enrollment of Robert F. Wyly as a citizen by intermarriage of the Cherokee Nation. Further proceedings in the matter of said application were had at Tahlequah, Indian Territory, September 29, 1902, May 6, 1903 and at Muskogee, Indian Territory, January 10, 1907, January 24, 1907 and February 23, 1907.

THE EVIDENCE IN THIS CASE SHOWS: That the applicant herein, Robert F. Wyly, a white man, was married in accordance with Cherokee law February, 1858 to his wife, Mary J. Wyly, nee Buffington, who was at the time of said marriage a recognized citizen by blood of the Cherokee Nation, who is identified upon the Cherokee authenticated tribal roll of 1880, Delaware District No. 3042, as a native Cherokee. It is further shown that from the time of said marriage the said Robert F. Wyly and Mary J. Wyly resided together as husband and wife and continuously lived in the Cherokee Nation up to and including September 1, 1902. It is also shown that prior to his said marriage to Mary J. Wyly the said Robert F. Wyly had been married to a recognized citizen by blood of the Cherokee Nation, who, it is affirmatively shown, was dead at the time of his said marriage to the said Mary J. Wyly. Said applicant is identified upon the Cherokee authenticated tribal roll of 1880 and the Cherokee census roll of 1896 as an intermarried citizen of the Cherokee Nation.

IT IS, THEREFORE, ORDERED AND ADJUDGED: That in accordance with the decision of the Supreme Court of the United States, dated November 5, 1906, in the cases of Daniel Red Bird, et al. vs. the United States, Nos. 125, 126, 127, and 128, the said applicant, Robert F. Wyly, is entitled, under the provisions of Section Twenty-one of the Act of Congress approved June 28, 1898 (30 Stats. 495), to enrollment as a citizen by intermarriage of the Cherokee Nation, and his application for enrollment as such is accordingly granted.

Tams Bixby
Commissioner.

Dated at Muskogee, Indian Territory,
this   FEB 26 1907

<><><><><>

Form No. 2.

THE WESTERN UNION TELEGRAPH COMPANY.

——— INCORPORATED ———
24,000 OFFICES IN AMERICA.   CABLE SERVICE TO ALL THE WORLD.
ROBERT C. CLOWRY, President and General Manager.

Receiver's No.	Time Filed		Check

SEND the following message subject to the terms on back hereof, which are hereby agreed to.

Muskogee, Indian T., Jan. 21 90 7

To   Zoe A. Watts,

                Sallisaw, Indian Territory.

            You are directed to appear before the Commissioner

immediately with witnesses to establish the marriage of your

parents.

BIXBY
Commissioner

Paid.
O.B.C.R.

☞ READ THE NOTICE AND AGREEMENT ON BACK. ☜

(Copies of original documents from case.)

Form No. 260.

THE WESTERN UNION TELEGRAPH COMPANY.
——— INCORPORATED ———
23,000 OFFICES IN AMERICA.   CABLE SERVICE TO ALL THE WORLD.
ROBERT C. CLOWRY, President and General Manager.

Receiver's No.	Time Filed		Check

SEND the following message subject to the terms on back hereof, which are hereby agreed to.

Muskogee, Indian Territory, February 21, 1907

Percy Wyly,

        Tahlequah, Indian Territory.

            Evidence of marriage of Robert P. Wyly to Mary
J. Wyly according to Cherokee law, insufficient. If Rev.
J. F. Thompson can testify relative to said marriage, send
him to this office immediately.

Bixby,

Commissioner

O.B.C.R.Paid

☞ READ THE NOTICE AND AGREEMENT ON BACK. ☜

◇◇◇◇◇

Cherokee 5788

Muskogee, Indian Territory, February 26, 1907.

W. W. Hastings,
    Attorney for Cherokee Nation,
        Muskogee, Indian Territory.

Dear Sir:

    There is enclosed herewith a copy of the decision of the Commissioner to the Five Civilized Tribes, dated February 26, 1907, granting the application for the enrollment of Robert F. Wyly as a citizen by intermarriage of the Cherokee Nation.

Respectfully,

Encl. H943
  JMH

Commissioner.

◇◇◇◇◇

Cherokee 5788

Muskogee, Indian Territory, February 26, 1907.

The Commissioner to the Five Civilized Tribes,
    Muskogee, Indian Territory.

Sir:

    Receipt is acknowledged of the testimony and of your decision enrolling Robert F. Wyly as a citizen by intermarriage of the Cherokee Nation. Time for protesting said decision is waived, and I consent that said person may be placed upon the schedule immediately.

Respectfully,
W. W. Hastings
Attorney for Cherokee Nation.

◇◇◇◇◇

Cherokee 5788

Muskogee, Indian Territory, February 26, 1907.

Robert F. Wyly,
Tahlequah, Indian Territory.

Dear Sir:

There is enclosed herewith a copy of the decision of the Commissioner to the Five Civilized Tribes, dated February 26, 1907, granting the application for your enrollment as a citizen by intermarriage of the Cherokee Nation.

You will be advised when your name has been placed upon a schedule of citizens of the Cherokee Nation and approved by the Secretary of the Interior.

Respectfully,

Encl. H-125   Commissioner.
JMH

Cher IW 266

◇◇◇◇◇

FR

DEPARTMENT OF THE INTERIOR,

COMMISSIONER TO THE FIVE CIVILIZED TRIBES.

In the matter of the application for the enrollment of

ELVIRA RATLEY

as a citizen by intermarriage of the Cherokee Nation.

Cherokee 7335.

◇◇◇◇◇

Cherokee Intermarried White 1906
Volume IX

MEMORANDUM as to Eliza Goings.

STRAIGHT CHEROKEE CARD as to applicant, his wife Elvira, his child Sarah Ratley and his step-child Sampson Still.

* *

Department of the Interior,
Commission to the Five Civilized Tribes,
Muskogee, I. T. February, 20th 1901.

In the matter of the application of Wallace Ratley for the enrollment of himself, wife and one child of his own, a step-child named Sampson Still and one adopted child named Eliza Goings, as Cherokee citizens; he being first duly sworn before Commissioner T.B. Needles, testified as follows:

Q What is your name?   A. Wallace Ratley.
Q What is your age?   A. 60.
Q What is your post office address?   A. Campbell.
Q What district do you live in?   A Illinois.
Q Are you a recognized citizen of the Cherokee Nation?   A. Yes sir.
Q By blood or intermarriage?   A. By blood.
Q Whom do you desire to have enrolled?   A. Myself and family.
Q Have you a wife?   A. Yes sir.
Q How many children?   A. Three.
Q What is your wife's name?   A. Elvira.
Q Is she a Cherokee citizen by blood?   A. By marriage.
Q When were you married to her?   A. In 1886.
Q You say she is a white woman? A She was a citizen by marriage before I married her.
Q Have you no certificate of marriage?   A No sir.
Q What was her name before you married her?   A. Still.
Q What was her first husband's name?   A. Jack Still.
Q What are the names of these children?   A. The first one is a step child named Sampson Still.
Q How old?   A. 18.
Q Next child?   A. Sarah Ratley.
Q How old?   A. 13.
Q Next child?   A. She is an adopted child named Eliza Goings.
Q You say she is an adopted child?   A. Yes sir.
Q How old is she?   A. 8,
Q What is the next child's name?   A. That is all.
Q What is the name of Eliza Going's father?   A. Riley Goings.
Q Is he living?   A. Yes sir.
Q Is he a Cherokee by blood?   A. No sir.
Q What is the name of her mother?   A. Jane.

Q Is she living?   A. No sir.

Q Was she a Cherokee by blood?   A. No sir.

Q This child has no Cherokee blood in her then?   A. No sir just lives with me.

Upon an examination of the 1880 authenticated roll of the Cherokee Nation there is found the name of Wallace Ratcliff on page 575, #1584 in Illinois district. On page 584, #1773 thereof appears the name of Jack Still in Illinois district. On page 584, #1774 appears the name of Elvire[sic] Still in Illinois District.

Upon an examination of the 1896 census roll of the Cherokee Nation there is found the name of Wallace Ratcliff on page 895, #1575 in Illinois district.

Q You sign your name Ratley do you?   A. Yes sir.

Q Your wifes[sic] does not appear to be on the roll of 1896, so you know why?

A. I didn't have any then.

Q You said you married her in 1886?   A. Yes sir.

Q Have you been living with her ever since?   A. Yes sir.

Q You were living with her in 1896 were you not?   A. Yes sir.

Q Dont[sic] you know why her name is not on the roll of 1896?   A. No sir.

Upon an examination of the 1896 census roll of 1896[sic] there is found on page 905, #1850 the name of Samson Still in Illinois district.

Q Who was the mother is Sampson Still?   A. My present wife Elvira.

Upon an examination of the 1896 census roll page 895, #1579 appears the name of Sarah Ratcliff in Illinois district.

Q Did I understand you to say that the mother and father of Eliza Goings are white people?   A. Yes sir.

Q How long have you lived in the Cherokee Nation?   A. All my life.

Q Are these children, Sampson Still and Sarah Ratley both living now?   A. Yes sir.

Q Did Elvira Still live with her first husband continuously until his death?   A. Yes sir.

By Com'r Needles,-

The name of Wallace Ratley is found on the authenticated roll of 1880 and is identified as Wallace Ratcliff; he also appears on the census roll of 1896 as Wallace Ratcliff. He avers that he is married to one Elvira Still a non-citizen, but a citizen by intermarriage, she having married one Jack Still a Cherokee citizen by blood and lived with him until his death, and the name of said Jack Still is found on the authenticated roll of 1880, and the name of Elvira Still, the present wife of Wallace Ratley is found on the authenticated roll of 1880 as an intermarried white. The name of the step child, Sampson Still is found on the census roll of 1896. Said Sampson Still is identified as the child of Jack and Elvira Still, whose names appear on the authenticated roll of 1880. The name of Sarah Ratley appears on the 1896 census roll as Sarah Ratcliff; she is identified as the child of Wallace and Elvira Ratley. They are all duly identified and make satisfactory proof as to residence, consequently the said Wallace Ratley, the child of his wife by her former husband, and his own child will be listed for enrollment as Cherokee citizens by blood, and his wife Elvira will be listed for enrollment as a Cherokee citizen by intermarriage. The applicant also applies for the enrollment of Eliza Goings, whom he avers is an adopted child, and avers that the parents of this child are white people, consequently the application for enrollment as to said Eliza Goings will be refused for want of jurisdiction, her name not appearing on any of the rolls of the Cherokee Nation, and no proof being made as to her being a citizen.

= =

Chas. von Weise, being sworn states that as stenographer to the Commission to the Five Civilized Tribes he reported in full all the proceedings in the above cause and that the foregoing is a full, true and correct transcript of his stenographic notes therein.

Chas von Weise

Subscribed and sworn to before me this the 23rd of February, 1901.

T B Needles

Commissioner.

◇◇◇◇◇

Cherokee 7335.

DEPARTMENT OF THE INTERIOR,
COMMISSION TO THE FIVE CIVILIZED TRIBES.
Muskogee, I. T. October 13, 1902.

In the matter of the application of Wallace Ratley, for the enrollment of himself, his child, Sarah Ratley and his step-child, Sampson Still, as citizens by blood of the Cherokee Nation, and for the enrollment of his wife, Elvira Ratley as a citizen by intermarriage of said Nation.

Elvira Ratley, being first duly sworn and examined by the Commission, testified as follows:

Q What is your name?   A Elvira Ratley.
Q How old are you?   A About 35.
Q 35 are you?   A Yes sir.
Q When were you born, do you know?   A No sir, I don't know.
Q Are you as old as 40 do you think?   A Yes I guess I am.
Q What is your postoffice?   A Illinois, (Campbell).
Q You are a white woman?   A I don't claim it, I am just an adopted citizen.
Q Your don't claim any Indian blood?   A Yes sir.
Q But you are claiming as an intermarried citizen?   A Yes sir.

Q Were you on the 1880 roll?   A Yes sir.

Q How were you on that roll; intermarried?   A Yes sir.

Q What was your husband's name?   A Jack Still.

Q Was he your husband in 1880?   A Yes sir.

Q Is he dead?   A Yes sir.

Q How long has he been dead?   A I don't know just the exact date, about 15 years.

Q You married again?   A Married Wallace Ratley.

Q When did you marry him?   A About 12 years ago.

Q Is he a Cherokee by blood?   A Yes sir.

Q Have you lived with your husband Wallace Ratley for the last 12 years?   A Yes sir.

Q Never separated?   A No sir.

Q You were never separated from your first husband?   A No sir, lived with him until he died.

Q How many children have you?   A Got five.

Q How many living at home with you?   A Four.

Q That is, your children?   A Yes sir.

Q Has your husband any children?   A No sir, he aint[sic] got any children; his boy died.

Q What was that child's name?   A Allen Ratley.

Q Sampson Still and Sarah Ratley are your children?   A Yes sir.

Q Are they living at home?   A Yes sir.

Q Lived in the Cherokee Nation all their lives?   A Yes sir.

Q Your husband is living?   A Yes sir he is living, he is at home.

Q Where are your other children?   A I have got one of them with me here, my oldest boy.

Q Three of your children are over 21?   A Yes sir.

R. Palmer, being first duly sworn, states that as stenographer to the Commission to the Five Civilized Tribes, he correctly recorded the testimony and proceedings in this case and that the foregoing is a true and correct transcript of his stenographic notes thereof.

R. Palmer

Subscribed and sworn to before me this 18th day of December, 1902.

BC Jones
Notary Public.

◇◇◇◇◇

PGR
Cherokee 7335.

DEPARTMENT OF THE INTERIOR,
COMMISSION TO THE FIVE CIVILIZED TRIBES,
MUSKOGEE, IND. TER., OCT. 16, 1902.

In the matter of the application for the enrollment of Wallace Ratley et al. as citizens of the Cherokee Nation:

SUPPLEMENTAL STATEMENT.

An examination of the 1896 census roll of the Cherokee Nation shows that Elvira Ratley is identified on that roll, at page 934, #173, Illinois District, as Elvire Ratcliff.

It is ordered that copies of this statement be filed with and made a part of the record in this case.

C. R. Breckinridge
Commissioner.

◇◇◇◇◇

F.R.

Cherokee 7335

DEPARTMENT OF THE INTERIOR,
COMMISSIONER TO THE FIVE CIVILIZED TRIBES
Muskogee, I. T. February 23, 1907.

In the matter of the application for the enrollment of Elvira Ratley as a citizen by intermarriage of the Cherokee Nation.

Elvira Ratley being first duly sworn by Frances R. Lane, a Notary Public for the Western District of Indian Territory, testified as follows:

By the Commissioner:
Q What is your name?   A Elvira Ratley.
Q What is your age?   A I don't know; forty though.
Q What is your postoffice address?   A Campbell, I. T., Illinois District.
Q You are a white woman?   A I don't claim it but I guess I am; I never proved any rights.
Q What Indian blood do you claim to have?   A Cherokee.
Q You are the same person who made application before the Commission to the Five Civilized Tribes at Muskogee, I. T., in February, 1901, for enrollment as a citizen by intermarraige[sic] of the Cherokee nation?   A Yes sir.

Q   What is the name of the Cherokee citizen through whom you claim intermarried rights?   A Jack Still.

Q When were you married to Jack Still?   A A[sic] I don't know as I can tell you the right date or not.

Q About what year was it?   A About in 1870 of 78; somewhere along there.

Q You have not any record by which you can fix that date?

A No, there was no license given then.

Q You have no family records or family bible showing the date?

A No, I aint[sic]; nothing at all.

Q Where were you married to Jack Still?   A Greenleaf.

Q In what district?   A Illinois.

Q In the Cherokee Nation?   A Yes, it was Judge Thornton.

Q   At the time of your marriage to Jack Still he was a recognized by blood of the Cherokee nation?   A Yes, always had been.

Q Is Jack Still dead?   A Yes sir, he has been dead 20 years.

Q Were there any children born to you and Jack Still?

A I have got four boys, Still boys.

Q What is the name of the oldest one?   A David.

Q Is he living at this time?   A Yes sir.

Q How old is he?   A He is along in the thirties, I guess.

Q Has he been enrolled as a citizen by blood of the Cherokee Nation?   A Yes, all of them.

Q What is the name of the next one?   A William.

Q And the next one?   A Sam.

Q How long had you been married to Jack Still at the time your oldest child, David Still, was born?   A I don't remember just how old he was when he died.

Q Do you remember how long you had been married to him at the time this child was born?   A No, I don't really. Must have been about four years old though --I don't understand.

Q I man[sic], how long after you were married to Jack still until this first child was born?

A I don't remember; a year I guess; there is one dead, 18 month old, older than him.

Q What is the name of the older one?   A Isiah. He died when he was 18 months old, the first one. He never was enrolled.

> The name of Jack Still appears on the Cherokee authenticated tribal roll of 1880, Illinois District, page 584, opposite No. 1773 as a native Cherokee. This name is followed by the name of Elvin Still who, it is presumed is the same as the applicant in this case, opposite No. 1774, as an adopted white, and she is shown to have been 27 years old at that time. The name of Davis[sic] Still also appears on said roll opposite No. 1880. David Still is identified as a native Cherokee and his age is given as four years at the time of the making of said roll.

Q You say that David Still was not the first child born to you and Jack Still?

A No, I had one dead 18 months old before David; little boy.

Q Were you ever married before you married Jack Still?   A Yes, I was married but I didn't marry no Cherokee.
Q What was the name of your first husband?   A Goings.
Q Was Goings living at the time you married Still?   A No sir.
Q Goings was the only husband you had before you married Jack Still?   A Yes, he was all the one I had, and he died and Jack Still married me.
Q Was Jack Still married before he married you?   A Yes, he had a family of little children.
Q How many times had he been married before he married you?   A One time.
Q Was his first wife living when he married you?   A No, she was dead.
Q What is the name of his oldest child by his first wife?   A Lois.
Q What was the name of the other children?   A Jonas and Robert and a girl, Mary. Mary was the oldest.

> The names of Mary Still, Noah Still, James Still and R[sic] Robert Still, whose ages are given as 22, 21, 20 and 10 years respectively, are identified on the Cherokee authenticated tribal roll of 1880, Illinois District, page 584, opposite Nos. 1775, 1776, 1777, 1778, as native Cherokees

Q After the death of Jack Still, did you marry again?   A Yes sir
Q What was the name of that husband?   A Wallace Ratley
Q When were you married to Wallace Ratley?   A We married in a yar[sic] after Jack Still died. We have been married about 20 years I guess.
Q Was Mr. Ratley at the time of your marriage to him, a recognized citizen of the Cherokee Nation, by blood?   A Yes sir.
Q Where were you married to Wallace Ratley?   A Webbers Falls.
Q That is in what District?   A Canadian.
Q Who performed the marriage ceremony?   A Rocky Smith, District Judge.
Q You have no documentary evidence showing that marriage?
A No, I have not; we didn't get any then like we do now.
Q You have livd[sic] together as husband and wife continuously in the Cherokee nation from the time of your marriage to Jack Still until the present time?   A Yes, living right on Jack Still's own place, where he died at.
Q Can you say whether you had been married to Jack Still as much as one year or two years at the time your child David Still was born?   A No, I had one child die before David, 18 months old. This is Jack Still's child, and that child was our first child, a boy; he died.
Q Well, in other words, I am trying to find out how long you had been maried[sic] to Jack Still when David was born?   A I guess it had been about thre[sic] years; two years anyhow.
Q Is there anybody here who was present at your marriage to Jack Still that would know anything about the date of it?
A Nobody went with us. Me and him went alone.
Q There were no witnesses?   A No, Cherokees didn't have to have any then, no certificate nor nothing like that.

Witness excused.

Cherokee Intermarried White 1906
Volume IX

Jane Glenn, being first duly sworn by Frances R. Lane, a Notary Public for the Western District of Indian Territory, testified as follows:

By the Commissioner:
Q What is your name?   A Jane Glenn.
Q How old are you?   A Forty-six.
Q What is your postoffice address?   A Campbell, I. T.
Q Are you a citizen of the Cherokee Nation?   A I reckon I aint[sic], now.
Q You are not a citizen by blood then?   [sic] No, I ought to be.
Q How long have you known Elvira Ratley, the applicant in this case?   A Forty-six years. All my life.
Q Do you know when she married a man by the name of Going?   A Yes sir.
Q About when was that?   A Its[sic] been so long ago; I was small then.
Q Going was a white man was he?
A He was a Cherokee man, but he was not a citizen.
Q Do you know about when he died?   A He has been dead about 39 years.
Q After his death did Mrs. Ratley marry again?   A Yes sir.
Q What was her second husband's name? A Jack Still.
Q When did she marry Jack Still?   A About 37 or 38 years ago. I don't remember which.
Q Where were they married?   [sic] At Garfield.
Q In the Cherokee nation?   A Yes, In greenleaf[sic].
Q You didn't see them married?   A No sir.
Q How near were you living to them at that time?   A We was living together, but I didn't go with them. We was right in the same settlement.
Q It was the understanding in the community that they were married?   A Yes sir.
Q And from that time on did they live together as husband and wife until Jack Still died?
A Yes sir.
Q How do you fix the date of their marriage as having been 37 or 38 years ago?
A Thirty-nine years ago we came to this country and they married the next year after we came.
Q Do you know the name of the oldest child that was born to Mrs. Ratley and Jack Still?
A Yes sir.
Q What was that child's name?   A Isiah.
Q How long had Jack Still and Mrs. Ratley been married when Isiah was born?
A About two years.
Q What was the name of the next child?   A David.
Q How long was it after the birth of Isiah until David was born?   A I don't know whether it was 3 or 4 years.
Q How long as best you can remember from the time of the marriage of Jack Still and Mrs. Ratley until David Still was born?   A About four years; three or four years; three anyway, if not four.
Q After the death of Jack Still, Mrs. Ratley married again?   A Yes sir.
Q What was the name of her third husband? A Wallace Ratley.

Q She is living with him at this time?   A Yes sir.
Q She has lived with him continuously from the time of their marriage until the present time?   A Yes sir.
Q She never had any other husbands than these three you have named, Going, Still and Ratley?   A That's all.
Q She was never seaprated[sic] from any of them?   A No sir.
Q Were you living in the same neighborhood with these people when David Still was born?   A No. I was living down in Sequoyah district when David was born.
Q Did you see these people along about the time of David's birth?   A I saw him when he was a little baby, 3 or 4 months old
Q And the best you remember, at that time they had been married 3 or 4 years when David was born?   A Yes sir.

Witness excused.

Wallace Ratley being first duly sworn by Frances R. Lane, a Notary Public for the Western District of Indian Territory, testified as follows:

By the Commissioner:
Q What is your name?   A Wallace Ratley.
Q Your age?   A Sixty-five years.
Q Your postoffice address?   A Campbell, I. T.
Q You are the husband of Elvira Ratley, the applicant in this case?   A Yes sir.
Q When were you married to her?   A It has been about 1885.

Q Were you married before you married her?   A I had been married. My wife was dead, though.
Q Your first wife was dead at the time you married Elvira?   A Yes sir.
Q Elvira Ratley had been married before she married you?   A Yes sir.
Q Do you know the name of her former husband?   A Jack Still.
Q Do you know when she was married to Jack Still?   A No, I couldn't give no correct answer about it. It was, I think rough guessing, in 1870 or '71; somewhere along there.
Q Were you living there in the same neighborhood with these people a few years after they were married?   Three or 4 years?   A Yes, before that too.
Q Do you know when David Still was born?   A No, I remember about the birth of the child, but I don't remember just when
Q About how long had Jack Still and Mrs. Ratley been married when David was born?
A I don't know; must have been three or four years--2 or 3 years. There was a child born betwixt David and the time of their marriage.
Q Jack Still died before you married Mrs. Ratley?   A Yes sir.
Q You and Mrs. Ratley then lived together as husband and wife and lived continuously in the Cherokee Nation from the time of that marriage until the present time?
A Yes sir.
Q You are a citizen by blood of the Cherokee Nation?   A Yes sir.
Q Always been recognized as such?   A Yes sir.

Q Were you born in the Cherokee nation?   A No, I was born in the old Cherokee nation.

Q When did you come to this country?   A I was five years old when I come to this country. I don't know what year it was. I was born in 1839.

Q Came here along in the forties sometime?   A Yes sir, been raised right up here.

Q Always been a recognized citizen of the Cherokee Nation?   A Yes sir.

Witness excused.

Elvira Ratley Recalled:

By the Commissioner:

Q Did Jack still have a son by the name of Sampson Still?

A Yes, that's my boy, my and his boy. We had four boys.

Q You say that Mary Still was Jack's oldest child?   A Yes, by his forst[sic] wife.

Q How old was Mary Still at the time you and Jack Still were married?   A I don't know. She must have been about 13 or 14 when we married. She was big enough to do a little house work.

Q How big was Noah Still when you were married?   A He was not very large. Big enough to pack in a little wood.

Q How old do you think?   A I don't know how old he was

Q Was he as much as 10 or 12 years old?   A Yes, I think he was.

Q And James Still was just about a year younger was he?--Was there a child named James?   A That's a new name to me.

Q You don't know James?   A No sir.

Q How old was Robert Still?   A He was 21 when he died.

Q But Robert Still, that was a child by his first wife?   A Yes sir.

Q How old was Robert Still at the time you married Jack Still?

A I don't know how old he was--7 or 8 years old I reckon. They was all little; I raised them from little boys; there was not any of them very large. But their ages, I could not remember them.

Witness excused.

The applicant Elvira Ratley and her husband, Wallace Ratley are identified on the Cherokee Census roll of 1896, Illinois District, opposite Nos. 173 and 1575, respectively.

Frances R. Lane upon oath states that as stenographer to the Commission to the Five Civilized Tribes she reported the testimony in the above entitled cause and that the foregoing is an accurate transcript of her stenographic notes thereof.

Frances R Lane

Cherokee Intermarried White 1906
Volume IX

Subscribed and sworn to before me this February 23, 1907.

Walter W. Chappell
Notary Public.

◇◇◇◇◇

F.R.   Cherokee 7335.

DEPARTMENT OF THE INTERIOR,

COMMISSIONER TO THE FIVE CIVILIZED TRIBES.

In the matter of the application for the enrollment of Elvira Ratley as a citizen by intermarriage of the Cherokee Nation.

D E C I S I O N

THE RECORDS IN THIS OFFICE SHOW: That at Muskogee, Indian Territory, February 20, 1902, application was received by the Commission to the Five Civilized Tribes for the enrollment of Elvira Ratley as a citizen by intermarriage of the Cherokee Nation. Further proceedings in the matter of said application were had at Muskogee, Indian Territory, October 13, 1902, and February 23, 1907.

THE EVIDENCE IN THIS CASE SHOWS: That the applicant herein, Elvira Ratley, claims the right to enrollment as a citizen by intermarriage of the Cherokee Nation by virtue of her marriage, in about the year 1873, to one Jack Still, who was at the time of said marriage a recognized citizen by blood of the Cherokee Nation, who is identified on the Cherokee authenticated tribal roll of 1880, Illinois District, page 584, opposite No. 1773, as a Native Cherokee. The said Jack Still and the applicant herein resided together as husband and wife from the time of their said marriage until the death of Jack still in about the year 1885.

It further appears that in about the year 1886 the applicant was lawfully married to one Wallace Ratley, who was at the time of said marriage a recognized citizen by blood of the Cherokee Nation, who is identified on the Cherokee authenticated tribal roll of 1880, Illinois District, page 575, opposite No. 1584, as a Native Cherokee, and whose name is included on the approved partial roll of citizens by blood of the Cherokee Nation opposite No. 17427. Since the time of their said marriage the said Wallace Ratley and Elvira Ratley have resided together as husband and wife.

It is further shown that the applicant, since her marriage to her husband, Jack Still, in about 1873, has continuously lived in the Cherokee Nation up to and including September 1, 1902.

The date of applicant's marriage to Jack Still is not definitely shown by the record herein. It is shown, however, by the testimony of the applicant taken at Muskogee, Indian Territory, on February 23, 1907, that she had been married to Jack Still about three years when her son, David Still, was born. She further testified that Mary Still, a daughter of Jack Still by a former wife, was about fourteen years of age at the time of her marriage to Jack Still. The applicant's testimony in this respect is corroborated by the testimony of her present husband, Wallace Ratley, and one Jane Glenn, taken on the same date.

It appears from an examination of the Cherokee authenticated tribal roll of 1880 that said Mary Still and David Still are identified on said roll, Illinois District, page 584, opposite Nos. 1775 and 1779, respectively, as Native Cherokees. The said Mary and David Still are also shown to have been 22 and 4 years of age, respectively, at the date of the making of said roll.

The applicant is identified on the Cherokee authenticated tribal roll of 1880 and the Cherokee Census Roll of 1896 as an intermarried citizen of the Cherokee Nation.

I am, therefore, of the opinion that the preponderance of the evidence establishes that the applicant, Elvira Ratley, was married to her husband, Jack Still, prior to November 1, 1875.

IT IS, THEREFORE, ORDERED AND ADJUDGED: That in accordance with the decision of the Supreme Court of the United States, dated November 5, 1906, in the cases of Daniel Red Bird et al., vs. the United States, Nos. 125, 126, 127, and 128, the said applicant, Elvira Ratley, is entitled, under the provisions of Section 21 of the Act of Congress approved June 28, 1898 (30 Stats. 495), to enrollment as a citizen by intermarriage of the Cherokee Nation, and her application for enrollment as such is accordingly granted.

Tams Bixby
Commissioner.

Dated at Muskogee, Indian Territory,
this _____

◇◇◇◇◇

(Copy of original document from case.)

Translation: *(Typed as given.)*

Dated   Muskogee I T
To Elvira Ratly Care Wallace Ratly
          Illinois I T
It is necessary that you appear before Commissioner in Charge. Muskogee not later than Feby twenty third with witnesses to testify in your intermarried citizenship case testimony required to your marritial to Jack Still. Bixby Commissioner

◇◇◇◇◇

Muskogee, Indian Territory, February 20, 1907.

Elvina[sic] Ratley,
     c/o Wallace Ratley,
          Illinois Station, Indian Territory.

Dear Madam:

          This office today wired you as follows:

          "It is necessary that you appear before Commissioner in Charge.
          Muskogee not later than February twenty-third with witnesses to
          testify in your intermarried citizenship case. Testimony required as
          to your marriage to Jack Still."

and this will confirm same.

280

On November 6, 1906, the Supreme Court of the United States held that white persons who intermarried with Cherokee citizens, according to Cherokee law, prior to November 1, 1875, are entitled to enrollment and allotments of land as citizens of the Cherokee Nation.

You are advised that to properly determine your right to enrollment as a citizen by intermarriage of the Cherokee Nation, it will be necessary for you to appear on or prior to February 23, 1907, before the Commissioner for the purpose of giving testimony as to the date of your marriage, and whether or not your husband, by reason of your marriage to whom you claim the right to enrollment as a citizen by intermarriage of the Cherokee Nation, was a recognized Cherokee citizen at the time of your marriage to him.

Respectfully,

Commissioner.

(SPECIAL)

◇◇◇◇◇

Cherokee

7335.

Muskogee, Indian Territory, February 26, 1907.

W. W. Hastings,
    Attorney for the Cherokee Nation,
        Muskogee, Indian Territory.

Dear Sir:

There is enclosed herewith a copy of the decision of the Commissioner to the Five Civilized Tribes, dated February 26, 1907, granting the application for the enrollment of Elvira Ratley as a citizen by intermarriage of the Cherokee Nation.

Respectfully,

Encl. HJ-116.
    HJC

Commissioner.

◇◇◇◇◇

Cherokee
7335.

Muskogee, Indian Territory, February 26, 1907.

The Commissioner to the Five Civilized Tribes,
Muskogee, Indian Territory.

Dear Sir:

Receipt is acknowledged of the testimony and of your decision enrolling Elvira Ratley as a citizen by intermarriage of the Cherokee Nation. Time for protesting said decision is waived, and I consent that said person may be placed upon the schedule immediately.

Respectfully,
W. W. Hastings
Attorney for Cherokee Nation

◇◇◇◇◇

Cherokee
7335.

Muskogee, Indian Territory, February 26, 1907.

Elvira Ratley,
Campbell, Indian Territory.

Dear Madam:

There is enclosed herewith a copy of the decision of the Commissioner to the Five Civilized Tribes, dated February 26, 1907, granting your application for enrollment as a citizen by intermarriage of the Cherokee Nation.

You will be advised when your name has been placed upon a schedule of citizens of the Cherokee Nation and approved by the Secretary of the Interior.

Respectfully,

Encl. HJ-115.
HJC

Commissioner.

◇◇◇◇◇

(Copy of original document from case.)

www.ingramcontent.com/pod-product-compliance
Lightning Source LLC
Chambersburg PA
CBHW020246030426
42336CB00010B/644